Published by Straight Talk Books
P.O. Box 301, Milwaukee, WI 53201
800.661.3311 · timeofgrace.org

Cover image: Pearl/Lightstock

Printed in the United States of America
ISBN: 978-1-949488-23-4

seeds of joy

Daily devotions for a joy-filled life

Introduction

Joy. Who doesn't want more of it? If joy was for sale, I bet you would buy truckloads of it and tell your loved ones to race to the store before it was sold out.

But joy is not for sale, because it's not something you buy. Joy is something you grow.

"The fruit of the Spirit is . . . joy" (Galatians 5:22).

Thankfully, God doesn't make us guess how the Holy Spirit makes joy grow. That sacred work happens in our hearts when we meditate on the holy words that we've seen and heard. When we give God's verses the time they deserve and wrestle with them in our hearts, the Spirit waters the seeds that grow into the spiritual happiness that we call joy.

That's why I'm grateful you've picked up this book.

This book won't make you joyful by osmosis. Nor will it change you via page flipping or distracted skimming. But if you take time—quality and quantity time— the words in this book will push the hopelessness out of your heart.

Instead, joy will grow out of the trustworthy promises of our glorious God.

Happy meditating!

Pastor Mike Novotny

january

He put a new song in my mouth,
a hymn of praise to our God.
Many will see and fear the Lᴏʀᴅ
and put their trust in him.

Psalm 40:3

Take the Baptism plunge

New Year's Day

Pastor Daron Lindemann

When I lived in the Milwaukee area, headline news on New Year's Day announced the annual Polar Plunge. Every year people brave the frigid climate and 30-something degree Lake Michigan water to prove that they're tougher than winter.

It can also prove resolve. "Now I know he's committed if he's doing this with me," a young lady commented on a local news report about her fiancé who took the plunge with her. Taking a polar plunge makes a statement that you're a person who is committed.

The Bible tells us about a similar plunge that did not take place in the frigid waters of Lake Michigan but the fertile waters of the Jordan River. Jesus' baptism made a statement of commitment that changes your life.

The Son of God committed to a mission of humble obedience and mercy for sinners when he walked into the water.

God the Holy Spirit committed to tearing open heaven—at Jesus' baptism and every baptism including yours—descending with heavenly gifts that equip the baptized for acts of faith and love.

God the Father committed to his Son and to every one of his children baptized in the name of the triune God: "I love you." **"With you I am well pleased"** (Luke 3:22).

Take the Baptism plunge. Use your baptism to drown your shame, despair, and fear. Rise out of the water with Jesus, encouraged by the Father's love and with the Spirit's gifts.

Immense patience
Pastor Mark Jeske

One of the unique terms that the Bible uses to describe the Holy Spirit is *Paraclete*, derived from a word in the Greek original that means "Encourager." The Spirit does for us what good coaches do for their athletes: he trains us, encourages us, scolds us, disciplines us, and cheers us on in order to develop our potential to be useful to his agenda.

That process often takes a long time. We are works in progress, and thankfully God does not possess a hair-trigger temper. St. Paul (who ashamedly admitted to being a blasphemer before his conversion) called God's patience with him *immense*: **"For that very reason I was shown mercy so that in me, the worst of sinners, Christ Jesus might display his immense patience as an example for those who would believe in him and receive eternal life"** (1 Timothy 1:16).

Isn't there great comfort to be found in God's great patience with us? By this I don't mean to gloat at how much sinful and selfish behavior we can get away with. I don't mean to excuse those who put off repentance indefinitely, thinking they have all the time in the world. I do mean to arouse within us all a mighty appreciation for the gospel of Christ. He really does love us! He really does want us all to believe his promises! He really does want us to grow in spiritual knowledge and service.

And he really does want us to spend eternity with him.

The sin that kills friendship

Pastor Mike Novotny

My wife is amazed at how men can fight and still be friends. Guys can get into an argument, throw a few punches, apologize, and immediately go out for appetizers and drinks (with ice packs still on their faces). Apparently, in my wife's experience, things are a touch more complicated for our sisters in the faith . . .

Some friends can move past a few punches almost immediately, but few can survive the sin that kills friendships. **"A gossip separates close friends,"** writes King Solomon (Proverbs 16:28). A gossip pushes the nuclear button on even the strongest relationships. Why? Because friendships are built upon honesty. What truly draws us together is being real, opening up, confessing our weaknesses, and bearing each other's burdens. But when I gossip, when I embarrass you instead of protecting you, you will learn to fake it in front of me, if for no other reason than self-preservation.

Can I encourage you today to take gossip as seriously as Scripture does, whether it comes in the form of a whispered conversation, an email shared among snarky friends, or an "I just need some extra advice" cover? Words of gossip have the power to kill one of God's greatest gifts as quickly as a fire can burn down a forest that took a generation to grow.

Instead, talk about something even more interesting—the bottomless blessings of knowing Jesus. **"Praise the Lord, my soul, and forget not all his benefits"** (Psalm 103:2).

Stubbornly holding on

Diana Kerr

When my son, Harrington, was younger, he loved crawling into his mama's lap. He'd look up at me as he played, I'd put my arms out toward him, he'd crawl excitedly over and up into my lap, and I'd scoop him up.

Sometimes he'd try to crawl while clutching a toy at the same time. It didn't work. He couldn't manage both holding onto a toy and climbing into my lap. The toy got in the way. He had to choose.

It struck me one day as I watched him wrestle stubbornly with not wanting to set down his toy how I act just like Harrington on a daily basis. God's always there for me, arms open, smiling at me, excited to be close. But I let stuff get in the way. I want the best of both worlds. I want intimacy with God *and* I want to hang onto everything worldly. God's love doesn't waver, but my choices distance me from him.

I want to embrace James' words: **"Come near to God and he will come near to you"** (James 4:8). Like James encourages in the verses that follow this one, I want to repent and purify my heart. I want to give up the illusion that I can love God and the world at the same time. I can't do these things on my own, but I know God wants to help. Then there's a final promise that fits the illustration with my little boy so perfectly: **"Humble yourselves before the Lord, *and he will lift you up*"** (verse 10).

Sometimes God hides himself

Pastor Mark Jeske

Okay, it's a paradox, but it's an important one, one you need to embrace and trust.

Sometimes God is obvious and accessible. His Word speaks clearly on what he has done to rescue a broken and fallen mankind. The work of Christ is narrated and explained in the clearest possible language, and Christ's mercy is extended to all through Word and sacrament.

But God does not always make clear what he is going to do in the future. **"Truly you are a God who has been hiding himself"** (Isaiah 45:15). God feels absolutely no obligation to tip his cards. Our information is on a need-to-know basis. Even Elisha, one of the greatest of his prophets, had to wait with the rest for clarity and outcomes: **"When she reached the man of God [i.e., Elisha] at the mountain, she took hold of his feet. Gehazi came over to push her away, but the man of God said, 'Leave her alone! She is in bitter distress, but the LORD has hidden it from me and has not told me why'"** (2 Kings 4:27).

Does God's reticence disappoint you? Don't let it. Parents do not always feel obligated to explain themselves to their children, and they know also that their children are not always ready for the realities of the adult world.

The time of full disclosure will soon be here. Paul said, **"Now I know in part; then I shall know fully, even as I am fully known"** (1 Corinthians 13:12).

Seven things I learned from the Magi

Pastor Daron Lindemann

On January 6, Christians celebrate the Epiphany of our Lord. The account of the Magi following the star to visit Jesus with gifts of gold, incense, and myrrh teaches us that salvation through Jesus is revealed to all people. Here are seven more things I learned from this event recorded in Matthew chapter 2.

Even after consulting seminary professors, Greek lexicons, and Hebrew dictionaries, I still don't know whether to say "mey-jahy" or "madge-eye." A thoughtful friend suggested, "Just call them wise men."

Their profession (studying the stars) opened possibilities for their faith. Don't limit what God can do for you or others through your work.

Even the stars bow down to Jesus. All creation worships him.

Foreign Magi working in a pagan setting knew about a king of the Jews because some believer at some time had the courage to say something to someone about God's promise to send a Savior. You never know where your witnessing will lead. Say something to someone today.

They worshiped Jesus. Not people, places, or things.

Maybe we call the men wise because they stopped and asked for directions. And they listened. What directions does God have for you if you'd only stop, ask, and listen to the guidance he has in his Word (which, according to 2 Peter 1:19, is your personal guiding star)?

Jews today who are still waiting for a messiah should know that their own religious leaders pointed the Magi to Bethlehem to find the Messiah.

The man who preached to 20 million

Pastor Mike Novotny

One day a reporter went to witness the most famous man on earth in action. Walter Maier, the Lutheran radio preacher whose sermons reached 40,000,000 ears every week, was about to record another message. When the reporter arrived at the studio, however, he didn't see Maier. He looked into the recording booth and saw nothing but an empty room. But the tour guide smiled at the reporter, "Look down." The reporter took a step closer and saw the celebrity on the floor of the studio, on his face, begging God to bless his message.

I love that story. It reminds us all to stay humble, no matter how successful we are in ministry, business, or life. Even more, it reminds us of Jesus. Despite the notoriety and the size of his miracle-seeking crowds, where do we find Jesus at the end of his life? Matthew tells us, **"Going a little farther,** [Jesus] **fell with his face to the ground and prayed"** (Matthew 26:39).

Jesus stayed humble. As our sinless Savior, he avoided the proud assumption that he could handle things without prayer. Thus, when he died the next day, he had a perfect life to give for you, a sacrifice that would make God's face shine with approval every time he thought of you.

So imitate Maier as you humbly pray today, and worship your Savior for praying his way to your salvation!

Love your work
Pastor Mark Jeske

You know, being a working stiff isn't so bad when you like your boss, when the job is pleasant, when you have terrific coworkers, and when the pay is more than you deserve. It gets really hard, though, when you can't stand your boss, the work is monotonous and unfulfilling, you have to work with fools, and the pay is terrible. But what a great way to show your faith!

Scripture calls on Christians to love their work even when, *especially* when, their work is unlovable: **"Obey your earthly masters in everything; and do it, not only when their eye is on you and to curry their favor, but with sincerity of heart and reverence for the Lord. Whatever you do, work at it with all your heart, as working for the Lord, not for human masters, since you know that you will receive an inheritance from the Lord as a reward. It is the Lord Christ you are serving"** (Colossians 3:22-24).

Those golden verses have the key to everything: "as working for the Lord." When pleasing your Savior is your number-one mission each day, it changes everything. You are freed from the pressure of deciding if you feel like putting forth your best effort. Christians work hard all the time, especially when no one's watching, especially when you don't like your boss.

Work with all your heart—maybe even singing quietly to yourself—because after all you're doing it for your Lord Jesus. He sees. He remembers.

Look for fullness
Jason Nelson

I'd like you to think about something I'm wrestling with. How do you see the Bible? Is it half empty, or is it full? Are you a stickler for the rules, or is your favorite commandment, "Love one another"? Do its warnings urge us toward good deeds, or are they a destiny we must fulfill? I suppose we could bring doomsday on ourselves if enough people believe the Bible says it should happen soon. Do you keep the commandments because you are afraid not to or because you really want to? Are you crabby because nothing is perfect, or are you happy to see beauty where you least expect to find it? Do you think being a Christian won't pay off until you die, or are you enjoying yourself now because your faith adorns your walk with good character? Is your life half empty, or is it full?

When you read the Bible, are you looking for the fullness of God? **"For in Christ all the fullness of the Deity lives in bodily form, and in Christ you have been brought to fullness. He is the head over every power and authority"** (Colossians 2:9,10). Jesus is the fullness of God, and he is God's Word brought to vivid life. He is the embodiment of God's love for us. When you're not sure what to focus on in the Bible, focus on Christ. Jesus' life and work and teachings and example make everything in the Bible complete. And he makes us complete.

I am a friend of God!

Pastor Mike Novotny

How many friends do you have? I suppose your answer to that question depends on your definition of the word *friend*. In our day, when so many of us are lonely and craving friendship, we slap the word *friend* on anyone who isn't our enemy and pray our loneliness goes away.

But I'm guessing you've figured out that it takes more than two clicks and a vague digital connection to fill the friendship space in your heart. What you crave is someone who is there for you, real with you, supportive of you, and makes your days better. I'm guessing you want a true friend, a preferred companion, to steal the dictionary's definition.

Can I share some good advice with you? According to psychologist Debra Oswald, you can improve your friendships this week. If you are (1) willing to confess your struggles, (2) ready to bear others' burdens, (3) open to investing time to deepen your relationships, and (4) up for being generally positive (instead of the person who vents, complains, and grumbles about the government, your health, etc.), you could soon enjoy an actual friendship.

Can I share some good news with you? According to John, Jesus is your friend: **"I have called you friends,"** Jesus told his followers (John 15:15). If Dr. Oswald's four steps are right, Jesus accepts you despite your weaknesses, bears your heaviest burdens, makes time to listen to your prayers, and speaks multiple words of comfort for every one word of critique. Just think what this sentence means—You are a friend of God!

Unload your worries

Diana Kerr

"Cast all your anxiety on him because he cares for you" (1 Peter 5:7). Most of us have heard this verse *many* times. Personally, I've unfortunately allowed it to become one of those quaint, little Christian one-liners that has lost its power.

Let's dissect this verse a little and change that. Let's start with *cast*, a word we use when talking about actors, fishing, or broken bones, but rarely in this context. Here, *cast* means "to throw upon or place upon." My mind envisions dumping things on God, the way you do when you wrangle too many grocery bags into the house and unload the weight on the counter with a sigh of relief.

On to the mention of *anxiety*. In the original Greek, this is the same word as the word *worries* in the parable of the sower where it says that **"the worries of this life and the deceitfulness of wealth choke the word, making it unfruitful"** (Matthew 13:22). Casting anxiety on God isn't just beneficial for our emotional health, but it can actually help us from falling away in tough times.

There's so much more to say, but here's a final thought: Most of us dump our anxiety on other people, but that's not what's encouraged here. This verse encourages us to cast our anxiety on *God*. Why? Because he cares for you. I know, it sounds flowery, but think about the gravity of how much God loves you. To death. Literally.

Worried? Throw it on God.

A contrarian's playbook

Jason Nelson

I've read that Jesus is the greatest contrarian in history. People see him going against the grain and doing the unexpected. On that basis, they argue for a more tolerant society or a theocratic state. But is that what he was about? I'm up for looking at things another way, so let's put Jesus through a playbook for being a contrarian.

Learn the rules. Jesus grew in wisdom and favor with God and men because **"they found him in the temple courts, sitting among the teachers, listening to them and asking them questions. Everyone who heard him was amazed at his understanding and his answers"** (Luke 2:46,47). Jesus knew exactly what the law required.

Follow the rules. The will of God wasn't a theory for Jesus. He was a compelling Messiah because he subjected himself to the ultimate conclusion of everything God expected. **"Being found in appearance as a man, he humbled himself by becoming obedient to death— even death on a cross!"** (Philippians 2:8).

Break the rules. When people still questioned his authority, he exceeded every limitation on life as we know it. **"Destroy this temple, and I will raise it again in three days"** (John 2:19). Jesus' ministry, death, and resurrection were total departures from conventional wisdom. **"After he was raised from the dead, his disciples recalled what he had said. Then they believed the scripture and the words that Jesus had spoken"** (John 2:22). Jesus is someone you can believe in. That's as contrarian as it gets.

Painful memories

Pastor Mark Jeske

Our capacity for memory is a wonderful thing, isn't it? In the 3 pounds of tissue and chemicals within our skull are beautiful images, great music, mental videos of happy family times, and the skills we need to earn a living.

Alas, we remember our failures too. Not only do I need God to forget about them, *I* want to forget about them. What do you do when those old shameful words and actions keep coming back to haunt you? Do what St. Paul did. Although he had a terrible vault of violent and ungodly acts in his past, he found comfort in the free and full forgiveness of Jesus Christ, who takes our sins away as far as east is from west: **"I thank Christ Jesus our Lord, who has given me strength, that he considered me trustworthy, appointing me to his service. Even though I was once a blasphemer and a persecutor and a violent man, I was shown mercy because I acted in ignorance and unbelief"** (1 Timothy 1:12,13).

It may be that God allows us to remember our rebellious and evil deeds of the past to keep us humble . . . to remind us that we are saved by God's grace, not our works . . . to keep a judgmental spirit from arising in our minds . . . to keep our voices and hearts soft as we deal with the other fools and sinners around us.

Look ahead. The pain will be gone in heaven.

Did Jesus play favorites?

Pastor Mike Novotny

Do you think Thomas was offended when Jesus didn't give him one of the three VIP passes to get a glimpse of glory on the Mount of Transfiguration (Matthew 17:1)? Do you think Andrew and Matthew grumbled when Jesus chose Peter, James, and John to pray with him in the Garden of Gethsemane while they and the other apostles waited outside (Matthew 26:37)?

I don't know how they felt, but I know Jesus did not sin. That fact fascinates me, since it proves that being close friends with only a few is Christ-like and not cliquish. Jesus preferred the 12 apostles to the crowds of thousands, the "inner three" to the Twelve, and "the one whom Jesus loved" to Peter and James. And yet he did not sin a single time! Apparently, you can be close with some without being cliquey toward the rest.

Do you recognize this key distinction? *Fellowship* is the love you show to every brother and sister in your church family. It's when you push pause on your little circle of friends and open up your arms to welcome those who might not get invited out for coffee, dinner, and drinks. God, help us remember that next Sunday!

Friendship, on the other hand, is your smaller circle of "Peters, Jameses, and Johns." It's the few people whom you do life with—confessing sins, bearing burdens, and investing extra hours of your limited time.

Remember that distinction and you will imitate your Savior who loved all but was friends with only a few.

It's all in the attitude
Jason Nelson

There are three outlooks on life I know don't work.

1. Clinging to the past (because there is no future in it)
2. Pessimism (because there is no incentive for hope)
3. Conspiracy theories (because the dark side isn't that well organized)

After years of gathering anecdotal evidence by watching people, I've observed that various leaders who expressed these attitudes all seemed to have struggling operations. There's something that flows from our attitudes to the outcomes in our lives. Warren Buffett is one of the most optimistic people I follow, and he's got the goods to back it up.

Out of all the available attitudes, there is one that consistently works: **"Have the same attitude that Christ Jesus had"** (Philippians 2:5 GW). God never qualified this expectation by saying he would understand if under certain circumstances we would have lousy attitudes. He makes no exceptions. The genius of God is in the fact that we are always in the process of acquiring Christ's attitude. That means we need to think about Jesus a lot: what he did for us and what he would do if he were in our situations. The Bible gives us clear accounts of both. And the Holy Spirit enables us to absorb Jesus' atoning work and exemplary life into our own attitudes and press them into every corner of our being. That is the attitude that will work for us today, tomorrow, and forever.

Jesus served time to free me
Pastor Daron Lindemann

I think about time a lot at the beginning of a new year. How do I use time? How do I manage it? Or, well, does time use and manage me?

I have regrets about my undone to-do lists and missed opportunities of the past. I want to get everything done, but I never have enough time to do it. That leaves me with only two options.

1. I must be infinite. I must be better than the best superhero, able to do everything, be everywhere, and get it all done. Since this is impossible, the better choice is . . .

2. I let Jesus be infinite. He's everywhere and over everything. He's eternal. But he became finite! Limited. Subject to time's control.

Time kept Jesus in Mary's womb for about nine months. Time initiated puberty. Time called him to Jerusalem, where he suffered and died and then rose.

As we try hard to be infinite but cannot, the One who is infinite became finite, became limited, a servant of time. Why? This Bible verse says it all: **"But when the set time had fully come, God sent his Son, born of a woman, born under the law, to redeem those under the law"** (Galatians 4:4,5).

Jesus served time to redeem us. We who are finite do not need to become infinite because Jesus, who is infinite, became finite to save us, to forgive us, and to set us free.

Ladies, we men need you

Pastor Mike Novotny

There are few things as statistically powerful as a man who loves Jesus. Perhaps you've read the studies concerning the impact men have on their families. Give a kid a dad who talks about God every day and tucks him in every night, and that child has a distinct advantage economically, socially, and spiritually.

Perhaps that's why Deborah, one of the strongest women in the Old Testament, once sang, **"When the princes in Israel take the lead, when the people willingly offer themselves—praise the Lord!"** (Judges 5:2). In the lackluster generations of the Judges, Deborah pushed the "princes" in Israel to step up in faith and lead the people toward God.

If you are a husband or a father, please remember this unique calling God has given you. Today you will lead the people in your life toward something and Someone. Take advantage of this "limited time offer" that God has given you to make that Someone the Savior of the world!

And if you're a woman (married, single, divorced, or widowed), join Deborah's song and spur the men in your life to love the Lord with all their hearts and to find all their hearts need in his unconditional love. We men so often forget about God in the pursuit of here-and-now success. We need you to pray for us and to push us forward. Because, as Deborah says, a man of faith is reason to praise the Lord!

Miracles are easy for God

Pastor Mark Jeske

In some ways, bringing water to arid Southern California is one of America's greatest engineering achievements. Over the course of many decades, government entities have spent billions of dollars to establish huge reservoirs in the mountains and hundreds of miles of aqueducts to bring enough fresh water to support a population of 15 million people in the valleys around Los Angeles.

God once did approximately the same thing in a day by simply speaking his powerful Word. He decided, as a gift, not only to keep the waterless army of the Israelites alive after they had been marching in the desert for a week, but he guaranteed them a victory over their feared Moabite enemies. The prophet Elisha told the Israelite commanders that God wouldn't even have to break out a sweat to do it: **"This is what the Lord says: You will see neither wind nor rain, yet this valley will be filled with water, and you, your cattle and your other animals will drink.** *This is an easy thing* **in the eyes of the Lord; he will also deliver Moab into your hands"** (2 Kings 3:17,18).

Think what that means! Every molecule of matter on earth was made out of nothing by God, and he is fully capable of repeating that creative act at any time of his choosing. It's *easy* for him! He just thinks of what he wants and then wills it into existence.

There are no limits to his power to take care of the needs of his believers.

What am I—chopped liver?

Pastor Mark Jeske

"Hey! I'm talking to you!" I wonder how many frustrated parents have burst out those words to a sullen teenager. Has that phrase ever been heard in your home? Communication can't happen unless both parties are engaged in the conversation.

Our God earnestly desires a relationship with all his human creatures, but it can't happen without communication. The heart-faith that bonds us to our Maker is created and fueled by his Word, and when people lose interest in the Word, they begin to die spiritually. It's been going on forever. An example from the time of the kings of Judah: **"The LORD spoke to Manasseh and his people, but they paid no attention"** (2 Chronicles 33:10). God must have felt even less important than chopped liver.

Why do people blow him off? Because they can. After they've committed their various acts of defiance *and nothing bad happened to them*, they assume that they are sovereign agents on their own. They revel in their "freedom" and lack of accountability. But that "declaration of independence" from God is actually spiritual suicide.

This is a big deal for you. Only those connected to Christ by faith will receive forgiveness of their sins, survive the great judgment, and be invited into heaven. God has spoken to *you* through his Word, revealing the blessed path of salvation. But only *you* can control the attention you choose to give it.

Choose to pray for your leaders

Pastor Mark Jeske

May I admit that when I pray for people, I find it easiest to pray for myself? I'm not proud of saying that, but it doesn't just naturally occur to me to pray for people wealthier and more powerful than I am.

But here's a challenge: God loads our prayers with power, and he invites us, even commands us, to pray for the powerful (and usually wealthy) people who lead our cities, states, and country: **"I urge, then, first of all, that petitions, prayers, intercession and thanksgiving be made for all people—for kings and all those in authority, that we may live peaceful and quiet lives in all godliness and holiness. This is good, and pleases God our Savior"** (1 Timothy 2:1-3).

What good can prayer for our leaders do? It can bring wisdom from heaven to augment their own. When King Solomon was granted one "magic" wish, he asked for wisdom, since he was overwhelmed with the pressure of governing and knew he needed God's help. We can pray for patience in our leaders, for good judgment, for compassion for those who are weak or suffering, for integrity in their deeds and honesty in their talk, and for hearts of service. You can choose to pray for people you voted against, and even pray for leaders who may not be Christians, since the church sometimes has to make its way in places where the believers are in the great minority.

Will you do it today?

A word to impulsive people

Pastor Mike Novotny

The reformer Martin Luther once said, "All of us are either a Jacob or an Esau." If you know the story of those twin brothers from Genesis chapters 25-32, you realize Luther was giving us a warning, not a compliment.

Jacob was that crafty momma's boy who used his brain to outmatch his brother's brawn. Esau was that impulsive hunter who could kill the beasts of the field but couldn't kill his own impatience. Yet both brothers had this in common—they were impulsive. They were not willing to wait for God's blessing at God's time. They cut corners. They sinned.

The New Testament warns us about this kind of behavior: **"See that no one is . . . godless like Esau, who for a single meal sold his inheritance rights as the oldest son"** (Hebrews 12:16). Don't be like Esau and trade something as sacred as your character, your integrity, your clean conscience, or your spiritual inheritance for something as temporary as a bowl of soup.

The great deceiver will try to convince you that you need to sin. You *need* to. You can't live without doing this or saying that. At the same time, the Spirit of Jesus (who is "the Truth") will remind you that you can have a fulfilling, joy-saturated, good life with God, that everything is yours in Jesus Christ, your Savior. I pray you listen to the Spirit today and trust the patient path of God in a corner-cutting world.

Code of conduct

Jason Nelson

I don't think God gave anyone authority to dictate sub-commandments. I don't think there's a First Commandment subsection A.1.b.ii that we need to follow to prove loyalty to Christ. Man-made expectations complicate Christianity. They burden the consciences of longtimers in the faith and confuse newcomers who are trying to make sense of it all and do the right thing. There are clear teachings in the Bible that dwell in the hearts of all followers of Jesus. Blest be those ties that bind us to our Lord and one another.

The Bible unclutters the path of discipleship. **"Whatever happens, conduct yourselves in a manner worthy of the gospel of Christ"** (Philippians 1:27). That is the sweeping summary of what God expects. Everyday people who are familiar with the Scriptures know what is worthy of Christ. **"Or, say, one person thinks that some days should be set aside as holy and another thinks that each day is pretty much like any other. There are good reasons either way. So, each person is free to follow the convictions of conscience"** (Romans 14:5 MSG). Our own consciences, informed by God's Word, arbitrate what is permissible for each of us.

In good conscience, we can embrace others who relate to God in simpler ways or more magnificent ways than we do because there is only one answer to this question: What must I do to be saved? It's this: Believe in the Lord Jesus Christ.

The church is people
Pastor Mark Jeske

People can be forgiven for thinking of the church as real estate or buildings. After all, those are seemingly the most permanent features of the organization. It's what you see when you drive past. People come and people go, but the geographic location gives the church a sense of "place," and the building provides a sense of "home."

And yet, the church is really the people. Churches move—perhaps to be able to grow, perhaps because of persecution, perhaps because of immigration and new opportunities. The people matter more than the buildings. Listen to Paul talk about the true church in Rome at his time: **"Greet Priscilla and Aquila, my fellow workers in Christ Jesus. They risked their lives for me. Not only I but all the churches of the Gentiles are grateful to them. Greet also the church that meets at their house"** (Romans 16:3-5).

God's kingdom is not a geographic location or an inventory of assets but, rather, his gracious rule in people's hearts. It is people, not buildings, for whom Jesus Christ died and rose again. Your congregation's true mission is not preservation and expansion of the physical plant but connecting with people through the gospel. The next time you are worshiping in your congregation, look around you and enjoy the decorations and architectural beauty. But enjoy the people even more. It is their energy and creativity and loyalty and love that really hold the place together.

Love them. Appreciate them. Thank them.

The weight of sin
Diana Kerr

I'm fascinated by the fact that all the toppings at a frozen yogurt shop cost you the same amount per pound. Clearly the breakfast cereal toppings or gummy bears cost the owners less per pound than the nuts and fruit, right? I load up on pecans and fruit because, hey, when they weigh my bowl, it will all cost me the same. Outside of the froyo shop, that logic doesn't make sense, but in there, the price is equal.

When it comes to sin, though, we're really good at weighing it unevenly, aren't we? I get it. It's almost impossible not to. According to society and our justice system, sin isn't created equal. But in God's court, sin is sin. It all weighs the same, and we've all been charged equally: **"All have sinned and fall short of the glory of God"** (Romans 3:23) and **"The wages of sin is death"** (Romans 6:23).

Yep. One sin, even one tiny sin, separates me from God, and the price is death. (I need to remember this when I'm smugly thinking I'm better than others.) To God, the cost for an ever-so-slightly snarky comment toward someone is the exact same as the cost for a grotesque sexual sin.

That's heavy news without the gospel, but here it is: **"Our old self was crucified with him. . . . Anyone who has died has been set free from sin"** (Romans 6:6,7). Miraculously, mercifully, Jesus paid the cost through death, and his death counts for us. Our sins' weight was crushing, but now we're light and free.

Our *Father*

Pastor Mike Novotny

I never thought I would be the guy to stare at children while they sleep. But I do. When I get home late from work or from soccer, I sneak into my daughters' bedrooms and I just stare. Sometimes I sit down on the carpet and just look at their bare feet sticking out from the fuzzy pink blankets. Or I fix my eyes on their little faces snuggled up against their favorite "stuffy." There are few things more beautiful or more emotional for me than those two girls.

Which is why I adore Jesus' prayer. When his disciples begged him for a tutorial on talking to God, Jesus didn't say, "Pray like this—Our King in heaven." Nor did he instruct them to say, "Our Judge in heaven." No, he gave them a pattern for prayer that stirs our hearts. Jesus said, **"This, then, is how you should pray: 'Our *Father* in heaven'"** (Matthew 6:9). What a word! God is your *Father*. You are his child. Incredible, isn't it?

After all you've done wrong. After all you've failed to do right. After all you've struggled with, indulged in, or been too scared to stand up for. After all of it, God is not ashamed to call you his kid. He feels the way I feel when I sit on the carpet and stare at my kids. Love swells up in his heart. Emotion floods his mind. You are not a minion to God. Not a name or a number. You are infinitely valuable. If you could only see your Father's face when he looks down upon you!

Our Father In *heaven*
Pastor Mike Novotny

I accidentally threw my dad under the bus the other day. I was trying to tell a fictional, first-person story about a guy with a bad father, so I said, "I never had a dad who was loving . . . " The church got awkwardly quiet. They thought I was talking about my own father. Even worse, my dad goes to our church!

By God's grace, I had (and still have) a really good dad. He traveled crazy distances to watch me play soccer. He supported my desire for ministry even before he was a churchgoing guy. And he is a wonderful grandpa to my girls.

But I know not everyone has a dad like that. Maybe your dad was demanding and gruff. Maybe he was ashamed of you. Maybe he was a hypocrite who went to church, went home, and hurt your mom. Maybe he showed up for your conception and then bailed for the rest of your story.

If so, I want to introduce you to a prayer Jesus taught. It starts, **"Our Father in heaven"** (Matthew 6:9). I love those last two words—*in heaven*. Our God is not an earthly father. Not a flawed, sinful man who fails us in scarring ways. No, God is a Father who is in heaven, where sin cannot exist. He is holy. It is impossible for him to break a promise to you.

Pray that prayer often. Say those words slowly. Having a great father can change your life in powerful ways. Thankfully, you have one. Because he is not just our Father. He is our Father in heaven.

Our Father in *heaven* (Part 2)

Pastor Mike Novotny

My daughters are still at that priceless stage where they adore their daddy. When I come home from work, they drop everything and sprint, squealing, to squeeze their arms around Daddy's legs. (They'll do that when they're 16, right?) They love their father. Why wouldn't they? I have loved them first, in a million different ways.

Loving God can be a bit more challenging. Because even Jesus admitted that we pray to **"our Father in heaven"** (Matthew 6:9). *In heaven* means he's not on earth. He's not visible or touchable. Therefore, believing our Father loves us and accepts us, despite our sins, can be a great challenge for our faith.

That is precisely why our Father gives fathers . . . and mothers . . . and friends. Good people are great glimpses of the best Father. Whenever your dad lends you some money in your time of need. Whenever your mom lends her ear and just listens to your struggles. Whenever your friends make you laugh and invite you to hang out. Every time someone on earth is kind, patient, selfless, and forgiving, they are helping us to know, in a deeply personal way, the expression that is on our heavenly Father's face.

Today you will not be able to see your Father. Unless you see by faith. By faith, you see God's face when you look at their faces, a glimpse of his glory. Now I'm off to give two little girls a glimpse of their Father who is in heaven. They can't yet see his face, but they can see mine.

Our Father in heaven

Pastor Mike Novotny

Once upon a time, Billy had the best dad. Billy's dad valued his family more than his career. He leveraged those early years, the ones that pass so quickly, to shape his son with God's love and give the boy a glimpse of God the Father—present, kind, forgiving, encouraging. Billy grew up loved, protected, and blessed by his dad.

What do you feel as you read about Billy's father? I'm guessing something like, "Good for Billy." Because stories about even the best fathers mean nothing to us when it's *his* father or *her* father or *their* father. The only father that means much to us is *our* father.

Which is why I love Jesus' prayer. He taught us to pray, **"*Our* Father in heaven"** (Matthew 6:9). That has to be the most beautiful possessive pronoun in the history of grammar! This ever-present, always-compassionate, relentlessly forgiving Father is *our* Father. We are his children. You are his dear daughter. You are his precious son.

Do you know what that means? If you tried to call up Warren Buffet and ask for money, he wouldn't take your call. He's not your father. But if you called to God in prayer and asked for anything in Jesus' name—for endurance against cancer, for the ability to forgive your critics, for courage to share your faith—he would listen. He would give you his full attention. He would care. He would either give you exactly what you wanted or something even better. That's the power of having *our* Father in heaven.

Chased by the Shepherd

Jason Nelson

Sometimes it feels like we got away. It seems like we outmaneuvered God somehow or that circumstances we couldn't control put us out of reach of his protection and healing. Those are hard times. We can't pretend they're not hard times. We just can't see any relief at the end of the rainbow. We can't even see the rainbow. Then we realize our Shepherd is willing to be unconventional. Sometimes he lets the sheep go first. He chooses not to be out front in a pillar of blazing hope. Sometimes he catches up with us from behind. We learn this the hard way over a lifetime of faith. **"Even when the way goes through Death Valley . . . your beauty and love chase after me every day of my life"** (Psalm 23:4,6 MSG). Even when we want to look forward, and believe in looking forward, sometimes we can only go on by remembering God's past mercy to us.

The Lord is our Good Shepherd who gives us all those nice things we cherish: green pastures, quiet waters, overflowing cups. What makes him an absolutely Great Shepherd is that he relentlessly, without interruption, pursues us in his grace. His goodness and mercy are always following us; always closing in on us; always on the verge of overcoming our pain, heartache, loss, and grief. We know from past experience he will catch up. And we will dwell in the house of the Lord forever.

Who, me? Pessimistic?

Pastor Mark Jeske

A woman I know has the habit of giving people only one chance. If disappointed even once, she will drop the person from her life, including the modern-day form of excommunication: unfriending on Facebook. I wonder if people see that in me. Am I like that?

Being cynical and pessimistic has a certain logic, doesn't it? If you wall off your heart after one disappointment, you think you can't get hurt again. If you assume all people are jerks, you won't be surprised when they act like jerks. And since most people's words and actions can be interpreted in various ways, you can always ascribe negative motivation, that they're just using you.

What a lonely way to live! It's also a mind-set that could destroy a family. Relationships can't last without trust. Trust is earned, but trust also has to be given, and preferably given in advance. If every disappointment in a marriage destroyed all trust in one or both hearts, no marriage could last. St. Paul has wise words for us: Love **"always trusts, always hopes"** (1 Corinthians 13:7). It sure does. Now here's the question: Will you believe that that statement applies to you and choose to trust the people in your family? Always to assume the best explanation for their behaviors? To be willing to let go of yesterday's frustrations in the hope that tomorrow will be better?

When you trust and hope, you release trust and hope in others' hearts.

The fruit of self-control

Pastor Mike Novotny

I know better than to take a pint of ice cream to the couch. I know I shouldn't hold it in my hands until the edges get all melty. I know I shouldn't go digging for those chocolate-covered cow tracks like they are buried treasure. I know I shouldn't, but I still do. I lack self-control.

So where do we get the self-control we need to say no to temptation? When we could eat this or say that or dwell on this or sin like that, where can we find the power to say yes to God and no to sin?

The answer is found in Galatians 5—**"The fruit of the Spirit . . . is self-control"** (verses 22,23). Self-control is a *fruit*. It's grown. It doesn't just appear in our hearts. It's grown from a root. And that root is . . . Jesus. In the next verse, Paul says that you **"belong to Christ Jesus"** (verse 24). You belong to Jesus. You are his child. And he adores you.

That truth is powerful enough to produce a new spiritual power in you. When you realize that you belong to Jesus—loved by the Father, accepted into heaven, invited to the feast, chosen for the kingdom, valued in the mission, and filled with the Spirit—you find a deep sense of satisfaction and joy. A contentment so deep that sin starts to lose its grip.

Self-control is, admittedly, hard to grow. But the soil of God's love in Christ is rich enough to produce all the self-control you need.

february

He has given us this command:
Anyone who loves God must also
love their brother and sister.

1 John 4:21

Adulting is hard
Diana Kerr

I love that the verb *adulting* is now officially in multiple reputable dictionaries. I know you're curious about the definition, so here's Oxford's: "The practice of behaving in a way characteristic of a responsible adult, especially the accomplishment of mundane but necessary tasks."

In case you're not familiar with this word, adulting is not generally viewed as a positive thing. "Adulting is hard" is a common sentiment I hear (and sometimes feel myself).

What's tough about adult life is that a lot of the burden rests on you. Being a grown-up requires a lot of work, and it can feel a little lonely. When your whole family's got the flu, who's there to take care of *you*, the mom? When your business is in crisis but you're the boss, who's there to give *you* a pep talk? How do you grieve a death when the person who typically comforts you is the one in the coffin? It's easy to lose heart or even your faith.

I know you know that you're not carrying the load yourself, but I want to remind you. Jesus is tending to you—your spiritual life and your earthly life—with more care and compassion than you can imagine. Isaiah 40:11 says, **"He tends his flock like a shepherd: He gathers the lambs in his arms and carries them close to his heart; he gently leads those that have young."** (I love how those last few words encourage me as a mom of a toddler!) Adulting isn't easy, but a powerful, loving God is carrying me.

Love your God
Pastor Mark Jeske

A million songs and a million poems and a million stories have been written about the meaning of love. You may have your own personal definition. Your friends might say that love involves feelings of admiration, need, intimacy, and appreciation. The Bible teaches us that a higher form of love for one another involves commitment and a desire to serve—spending ourselves to make someone else's life better.

The Bible also invites, even commands, us to love God. How can we not? We wouldn't exist without his creative word. We would be doomed and damned without Christ. And we wouldn't even be believers in the first place without the patient work of the Spirit to regenerate us. All this our God did because he loves us personally. Individually. How can we not love him back?

The Bible shows us how to put that God-love into action: **"Everyone who believes that Jesus is the Christ is born of God, and everyone who loves the father loves his child as well. This is how we know that we love the children of God: by loving God and carrying out his commands. In fact, this is love for God: to keep his commands. And his commands are not burdensome, for everyone born of God overcomes the world"** (1 John 5:1-4).

Here's how you know when you are approaching that wonderful mind-set—when your prayers start to include the phrase, "Lord, it's not so much what I want. What matters is what you want."

Ask a woman how it feels

Pastor Mike Novotny

I had no clue what it was like to be a woman until I asked some women. In my research for an upcoming sermon, I asked over a dozen sisters in the faith, "What is it like to be a woman in church?"

The answers floored me. A few women shared stories of incredible men who empowered them, listened to them, and valued them. Too many others, however, wrote pages and pages (and pages) about the men who ignored them, belittled them, and treated them as second-class Christians. Their answers were not a cry to throw out those passages about the unique callings God has given, for example, to husbands and wives (Ephesians 5:22-33). Rather, they were a cry for women to be included. To be consulted. To be loved.

Those emails reminded me of some incredible wisdom from Jesus' brother James: **"Everyone should be quick to listen"** (1:19). It is so easy to assume we understand another person or group's situation, which is why James encourages us to assume that we don't. Instead, ask questions, listen well, and learn from what you hear.

There are people whose lives you do not understand. It might be the man you married. Or your smartphone-clutching grandkids. Or the neighbors whose skin color is different from yours. Perhaps you could do some research this week and ask them what their lives are like. Be quick to listen, and God will fill you with wisdom.

Love your country

Pastor Mark Jeske

It might be my imagination, but it sure seems to me that our country is getting more polarized every year. Politically, of course—election seasons seem to get nastier each cycle—but also socially, economically, racially, and across gender lines. Angry demonstrators call themselves "the Resistance." Football players and even cheerleaders and band members kneel during the national anthem to show how disgusted they are with their country.

There will always be a gap between the high ideals on which our country was founded and the actual reality of day-to-day life, but that doesn't justify contempt for our elected officials. Obedience to the law shouldn't be conditional on whether or not we like the political party that's running Congress.

Christ and the apostles lived in a political system that was far less free than ours, and they modeled for us the Christian way of civic life: **"Show proper respect to everyone . . . fear God, honor the emperor"** (1 Peter 2:17). The land of Israel, small and weak at their time, had not been a truly independent country for centuries, but God's church flourished anyway. The Roman Empire, though often violent and corrupt, provided some significant opportunities for the church to grow. Flawed government is better than chaos.

Think of how many Christians today live in countries far more oppressive than ours, and yet God is not calling the believers there to start political revolutions. Since we are citizens of an eternal kingdom in heaven, we don't have to try to get it all now.

What most married people forget
Pastor Mike Novotny

Do you know the difference between most dating couples and many married people? In a word—*effort*. When we date someone, we usually put in the effort. We shave our faces and our legs. We find the most flattering outfit and spritz some extra cologne on our necks. But give it a few years and a couple of kids, and a husband or wife might not even put in the effort to close the door before using the bathroom!

It's good for couples to remember the power of effort, which is what led them to the altar in the first place. This is the law of the harvest that Paul mentions to the Galatians: **"A man reaps what he sows"** (6:7). It's true in marriage and also true with God. Live for yourself and you will reap an eternity without God. Live for God, in repentance and faith, and you will reap eternal life thanks to the sacrifice of Jesus.

Which is one more reason why I love Jesus. Because Jesus always put in the effort. In his desire to unite you to God, he never took a day off. He never kicked up his feet, lived for himself, and gave into sin. Instead, his life was one of constant trying, ceaseless seeking, perfect love. Meditate for two minutes what that meant practically for Jesus. With every thought, every conversation, every person, and every choice, Jesus was sowing seeds that would grow into something beautiful—your perfect relationship with the Father.

Satan the rock climber

Diana Kerr

Ever been rock climbing? I scaled one of those fake rock walls once as a kid on a family vacation, so I'm about a 2 on a scale of 1 to 10 for my rock climbing expertise. But I do know this about rock climbing: You need footholds as you climb so you can push yourself off of them and move upward.

That rock climbing memory came to mind recently when I read Ephesians 4:27: **"Do not give the devil a foothold."** This section of Scripture talks a lot about anger and our words. And I suddenly pictured my sin giving the devil something to climb on to get closer to me. Every time I gossip, snap at someone, give someone the silent treatment, or hang onto resentment, I'm giving the devil opportunity. I provide footholds for him to scale the wall up to me and take over my heart, words, and actions.

These sins don't always seem serious, but the devil's an opportunist. He'll gladly take the small footholds we give him here and there and make the most of them for his own gain. If you're not convinced he's that dangerous, check the Bible for the countless stories where we see people's sin start with something seemingly harmless and spiral out of control.

Here's one way we can keep the devil away from us and others: **"Be kind and compassionate to one another, forgiving each other, just as in Christ God forgave you"** (Ephesians 4:32).

Teachers from hell
Pastor Mark Jeske

The digital revolution has brought enormous good to our world, but like every technological advance, it's brought bad things too. We can get news from around the world instantly, right as things are happening, with pictures, video, and comments, but we know that our devices are also awash in fake news. We can't always tell which is which. Just because information is on Twitter or YouTube or Facebook doesn't make it true.

Satan knows that the battlefield on which he hopes to win control of the human race is in our minds. And so he puts considerable thought and energy into spreading fake news about God. It's not a physical battle, with physical weapons against an enemy you can see. It is spiritual warfare. Satan's demon agents work just like spies, spreading disinformation: **"The Spirit clearly says that in later times some will abandon the faith and follow deceiving spirits and things taught by demons"** (1 Timothy 4:1). Teachers from hell!

How can mere mortals like you and me ever know the truth? How can we resist Satan himself? Realize that not every religious organization can be trusted—some are peddling a fake gospel. We have only one source of absolutely reliable information, and that is Holy Scripture. The Bible is *able* to make you wise for salvation. Hold onto it with a death grip! Read it! Listen to it! Believe it!

When you do, you will send the demons howling back to hell.

Manna must be fresh

Jason Nelson

"I will rain down bread from heaven for you. The people are to go out each day and gather enough for that day" (Exodus 16:4). The curious bread God dropped on his people to sustain them was gathered and eaten fresh every day. Only before the Sabbath could they tell the servers, "I'm gonna need a box for my leftovers." Otherwise, they couldn't take any home to warm up on a hot rock the next day because it would be way past its expiration date. God was making a point: "I will give you what you need today, and I will give you what you need again tomorrow. This is how relying on me works." He made that belief a habit by insisting that his people gather and consume this special bread every day.

The Bible is filled with promises of bread. There's bread for our physical well-being and bread for our spiritual security. We can read, mark, learn, and inwardly digest something fresh from God every day. We keep it fresh when we gather with our families or our Bible study groups and ask, "Where do we feel emptiness gnawing at us today?" Then we open our Bibles and find something that lifts our spirits and fills us with hope and encouragement. Jesus said, **"I am the bread of life"** (John 6:35). Brother, Sister, keep it fresh. **"For the bread of God is the bread that comes down from heaven and gives life to the world"** (John 6:33).

The tale of two women
Pastor Mike Novotny

"Pastor, I just need a little break," the college student told me. After two decades of going to church, she felt spiritually prepared to make church an occasional stop instead of a weekly habit. After all, she knew the stories, the lessons, and the big ideas of her sin and Jesus' salvation.

Contrast that with the 91-year-old woman I visited the other day. When I stepped into Jeanette's room at the nursing home, I saw the brightly colored Grace Moments book next to her bed, which she reads daily. Jeanette told me of her desire to get back to church and of her mission work to the nursing home staff (many of whom showed up for worship even before Jeanette was able to return!).

Jeanette reminds me of Jesus. At 12 years old, Jesus was in the temple, digging into the Word of God. At 30 years old, Jesus was at the temple, celebrating God's love at the Passover feast. At 33, Jesus went to the temple to become the perfect Passover Lamb and take away our sins. In other words, Jesus never took a break. Instead, like Jeanette, he sought God each day. He felt the temptation that college student was facing yet did not give in to it. **"We do not have a high priest who is unable to empathize with our weaknesses, but we have one who has been tempted in every way, just as we are—yet he did not sin"** (Hebrews 4:15). Thank God for Jesus!

You can learn to be content
Pastor Mark Jeske

Literature is full of stories that offer explanations of why things happen. Shakespeare presented Romeo and Juliet as star-crossed lovers, i.e., their deaths were driven by the "unlucky" positions of various heavenly bodies. The Greeks believed in three Fates, powerful women who controlled all human lives; the Romans believed in Fortuna, the goddess of luck. People talk about kismet and destiny, but these are just feeble attempts to explain away the actual twin drivers of our experiences: God's working and our own choices.

How you feel about your life is not out of your hands. Your life attitude is your choice! St. Paul discovered the secret to daily joy in living: **"I have learned to be content whatever the circumstances. I know what it is to be in need, and I know what it is to have plenty. I have learned the secret of being content in any and every situation, whether well fed or hungry, whether living in plenty or in want. I can do all this through him who gives me strength"** (Philippians 4:11-13).

Through the insights provided by Scripture, we can see that we actually deserve nothing, that all we have is a gift from God to bless us and give us a role in his agenda. We can banish envy and actually enjoy other people's prosperity. We can be proud of what we've accomplished and let go of our guilt at where we've failed.

We can enjoy each day, knowing that we are loved, forgiven, and immortal.

Why Ruth should be your favorite book of the Bible

Pastor Mike Novotny

I dare you to read Judges chapters 19-21. Go ahead; I'll wait. . . . Did you read it? Tell me that isn't the most messed up thing you've ever read in Scripture. A rape-loving city. A calloused man who hacks up his former lover into pieces. Kidnapping worshipers on the way to church. Seriously . . . that's messed up.

Which is why Ruth should be your favorite book of the Bible. Despite the absolute horror of those pages, the Bible goes on. Instead of ending the human experiment after Judges, God keeps working. The fact that there's a Ruth is proof that God is way more forgiving than we first believed. **"In the days when the judges ruled, there was a famine in the land"** (Ruth 1:1) should be words that make you stand up and cheer.

Because Ruth's sheer existence means your mess won't stop your Savior. God is so patient, so merciful, so forgiving that there is another page to your story. Maybe you've been trying to do things your way. Maybe you've justified your sharp, critical tongue and excused your meanness for decades. But it's not too late. You can cry out to Jesus. You can find forgiveness in his death and resurrection. You might assume God can't clean up your mess, but the broom of the cross is as wide as the grace of God is deep.

You are not beyond saving. Ruth is the proof.

It's great to be Jewish
Pastor Mark Jeske

Jewish people have suffered from anti-Semitism for thousands of years. Satan must have a bitter and permanent grudge against the nation that gave the world the Savior, the Champion who crushed his demonic serpent head. The world owes Jewish people an enormous debt of gratitude in that Jesus Christ was born a Jew, just as the Scriptures said he would be.

Christians have even more reason to appreciate Jewish people: **"What advantage, then, is there in being a Jew, or what value is there in circumcision? Much in every way! First of all, they have been entrusted with the very words of God"** (Romans 3:1,2). Almost every word of the Bible was written by a Jewish person, both Old and New Testaments. They alone were the guardians of the Word of God when the rest of the world had sunk into heathenism or no religion at all. In spite of their own spiritual ups and downs, the Israelites always had a faithful core that kept the faith and preserved the hope and promises of the gospel.

Almost everyone in the first generation of New Testament Christians was Jewish—they were the first evangelists and teachers. In Romans chapter 11, St. Paul calls them a sturdy olive tree trunk and root system that now support and nourish Gentile branches grafted on.

The children of Abraham deserve our appreciation and respect.

Standing invitations
Jason Nelson

When voices of influence contradict each other and you don't know whom to trust, you have a standing invitation from God: **"Come, my children, listen to me; I will teach you the fear of the Lord"** (Psalm 34:11).

When you feel like an orphan because no one resembles you in your values and you can't relate to the way other people approach life, you have a standing invitation to be part of God's family: **"Come, descendants of Jacob, let us walk in the light of the Lord"** (Isaiah 2:5).

When God gets tough with you because he doesn't want to lose you and you push him away out of sheer frustration, you have a standing invitation to embrace him again: **"Come, let us return to the Lord. He has torn us to pieces but he will heal us; he has injured us but he will bind up our wounds"** (Hosea 6:1).

When you think all roads lead nowhere because you've already taken them there, you have a standing invitation from God to find a new direction for your life: **"'Come, follow me,' Jesus said"** (Matthew 4:19).

When it seems like it will all end badly and there's nothing to look forward to, you have a standing invitation to the big reunion of the saints: **"Come, gather together for the great supper of God"** (Revelation 19:17).

There is etiquette for responding to God's gracious invitations. Simply say, *"O Lamb of God, I come. I come."*

Love is both roses and thorns

Pastor Daron Lindemann

If disciplining children is hard and at times hurts you more than it hurts them, it's love. If discussing your friend's bad behavior makes you uncomfortable but you do it anyway, it's love. If you volunteer and stick with it even when it becomes a hassle, it's love. If you make your pet peeve your own problem instead of everyone else's problem, it's love.

Love is not defined by how good it feels. Love's roses have thorns. **"This is love: that we walk in obedience to his commands"** (2 John 1:6).

God's commands can expect more than we want to give. These are the thorns of love, and we bristle as they touch our hearts. We feel pain; we flinch and step back. But God says, "Come near." We resist. We avoid. We turn away from those who need our love.

Think of this. God the Father said the same thing to his Son, Jesus. "Come near the thorns. They are thorns of love, my Son." And he did. They pierced him. The crown of thorns. The cross' nails. The stinging mockery and the piercing guilt of our sins.

"Come near," Jesus now says. "This is love. I died for it. I live for it. It's yours."

Believe that, and you'll learn what true love really is—outside of yourself, your heart, your feelings, and your own definition.

When God waits for you
Pastor Daron Lindemann

I grew up with a loving father who provided for me. Sometimes, though, he'd ask me to work for something.

For example, he gave me a lawn-mowing job in high school. He paid me to take care of the lawn at his office building. He wasn't going to do that work. That was my job, not his.

What in your life are you waiting for God to change? How much of it is your responsibility?

Sometimes we see the work that God has called us to do as something we want God to do. But there are things in your life that God isn't going to do for you. He wants you to do them. In Exodus 32:7 God told Moses, **"Go down, because your people, whom you brought up out of Egypt, have become corrupt."** God had something for Moses to do.

My dad also loaned me his shiny, blue Oldsmobile when I was in high school to take out my girlfriend (now my wife) on our first date. It was my job to put gas in it, clean it, and treat it well. But it wasn't my car; I didn't provide for the insurance or make car payments.

So even when you're at work doing what's yours to do, God's blessings are in it and on it.

Thank you, God, for valuing our contributions to this world and for calling us to work, but never leaving us alone!

Sounds like a prayer to me

Jason Nelson

Lord, I don't even know where to begin. I'm not sure how it all started or how to pick up the pieces of my messed-up life. I'm too tired to think, too stumped to put it into words.

Child, that sounds like a prayer to me. I hear it with my Spirit. I will do immeasurably more than you ask or imagine.

Lord, I want to come to you, but when I get on my knees, I should at least be able to start a conversation and offer you some suggestions for getting me out of this situation. That's how I did it last time. But I'm coming up empty. That's what I am—empty.

Child, that sounds like a prayer to me. I hear it with my Spirit. I will do immeasurably more than you ask or imagine.

Lord, maybe if I could cry or scream I would let off some steam and you would understand my frustration. That could be a starting point. You could take it from there. But all I have for you are these pathetic sighs.

Child, that sounds like a prayer to me. I hear it with my Spirit. I will do immeasurably more than you ask or imagine. This is how I know.

"The Spirit helps us in our weakness. For we do not know what to pray for as we ought, but the Spirit himself intercedes for us with groanings too deep for words" (Romans 8:26 ESV).

God-given tension
Pastor Mike Novotny

I rewrote my sermon six times. I was attempting to write a sermon about Deborah from Judges chapter 4, and the tension was tearing me apart. The tension between Deborah's leadership as a woman and her own desire to see men like Barak step up and lead (Judges 5:2).

After six tries and a few mentally agonizing days, however, a light bulb went on. The tension that I felt was . . . God-given. God came up with all the verses that made me feel so tense. God gifted Deborah with her passion and personality. AND God inspired those tough-to-apply verses about men in ministry. And, if there's one thing I've come to know about God, it's that he can be trusted in everything. **"Trust in the Lord with all your heart and lean not on your own understanding"** (Proverbs 3:5).

Maybe you've felt a similar tension with some teaching in the Bible. The tension between celebrating all Christians, no matter what their church or denomination, versus treasuring and defending every teaching in God's Word. The tension between honoring all those in authority versus calling out acts of injustice committed by the authorities. The tension between leveraging all of your gifts versus submitting to those whom God has called to lead you (even if they don't seem that gifted!).

In that tension, remember that all those Bible passages have a common source—God. The God who sent his only Son to remind us all that he is worthy of our trust.

Don't ever say, "just a layperson"

Pastor Mark Jeske

No Christians want weak pastors at their congregations. Church members want a pastor who is a good speaker; a hard worker; a good manager; and someone who is kind, attentive, honest, and competent. But our desire for building a culture that produces strong pastors should not result in a culture of weak laypeople. The church's vital mission needs strong lay leaders as much as it needs strong pastors.

God considers all believers to be his royal priests (see 1 Peter 2:9). But that's not just an honorific title. He is serious enough about putting you to work that his Spirit has generously distributed important personal gifts among the laity to serve the body of Christ and the world as his followers and leaders. **"I myself am convinced, my brothers and sisters, that you yourselves are full of goodness, filled with knowledge and competent to instruct one another"** (Romans 15:14).

Did you catch that? St. Paul wanted the lay Christians in the congregation in Rome to feel that he trusted their hearts and motives, that though always learning they still knew enough to get moving, and that they already had enough talent to be allowed to teach one another. Your pastors are not your bosses and overlords. They are your trainers and encouragers to help you develop your personal ministry for the Lord Jesus.

Don't ever say, "I am just a layperson."

A reminder of eternal importance
Diana Kerr

Ever seen someone struggling and helped them out? An elderly neighbor shoveling snow? A kid trying to sell cookies for a fundraiser? If you're a compassionate person, it's easy to see needs all around you.

Keep your eyes open for people's spiritual needs too. Every time I read Luke 13:24,25, I'm reminded there are people—even people I know and love—who won't be in heaven. Jesus said, **"Make every effort to enter through the narrow door, because many, I tell you, will try to enter and will not be able to. Once the owner of the house gets up and closes the door, you will stand outside knocking and pleading, 'Sir, open the door for us.' But he will answer, 'I don't know you or where you come from.'"**

Please keep tending to people's earthly needs, but tend to spiritual needs too. The news that people you love may not experience eternity with God should break your heart and spur you to action. You have the gift of eternal life; you know how incredible Jesus is. Not everyone else does. I know life is busy, I know it's hard to talk about your faith, I know that the Holy Spirit has to do his work and it's not all on you, but don't let these things get in the way. Paul's task is the same as yours: **"My only aim is to finish the race and complete the task the Lord Jesus has given me—the task of testifying to the good news of God's grace"** (Acts 20:24).

Friends confess
Pastor Mike Novotny

Most people are terrified to confess their sins to me. I guess that's the nature of sin—it prefers to hide in the dark rather than be dragged into the light. But what I wish everyone knew was the fact that I like people *better* when I hear how messed up they are! If they wouldn't be avoiding eye contact, they would see me nodding and smiling and saying, "Me too!"

Psychologist Debra Oswald believes the best way to start and deepen a friendship is through confession. Perhaps that's one of many reasons why James commands us, **"Confess your sins to each other"** (James 5:16). While we certainly can (and should!) confess our sins directly to God, there is relational power in opening up to a fellow Christian. Often that moment of vulnerability turns two people from fellow Christians into Christian friends.

Do you have relationships where you're that honest? Do you have a small, trusted group of friends who know the real you, the you who is insecure despite the college degree, overwhelmed despite the smiling profile pic, and worried despite the suburban lifestyle? Most important, do you have others who remind you of Jesus' forgiveness when you confess the real struggles of your life?

Today I am encouraging you to be real with others. Even more, I am asking God to bless you with friends who do more than give good advice but instead give the good news of God's love for real people like you.

Love your congregation

Pastor Mark Jeske

I've become a total perfectionist when it comes to dining out. There are so many entertainment choices these days that if a restaurant disappoints me with mediocre food, service, or ambience, I don't ever have to go back. One bad experience and I'm gone.

What if the evil one prompts me to view congregations like restaurants? If he can't keep me from going to church, at least he can ruin my enjoyment, keep my heart judgmental and proud, and whisper criticisms for all the shortcomings of the people, pastor, pews, parking, musicians, and even the restrooms.

Or is it just me? What's the talk like as you and your family drive home after a service? Is it open season on the previous hour? You know, if you look for disappointments, you will always find them. The worship leaders are as flawed and broken as you are. Here's a choice you can make: **"Love the family of believers"** (1 Peter 2:17). Perhaps God sent you to church that day not so much for your consumption but to be in a position to help somebody else.

How about a different conversation after the service: ask your friends and family what they loved . . . what built up their faith . . . a pleasant surprise . . . a story about a fellow worshiper . . . someone to pray for . . . happy memories from one of the hymns. The more you invest of yourself, the more you will get out of your fellowship.

If you listen for a spiritual insight, even just one, God will always provide one that you need.

Your God is beautifully complex
Diana Kerr

It's hard to surrender to the paradoxes in the Bible. Sometimes it frustrates me when things seem contradictory. Lately, I've been trying harder to embrace or even celebrate that tension.

The nature of God is one of those things that can seem paradoxical to me. You too? God is fierce and meek, harsh and gentle, just and merciful, mighty and humble.

Even though it's hard to wrap my mind around sometimes, I want a God who is all the things his Word says he is. I want that God who's so powerful he makes superheroes look pathetic *and* the God who's tenderhearted. I want the God who both disciplines me *and* loves me as his daughter.

In the Bible, the way Job's friend Eliphaz talked about God is incredible. He got it. Read Job chapter 5 and see how Eliphaz talked about God's miracles, his dominion over the world, the way he lovingly rescues the needy, the way he deals severely with bad guys . . . Eliphaz understood the complexity of God. **"He wounds, but he also binds up; he injures, but his hands also heal"** (Job 5:18).

Eliphaz encouraged Job, in the midst of Job's terrible suffering, to appeal to God. Why? Not because of one individual characteristic of God, but because God is a beautifully complex God—powerful, just, loving, and merciful. That's the same God who's on your side too. Embrace the full gamut of his amazing attributes. Your God is for you.

The first rule of holes

Jason Nelson

"Whoever digs a hole and scoops it out falls into the pit they have made" (Psalm 7:15). Stubbornness is one of our failings. We dress it up and call it stick-to-itiveness. We dig in as individuals and groups and rely on fallacies to explain why we don't stop self-defeating behavior. That's the stink smoldering out of the ashes of history. It is difficult to let go of story lines that put us deep in holes. The nagging voices in our heads and the chorus of those in the hole with us reinforce the narrative we have been operating with. We might even decorate our hole with artifacts commemorating the time-honored way we "dig." Our creed is, "This is who we are. This is how we do it. This hole is our brand." Endeavors fail because operators at the helm just can't see their way clear to reverse course. But eventually it becomes self-evident. "Hey, we are in a hole here. We need to stop digging."

The first rule of holes is stop digging. That takes an unfamiliar kind of determination. But it initiates renewal, including the one we need way down deep in our souls. When we recognize we're in over our heads, we're ready to drop the shovel and wash our hands of it. It's very straightforward. We don't need to redesign the shovel. We don't need to develop better digging techniques. We need God's power and grace to stop doing things that are not working.

The second rule of holes

Jason Nelson

The Spirit of God gives us the energy to get out of the holes we're in. Each message of perseverance in the Bible is an inspired variation of the second rule of holes. To get out of a hole, keep climbing. Warren Wiersbe said, "The bumps are what you climb on." **"Anyone who meets a testing challenge head-on and manages to stick it out is mighty fortunate. For such persons . . . the reward is life and more life"** (James 1:12 MSG).

A better life is the light at the top of the hole. Don't stay in a hole out of misguided conviction. There's only one direction to go—up. Getting out of a hole demands we lift our eyes from where they are focused—down. I can tell you what to expect. There will be stress. There will be strain. There will be letting go of some things you like. There will be opposition from others who want you to stay in the hole with them. There will be stumbles and falls when toeholds give way. It's rare to get out of a hole on the first try. But to get out of a hole keep climbing. Climb to daylight. Extend one hand of faith and then the other and lift yourself out of it. And then raise both hands to heaven. **"God has delivered me from going down to the pit, and I shall live to enjoy the light of life"** (Job 33:28).

Willing to wait for it?

Pastor Mike Novotny

Have you ever heard of the Stanford "marshmallow test"? A Stanford professor once offered kids a choice—They could eat a marshmallow now, or if they could wait, the kids would get two marshmallows later. Want to guess what happened? Most of the kids *tried* to wait. They covered their eyes. They tugged on their pigtails. One kid even petted the marshmallow like it was a stuffed animal! In the end, only one out of every three kids had the self-control to wait for the reward.

Life is just a bigger version of that experiment, isn't it? Satan offers us something sweet (like giving someone a piece of our mind or driving to the mall again despite 0 percent of our budget helping the poor), and we have to decide whether to wait for God's greater blessing or give in to the marshmallow of temptation.

This is where I'm amazed at Jesus. Starving in the desert, the deceiver used one of his oldest tricks, a promise of right-here, right-now pleasure. But Jesus replied, **"Away from me, Satan! For it is written: 'Worship the Lord your God, and serve him only'"** (Matthew 4:10). Jesus' willingness to wait was not just a good example for you to follow. It is your hope. Your salvation. Your perfection, to be later given to you at the cross.

I hope you are excited enough about future blessings to wait when you face today's temptation. But, no matter what you do, I know what Jesus did. He waited for the blessing of God. And that's good news for us all.

What's fellowship?
Pastor Mark Jeske

Every business has its own jargon, i.e., insider talk that makes total sense to the old guard and is confusing and embarrassing to the newbies. In the financial services industry, for instance, advisors might say, "I recommend a VA for long term and VUL for right-now coverage." But that wouldn't be a smart move if your client doesn't know what you're talking about.

There is a unique jargon found as well among gatherings of Christians. One unique word is *fellowship*, especially used as a verb, as in "We had a wonderful time fellowshiping yesterday." To which a new Christian might have responded, "Just exactly what were you people doing yesterday?"

Used as a noun, *fellowship* refers to the bond that believers have with each other and have with God. **"If you have any encouragement from being united with Christ, if any comfort from his love, if any common sharing in the Spirit, if any tenderness and compassion, then make my joy complete by being like-minded, having the same love, being one in spirit and of one mind. Do nothing out of selfish ambition or vain conceit. Rather, in humility value others above yourselves, not looking to your own interests but each of you to the interests of the others"** (Philippians 2:1-4).

Fellowship implies love, loyalty, service, respect, and appreciation, all proceeding from the common bond of faith in Christ. It is an absolute essential to any healthy congregation.

When the odds are against you

Pastor Mike Novotny

What are the odds that you'll resist temptation to-day? Um . . . yeah. We can quickly answer that question. Despite our willing spirits, our flesh is still weak. And the world is so persuasive. And the devil seems to know which bait works best with each of us. So we assume that sin will just happen.

But before we resign ourselves to spiritual failure, we should read Gideon's story. Facing a ruthless horde of 135,000 Midianites, God whittled down Israel's army to just 300 men. That's 1 Israelite to every 450 Midianites! But the presence of God has a way of messing with our math. **"When the three hundred trumpets sounded, the Lord caused the men throughout the** [Midianite] **camp to turn on each other with their swords. The army fled"** (Judges 7:22). Ha! Even the 300 Israelites stood around and watched God single-handedly take on the massive army of Midian.

How incredible that Israel's God is our God too. We might face 135,000 temptations today, but that same unstoppable God is with us. The Father is more pow-erful than the father of lies. The Son is stronger than your sinful nature. The Spirit is more persuasive than all your peers combined. The holy Trinity has a history of dominating the unholy three (the devil, the world, and our flesh).

So, fellow child of God, live with confidence today. You might sin, but you don't have to. You might be mightily tempted, but your God is mighty to save. With God, the odds are always in your favor.

Can children believe in Jesus?

Pastor Daron Lindemann

Do you know what kind of people really impress Jesus? Children. Little children. Even infants. They don't overanalyze. Their brains don't get in the way of the truth as much as adults' brains do.

"Truly I tell you, unless you change and become like little children, you will never enter the kingdom of heaven. Therefore, whoever takes the lowly position of this child is the greatest in the kingdom of heaven" (Matthew 18:3,4).

Jesus says that our adult thinking can get in the way of a fulfilling life connected to his kingdom, now and forever. He tells adults that we should stop complicating things and getting in our own way.

Be more like little children and toddlers. Humbly accept Jesus. Eagerly embrace Jesus. Quickly seek Jesus. Believe in Jesus with uncomplicated minds and underdeveloped egos.

Cognitive processing is related to faith, but it's not the same as faith. It can help faith. It can also hurt faith. What matters more than cognitive, conscious processing is believing. Awake or asleep. Adult or child. Baptism is the gift of God's saving grace that delivers such faith, even to infants.

This is why it's so good for adults to welcome infants—through Baptism—into a relationship with Jesus. In doing so, we welcome Jesus and his kingdom. And he approves: **"Whoever welcomes one such child in my name welcomes me"** (Matthew 18:5).

march

Christ Jesus who died—more than that,
who was raised to life—is at the right hand of God
and is also interceding for us.

Romans 8:34

Church jargon: Latin terms

Pastor Mark Jeske

If you want to study music, you have to learn some Italian. Can you say *adagio, andante, allegro*? If you want to be a ballet dancer, you need to learn some French to know how to say and execute a *pas de deux, plié,* and *brisé.* People all over the globe today need to learn a little English to be able to navigate the internet.

Most of the English-speaking world received its Christianity from Western Europe, where for a millennium and a half all worship services and most education was required to be conducted in Latin. And so it is not surprising that quite a bit of Latin terminology has persisted in church talk. Don't fight it. Learn it. It is efficient shorthand. The *Magnificat* is the song of Mary from Luke chapter 1. The *Agnus Dei* is a liturgical song just before Lord's Supper that echoes the gospel message of John the Baptist. The *Gloria in Excelsis Deo* is the song of the angels on Christmas Eve.

If the church is going to use its historic vocabulary, however, it needs to take seriously the need regularly to teach and explain so that its talk doesn't become frustrating jargon to newcomers. Those who know always need to bring more people into that knowledge. Like the evangelist Philip: The Ethiopian asked Philip, **"'Tell me, please, who is the prophet talking about, himself or someone else?' Then Philip began with that very passage of Scripture and told him the good news about Jesus"** (Acts 8:34,35).

Should you name your kid after a killer?

Pastor Mike Novotny

I normally wouldn't recommend naming your kid after the woman who murdered a man while he was sleeping. But when I met one of my wife's preschool students named Jael, I couldn't help but smile and think of the story.

"But Jael, Heber's wife, picked up a tent peg and a hammer and went quietly to [Sisera] **while he lay fast asleep, exhausted. She drove the peg through his temple into the ground, and he died"** (Judges 4:21). That verse isn't in any children's Bibles! Jael, that quiet tent-wife in northern Israel, seized her opportunity to put the murdering rapist named Sisera to death. Why would she do that? Because God directed the leaders of Israel to deliver the nation from Sisera, so Jael was doing God's will.

Where is the lesson for us? Perhaps that God saves in mysterious ways. He saved Israel from Sisera's cruel oppression through a tent peg. Just like he previously saved Israel from Pharaoh's cruel oppression through a Passover lamb and the salty waters of the Red Sea.

Just like he would later save you from sin's cruel oppression through a few "pegs" (nails) and a wooden cross. Your insecurity or pride or worry or spiritual forgetfulness might dominate you like Sisera dominated Israel, but God put those sins to death. He drove them into the cross, and that is where they will stay. Forever. So take a breath today. Your "Sisera" is dead. You are free to live with God's constant approval.

Thank God for Jael. Thank God even more for Jesus.

The Sunday school story

Jason Nelson

I can't remember her name, but I'll never forget what she taught me in that musty church basement. We started with Jesus stories and finished by memorizing the commandments. We said the first one over and over. The next week we said the first one again and then started on the second one. Turns out there were ten of them, and we learned them all.

The Sunday school story is an interesting chapter in Christian history. Sunday schools were started in England in the late-18th century by generous Christians. They wanted to provide education to poor children who were working in factories during the week. The kids and their families loved it. The idea spread to America, and nearly every denomination operated Sunday schools. When child labor was outlawed and public schools were established, Sunday schools limited their curriculum to religious studies. For over a century, going to Sunday school was a part of growing up for nearly every American child. Even parents who didn't go to church themselves took their kids to Sunday school until the 1960s when permissive parents let children decide for themselves if they wanted to go.

Sunday schools are still a great opportunity. There are still poor kids running around. Some of their families are new to America. They might like a place to go on Sunday morning that's warm and dry, where a kind lady could gather them in and give them some cookies and teach them something they will never forget.

My procrastination
Pastor Mark Jeske

I get a lot of laughs from "demotivation" posters—you know, the ones designed to look like inspirational office artwork but that instead have a subversive and ironic message. One of my favorites reads, "PROCRAS-TINATION—Hard work and discipline may pay off some-day, but laziness always pays off right now." Hahaha.

I laugh when I see that poster, but it's a nervous laugh. My insides know that I hate procrastination in myself. I know that putting off a job costs me a lot more energy in the long run, that I will feel depressed and guilty failing to meet deadlines, and that my excuses, while perhaps fooling others, fool neither God nor my own heart. I know that this is true: **"Sluggards do not plow in season, so at harvest time they look but find nothing"** (Proverbs 20:4).

How to break out of this rut? I find I have much better days when I start my morning with a devotion in the Word instead of putting it off till late. I do better when I ask God for help with my weaknesses.

Most of all, I do better when I stop the lying and self-justification and just tell the truth to God and myself. I really do love God, and it's refreshing and healthy to re-remember that I work for him in all I do.

Spiderwebs are flimsy and weak

Diana Kerr

I don't always get the picture language of the Bible. I'm not a farmer or a sailor or a soldier of ancient times. Often I don't fully appreciate Scripture's metaphors until I consult a commentary or really sit with the thought.

Here's something I *do* understand: Spiderwebs. I spent a lot of time as a kid playing outside and in basements, so I've encountered plenty of spiderwebs and cobwebs.

I'm sure spiders are proud of their webs, but to a human, they're flimsy and weak. We bat them away with minimal effort. No idiot would ever lean on a spider's web. I've never seen someone try to use a web as a hammock. That's ridiculous.

So Job 8:13-15 speaks right to me with a metaphor I (and I bet you too) can understand right away: **"Such is the destiny of all who forget God; so perishes the hope of the godless. What they trust in is fragile; what they rely on is a spider's web. They lean on the web, but it gives way; they cling to it, but it does not hold."**

I've been a Christian my whole life, but I've still forgotten God in a gazillion different moments. I've trusted him *at times*, but a lot of times I rely on stuff that's the equivalent of a spider's web. It always lets me down. God, give me the spiritual maturity to cling to you, my Rock, instead!

From dust to diamonds

Pastor Daron Lindemann

Did you know that one of the most cherished treasures in the world—a diamond—is nothing more than carbon dust that has been exposed to pressure? Transformed ashes.

In the good old days of black-and-white TV, long before Netflix, there was a TV series featuring Superman. In one episode, Superman clenches a lump of coal in his hand. He squeezes. He squeezes harder. Then there's smoke. And you guessed it. He opens his hand and the lump of coal is gone. Instead, there's a glistening diamond!

If you're glad right now for a superhero with such strength, then this will double your joy: In God's hand, the ashes of your repentance are not tossed away like dirty waste. He uses them. With some strength, some love, some pressure, the Lord God squeezes and shapes you. Transforms you.

"He raises the poor from the dust and lifts the needy from the ash heap; he seats them with princes and has them inherit a throne of honor" (1 Samuel 2:8).

Your destiny in God's saving grace is not the ash heap but a rich throne. Between the two is a humble faith that trusts while God squeezes. Sometimes hard. Sometimes there's smoke. In the end, God opens his hand and smiles at something so cherished that he's made. You.

The sum of our lives

Jason Nelson

I don't think I'm clinically depressed because I only feel sad in months that have an "r" in their names. I think it relates to the amount of light available at the curvature of the earth where I live, the amount of outdoor activity I can engage in, and the number of people available to keep me company. All of the above are in greater supply in the other months.

Sadness is a condition of our present outlook and not necessarily the antithesis of happiness. Happy people can have bouts of melancholy because they feel the difference between what they had and what they have. Low-level sadness is a fog that will lift. I don't think we can shop our way out of it or travel our way out of it, but I think we can meditate our way out of it by elevating our thoughts to the sum of our lives.

"As I lie on my bed, I remember you. Through the long hours of the night, I think about you. You have been my help. In the shadow of your wings, I sing joyfully. My soul clings to you. Your right hand supports me" (Psalm 63:6-8 GW).

Lord, when I add it all up, life is pretty good. My kids are okay, my grandkids are okay, and you are in the heavens. I have more than enough of everything. My life is full. Please help me feel that way. Thanks.

The biggest threat to your soul

Pastor Mike Novotny

Recently, a Christian blogger went public with a lifestyle that many Christians would consider a sin. In her post, she wrote, "What the world needs . . . is to watch one woman at a time live her truth without asking for permission or offering explanation. The most revolutionary thing a woman can do is not explain herself" (Heidi Stevens, "'Love Warrior's' Glennon Doyle Melton opens up about new love, Abby Wambach," *Chicago Tribune*, November 14, 2016).

Those words make me shiver. Because I see that same desire in the ugly part of my heart. I don't want to explain myself. I don't want to explain the time I "don't have" to help the homeless back on their feet. I don't want to back up with Bible passages how I react to people who are not nice to me.

And you? Do you openly invite others to hold you accountable to Jesus' standards? Do you test your motives by explaining your actions to others? Or do you push others away, assuming that your heart is an expert at knowing and living up to "your truth"?

When I read the book of Judges, I find that attitude across its pages. **"In those days Israel had no king; everyone did as they saw fit"** (Judges 21:25). Read Judges and you'll find out that the lack of authority does not lead to loving God and doing as he sees fit.

Can I challenge you today to ask a God-fearing, Bible-believing Christian to give you honest feedback about your faith? Because not explaining yourself is easy. But living under the authority of God's Word is the most revolutionary thing you can do.

Why God wants you to walk
Pastor Daron Lindemann

When my wife and I are riding our motorcycle, I like to go fast through the mountainous curves. That's a feel-good adrenaline rush. My wife, seated behind me, prefers to take in the scenery. It's hard for her to do that when she's holding on tightly as I lean the bike into a fast-paced curve. I try to remember this.

God knows it better than I. He told the Israelites that they should walk in the wilderness for 40 years. Why? Because this slower pace meant that they could discover some important things along the way. Things about God and themselves and faith and humility and God's faithfulness and love.

God worked it out so that Joseph and Mary had to walk to Bethlehem at the inconvenient last minute for Jesus' birth, then to Egypt, and then finally home to Nazareth. Jesus walked to Calvary carrying his own cross, and after he rose from the dead, he walked on the road to Emmaus with two disciples who would later exclaim, **"Were not our hearts burning within us while he** [Jesus] **talked with us on the road?"** (Luke 24:32).

Don't speed through life and miss it. Don't overload your schedule. Slow down. Walk more.

Be ready to discover something that's only discoverable before you get to the destination. It's not always about the fastest way from point A to point B. Sometimes, as we bikers like to say: the journey is the destination.

The glory all around you
Pastor Mike Novotny

"This is one of the best moments of my life." Those words ran through my head as I chased a baby sea turtle while snorkeling with my youngest daughter. Maya and I held hands and floated above one of God's many magnificent creatures until the speckled-shell turtle swam within arm's reach. My fingers grazed its back, and it dove to the seafloor for another mouthful of grassy lunch.

Wow! God is ridiculously good at his job, isn't he? The angels were right, **"The whole earth is full of** [God's] **glory"** (Isaiah 6:3). Notice the word *whole*. You don't have to chase a sea turtle to experience the glory of God. Lie down in your backyard and watch the clouds billow by, remembering that God sweeps away your sins in the same way (Isaiah 44:22). Grab a coffee and watch the birds eat breakfast at your feeder, thinking of how much God loves creatures that he didn't die for, which means he must love you infinitely more (Matthew 6). Watch your daughter's expression as she explores the world, recalling that you are not just a servant but a child of God (1 John 3).

In a million ways every day, God is revealing his power, his kindness, his wisdom, his love, and his character. Take a moment today to be mindful of his glory. And thank Jesus that his glorious death and resurrection made that wonderful God your Father.

Good leaders delegate

Pastor Mark Jeske

It's terrible to have a leader who doesn't do anything. But the reverse is worse—a leader who won't let go of anything. Why do people act like that? Maybe they have a control obsession. Maybe they're insecure and need huge amounts of attention. Maybe they can't trust anybody else. Maybe they think no one else can do it as well as they can. Maybe they are terrified that another person will do it better, that—gasp!—they aren't needed anymore.

Those leadership weaknesses hurt the larger group. They can stall the group's growth and development. They cheat other people out of the chance to develop their own skills. You know, congregations are human organizations too, and they are not immune to the disease of bad leadership.

Good leaders delegate. They respect and expect and inspect. They share, praise, and rebuke, just as Moses learned over three millennia ago: **"How can I bear your problems and your burdens and your disputes all by myself? Choose some wise, understanding and respected men from each of your tribes, and I will set them over you"** (Deuteronomy 1:12,13).

Is it your blessing to serve with a good leader? Have you ever taken the time to thank and encourage him or her?

Are you a leader? Do you find joy in lifting up other people to do jobs you used to do? Do you feed off the rush of being in charge, or have you cultivated the skill of making other people feel important?

The apple can fall far
Pastor Mike Novotny

Are you ever shocked that Jesus was Jewish? If that doesn't blow your mind, you haven't read the story of the Jewish people. It's the story of Abraham, the father of the Jews, who pimped out his wife. The story of Isaac, the dad who made his family dysfunctional by playing favorites with his kids. The story of Jacob, who repeated Isaac's error and made ten of his sons hate their brother Joseph. And yet Jesus came from that family!

Perhaps you come from a family as dysfunctional as Jesus'. Perhaps your parents divorced bitterly when you were seven. Perhaps Dad drank too much and Mom was a controlling woman. Perhaps your family never cared much for church or, if they did, never put the command to love one another into practice during the week.

But, as one author has put it, God can write straight with crooked pencils. Your Father can do wonderful things through people of imperfect pedigree. The author to the Hebrews says, **"Both the one who makes people holy and those who are made holy are of the same family. So Jesus is not ashamed to call them brothers and sisters"** (Hebrews 2:11).

Jesus is not ashamed of you, no matter what your dad was like. He makes you holy and calls you to a life of loving others, no matter what reputation your parents had in town. You are not just a child of your earthly family. You are a son or daughter of the King of kings, Jesus Christ! So live proudly as part of his royal family today!

Pattern recognition
Jason Nelson

I'm looking forward to the changing of the guard. I'm hoping that young people who aren't jaded by tribalism will go into church work and public service. So many churches and levels of government are behind the curve because religion and politics have been so divisive. The demands of party loyalty and denominational identity have fractured the ideals of one holy Christian church and one nation under God. The millennial generation has been turned off to both because they see the same old patterns in each.

Millennials are into pattern recognition. That's how Amazon knows what they might order next. They count blessings with big numbers, like stars in the sky and the limitlessness of the universe. Because they are seekers, they find things, like patterns in massive pools of health data that help them envision never-thought-of treatments for diseases. They chart progress on a global scale in causes like increased life expectancy, improved literacy, and reduced infant mortality. They share those values with tens of millions in their own generation around the world because they are interconnected like never before.

I pray they will seek God and accept his invitation. **"'Come on now, let's discuss this!' says the Lord. 'Though your sins are bright red, they will become as white as snow. Though they are dark red, they will become as white as wool'"** (Isaiah 1:18 GW). I pray they will not give up on church and state because the past is forgiven. I pray they will develop new patterns for both.

Where do I go with my loneliness?

Pastor Mark Jeske

Just because there are people all around you doesn't mean that you aren't lonely. In fact, one of the delusions that you might suffer from is to assume that everybody around you has it all together, has tons of friends, is financially secure, has a great family, and is really happy. You are the odd man or odd woman out. You can't trust anybody because you've been hurt before. Nobody likes you for who you are; nobody understands you.

Those things are almost certainly not true, but they seem very real. And in the showdown between your feelings and the logical part of your brain, feelings always win. Where do you go with your loneliness?

Go to your Father. He will hear your troubles without scorn or judgment. He will speak to you, if you let him, about his unconditional love and acceptance of you and about his free and full forgiveness of your sins. His fatherly heart hurts when you hurt, and he will hear and act on your prayers. Your Savior Jesus experienced a terribly lonely walk to the cross, and he can feel what you feel.

Here is his promise: **"God sets the lonely in families"** (Psalm 68:6). In his own way, at his own time, God will give you people in your life who will accept and love you, people with whom you can talk and serve and love.

Watch for them. They are God's answer to your prayers.

Mercy for sinners; judgment for scoffers

Pastor Mark Jeske

The biblical book of 2 Chronicles is the account of the monarchy of the kingdom of Israel and, after the division, the southern kingdom of Judah. Its final chapter summarizes the sad end to what had begun so brilliantly with King David and Solomon: **"The Lord, the God of their ancestors, sent word to them through his messengers again and again, because he had pity on his people and on his dwelling place. But they mocked God's messengers, despised his words and scoffed at his prophets until the wrath of the Lord was aroused against his people and there was no remedy"** (2 Chronicles 36:15,16).

In these summary verses, as really throughout the book, we see God's two-pronged strategy for his interactions with the human race: 1) mercy for sinners and 2) judgment for scoffers. His mercy is infinite, far greater than any of our sins or rebellions. But his wrath over being rejected is immense as well. God has great patience with our sins against his laws, but he absolutely will not allow his grace to be mocked. He was even willing to allow the Babylonians to destroy beautiful Jerusalem and his holy temple.

But even those terrible judgments had a plan of mercy behind them—in captivity in Babylon the Israelites repented of their sins. Second Chronicles ends with the hopeful announcement that the Jews were going to be allowed to return home.

God hasn't changed. Through faith in Christ, you will experience mercy, not judgment.

What's judgment day going to be like?
Pastor Mark Jeske

It pleases God to keep the veil drawn on what the end of time and life in heaven will be like. Mostly. Even though he is holding back on information about the Great Surprise, just like a parent who makes her kids wait until Christmas to unwrap presents, he does put out little bits of the puzzle to encourage us, keep us fired up, and help sustain us in our struggles.

St. Paul more than most was allowed to see what the end of time will be like and just how the long-suffering children of God will be reunited with their Father: **"The Lord himself will come down from heaven, with a loud command, with the voice of the archangel and with the trumpet call of God, and the dead in Christ will rise first. After that, we who are still alive and are left will be caught up together with them in the clouds to meet the Lord in the air. And so we will be with the Lord forever"** (1 Thessalonians 4:16,17).

Notice that for Christians, the return of Christ will bring no terrors. It will be like a family reunion. We will finally get to see and touch the One who was incarnate for us, lived for us, suffered and died for us, and rose again to guarantee our resurrection. We will also be gathered with the vast sea of other believers, the dear people with whom we will spend eternity.

Can't wait.

Friends with the world?

Pastor Mike Novotny

Ever heard of Simeon Stylites? Back in the A.D. 400s, Simeon decided the world was a spiritually dangerous place to live. So he constructed a small platform on top of a stone pillar and lived there . . . for over 30 years!

The idea of Christians escaping the tempting world persists even to our day. From parents who choose Christian education to keep their kids away from unbelievers to Christians who spend all of their free time worshiping, studying, serving, and playing sports with other members of the church, Simeon's spirit is alive and well. Some experts believe it takes only two to three years for new Christians to lose their friendships with their non-Christian former friends.

But listen to Jesus' prayer: **"My prayer is not that you take them out of the world but that you protect them from the evil one"** (John 17:15). Jesus did not want his followers to be separated from the world. Protected from temptation, yes. Isolated from unbelievers, no.

Why would that be? Because Jesus knew that faith comes from hearing the message, and so few have actually heard the message. Amidst all the noise, pop-up ads, and "be a good person" versions of Christianity, often all it takes for someone to actually hear the gospel of Jesus Christ is a friend who believes the gospel of Jesus Christ.

Is there a non-Christian you could invest in this week? Let your light shine so that those living in darkness might see your good deeds and praise our Father in heaven (Matthew 5:16)!

The Israelites aren't the only ones with a problem

Diana Kerr

Raise your hand if you've ever thought the children of Israel were pathetic. Me too. I mean, really people, God brought down supernatural plagues on your enemies, freed you from slavery, and parted a sea that you walked through, and you *still* doubted and whined?

Yep. They did. **"Now the people complained about their hardships in the hearing of the LORD, and when he heard them his anger was aroused"** (Numbers 11:1). God invites our cries for help, but he wasn't pleased with this situation.

It's easy to point out the obvious flaws in the Israelites and in other people's faith, but you can guess where I'm headed with this: I've definitely got a plank in my own eye to attend to. I've got plenty of thoughts and words that display my lack of gratitude and trust in God. You probably do too.

So let's be humble and learn from the Israelites since we need the help: 1) Practice gratitude. Focus on what God *has* given you instead of what he hasn't. 2) Avoid earthly tunnel vision. Keep your eyes on heaven and on God's bigger plan. He cares about your earthly problems, but he cares about your eternity more. 3) Remember how he's been faithful in the past to help you trust him in the present. Like Joshua said, **"Not one of all the good promises the LORD your God gave you has failed"** (Joshua 23:14).

By the way, focusing on my own sin makes me really thankful for two things: First of all, Jesus. Second, that my sins weren't recorded in the Bible like they were with the Israelites!

What does God look like?

Pastor Daron Lindemann

If God were to wait on your living room sofa for you to get home, what would you see when you walked through the door? A room filled with smoke and fire? A typical, handsome-looking American Jesus?

In ancient times, a person couldn't look at God and live. God's glory and holiness were too much. So when God appeared to people, he took an earthly form—as a cloud for the Israelites in the wilderness, as a weary traveler at Abraham's doorstep, as a thug picking a fight with Jacob.

But God wanted us to see the real God and not die. So he took on human nature, while totally remaining God. Full glory, but covered up by flesh. Jesus.

One of Jesus' disciples said, **"We have seen his glory"** (John 1:14). God appeared. People saw him, and nobody died. Well, except God. That's why he came. Jesus—God the Son—took on human flesh that would be beaten, nailed to a cross, and killed. That saving and sacrificial act for us paid the price for our sins. Now we can look at God and live.

There's a reason that believers around the world represent God with a cross. It's the best answer to these questions: What does God look like? What is the purpose of pain? Can I trust God? Does God forgive me? Where is God? Can I look at God and live?

Towel animals (aka, Jesus serves)

Pastor Mike Novotny

You know the service is good when housekeeping turns your bathroom towel into a sloth.

My extended family took a cruise recently and were delighted to learn that the housekeepers were trained to turn ordinary towels into extraordinary animals. After finding a towel bunny on our bed, my daughter wrote a passionate note in her second-grade font, "Please make me a sloth." And the housekeeper did! She even managed to make it hang from the drapes like it was in the wild!

That kind of over-the-top service reminds me of Jesus. He surprises us, doesn't he? He washed feet. He changed his plans for the scared dad of a dying girl. He chose a cross so we don't have to be scared of dying. **"The Son of Man did not come to be served, but to serve"** (Mark 10:45). No one would blame Jesus for ruling on a throne while we washed his feet. But—miracle of miracles—he humbled himself to serve.

I know of no greater comfort than to remember that the God who created the universe with a few words is in the service industry. Every day our Lord loves to serve us daily bread and hourly mercy. Just when you think you are blessed beyond what you deserve, you open your eyes and see the sun shining, the air conditioning running, a friend forgiving, a fellow Christian caring.

Or a sloth hanging from the drapes of Room 6152.

Working with clay

Jason Nelson

God is using us, and we may not even know it. **"Yet you, Lord, are our Father. We are the clay, you are the potter; we are all the work of your hand"** (Isaiah 64:8). We're the work of God's hand and do his work whether we realize it or not. Our good work is God's work. That fact is easy to overlook. But our lives are richer when we acknowledge it every day. Let's get started with a few questions. I know you will add more of your own. Just ask yourself, "Who would suffer if I didn't take care of them? What would die if I didn't water it? Who would feel lonely if I didn't greet them? Who wouldn't have a job if they didn't need to take care of me? What shape does God want me in today?"

We are clay with malleable properties. Sometimes we determine our own contours because that's how delicately the potter is holding us. We stretch to meet new opportunities and resist crushing pressures coming down on us. Sometimes we accept the shape we are in because that's how firmly the potter is holding us. There isn't much wiggle room. But every piece of clay, born or yet to be born, breathes in and breathes out the purposes of the potter. Someday, the potter will change well-used clay to dust and ashes and reshape it into what he always wanted it to be in the first place.

Decide to love your life
Pastor Mark Jeske

I'm ashamed to admit that I've done my share of complaining about my life. It's not too hard, you know, to find things to complain about—financial pressures, jerks at work, crime, aches and pains, and the huge army of disagreeable people that populates this planet. It's not too hard to envy and resent people who seem younger, richer, and more comfortable. We all want heaven on earth, and that means a bushel of disappointments every day.

But only if you've made a decision to let Satan steal your joy. Here's a better way—to look for God's daily gifts, even the small ones, and decide to enjoy your life: **"This is what I have observed to be good: that it is appropriate for people to eat, to drink and to find satisfaction in their toilsome labor under the sun during the few days of life God has given them—for this is their lot. Moreover, when God gives someone wealth and possessions, and the ability to enjoy them, to accept their lot and be happy in their toil—this is a gift of God. They seldom reflect on the days of their life, because God keeps them occupied with gladness of heart"** (Ecclesiastes 5:18-20). Good advice, Solomon. We deserve nothing from God, but for Jesus' sake he gives us so much!

Instead of burning out the lining of your stomach envying someone else's life, how about deciding to love yours?

Easy for God

Pastor Mike Novotny

The battles of the Bible make me laugh. Just when I'm expecting some *Saving Private Ryan/Braveheart/ Lord of the Rings* epic conflict, God shows up on the scene and ruins it.

Like in Judges chapter 4. Sisera, a sex-trafficking thug who murders and enslaves the people of Israel, shows up with nine hundred iron chariots. Chariots were like ancient tanks, and iron chariots would have destroyed Israel's brittle bronze swords. In other words, Israel stands no chance.

Until God shows up. After 14 nail-biting verses, Judges 4:15 says, **"The Lord routed Sisera and all his chariots."** Oh! One verse, one verb, one Lord and the battle is won. Nine hundred chariots are nothing for our all-powerful God.

That's good news for you. You might be facing nine hundred straight days of bitterness toward your ex. Or nine hundred straight weeks of trying to find peace in your problem-solving skills instead of God's power and plans. Or nine hundred angry questions for God in the midst of your back pain, depression, or cancer. You might have nine hundred million sins that make you think God is frustrated with you, if not completely disgusted.

But that's nothing to God. Because one day on a cross, the Lord Jesus showed up and routed all of your sins. He destroyed every single reason for God to be mad at you. One cross, one day, one sacrifice, one Jesus.

Just when you expect your sin to be too much for God, Jesus shows up and says, "That's nothing!"

A shout-out to "unslothy" women
Pastor Mike Novotny

The closest my wife gets to sloth is holding one. On a recent vacation, our family visited a sloth habitat in Honduras where my bride held on to God's coolest creation, the sloth. You need to YouTube some sloth videos today (I'm sure your boss won't mind). If you don't smile, you officially don't have a soul! In Spanish, sloths are called *perezosos*, which literally means, "lazy ones."

I thought of my wife's character as she held that creature. She is the opposite of a lazy woman. Unlike a sloth, she doesn't sleep 20+ hours each day. She is up before the sun to work out, read her Bible, and plan her day. She does a thousand and ten things for our family to keep us running on all cylinders. My Kim is quiet and reserved, but she fears the Lord. And, as the proverb puts it, **"A woman who fears the Lᴏʀᴅ is to be praised"** (Proverbs 31:30).

Do you know any hardworking women? Quiet or outspoken, introvert or life of the party, has God given you a mother, sister, daughter, or sister in the faith who is worthy of praise? Has Jesus blessed you with a woman who reminds you of grace and brings you back to God's perfect plans for your life?

Let's thank the Holy Spirit for producing such passion, love, and hard work in the women who make our physical and spiritual lives so much better.

God is in the wilderness

Pastor Daron Lindemann

What is your wilderness?

Nobody on this planet lives in such paradise that he or she never experiences the wilderness. Some of us know what loneliness or brokenness feels like. Some are wandering through unemployment or lost in secret sin that they aren't convinced anyone will understand.

Jesus was baptized by John. The Spirit's touch. The Father's voice. Within moments, perhaps while he was still dripping wet, **"the Spirit sent him out into the wilderness"** (Mark 1:12). The Spirit pushed Jesus in the direction of a desolate place where some don't survive! Literally, "sent him" means "threw him out" or "drove him away."

"And he was in the wilderness forty days, being tempted by Satan. He was with the wild animals, and angels attended him" (Mark 1:13).

The Holy Spirit pushed Jesus right into the waiting arms of Satan. So intensely painful and desperate was his struggle that angels came to assist and wild animals looked at him with sympathy. But know this: Jesus never left the Spirit's touch, and he still heard the Father's voice (through the Scriptures in his dialogue with the devil).

So Jesus conquered the wilderness for you. Your wilderness isn't ruled by Satan or your sins or fears or your circumstances or the powers of this world. Your wilderness is ruled by God—the Father's voice, the Son's tested triumph, and the Holy Spirit's touch. Don't be afraid. You're not lost. Your wilderness is never a random detour.

The gift you didn't know you gave

Jason Nelson

God bless you if you were a good kid. God bless you for not causing trouble. God bless you if creating drama for others wasn't your style. You gave your parents a priceless gift. It's at the top of the list of every nice thing you ever did for them. You spared them heartache. You gave them the gift of not having to worry about you or how you would turn out. You gave them peace of mind.

God bless you if you weren't such a good kid. God bless you for turning your life around. God bless you for changing your ways, taking care of yourself, and staying out of trouble. You are giving your parents a priceless gift. It's a gift that erases any memory of how upsetting it was during your worst times. Don't worry about how to make it up to them. You can't. You're giving them the only thing they want. You're giving them peace of mind because they don't have to worry about you or how you will turn out.

God bless you if you were a good kid or not such a good kid. Either way, the Sun of Righteousness rises on you with healing in his wings. **"He will change parents' attitudes toward their children and children's attitudes toward their parents"** (Malachi 4:6 GW). You can live in peace and love each other for it.

Lord, give me patience with you

Pastor Mark Jeske

Of all the many things I do that irritate my wife, known and unknown, near the top of the list must be her persistent complaint that I don't listen to her. Not to squirm out of that responsibility, but I fear that many wives would have the same lament. It may be that she wants my help with something. But of greatest urgency for her is that I pay attention to what is happening in her life and showing that I care about her situation. She needs me to resonate emotionally with what she is going through.

How frustrating to imagine that God is ignoring us. The prophet Habakkuk concluded that he was getting a divine brush-off, and he had the *nerve* to hurl a testy accusation against his Creator: **"How long, Lord, must I call for help, but you do not listen?"** (Habakkuk 1:2). From our vantage point millennia later, we know that everything turned out well for the believers. But at the time, stuck in the middle of their fears and dilemmas, the people didn't know that.

As Habakkuk reflected on the Lord's mighty deeds of the past and pondered his words and promises, he grew in his ability to trust his Father. His little prophecy ends on a happier note: **"I will rejoice in the Lord, I will be joyful in God my Savior. The Sovereign Lord is my strength; he makes my feet like the feet of a deer"** (Habakkuk 3:18,19).

So—do you have deer feet today?

I forget God's truths about money so easily

Diana Kerr

It's a weird feeling when you notice someone else's wealth and feel envy creeping in, isn't it? I hope you're immune from that, but I'd be lying if I said I don't feel it when someone I know upgrades her home or posts his extravagant vacation on social media.

I forget God's many warnings and wise words about money so easily. **"Cast but a glance at riches,"** Proverbs 23:5 says, **"and they are gone, for they will surely sprout wings and fly off to the sky like an eagle."** Psalm 49:16,17 encourages, **"Do not be overawed when others grow rich, when the splendor of their houses increases; for they will take nothing with them when they die."**

We all know that life is nothing compared to eternity and we can't take our stuff with us. But we live as if that's not the case. We get absorbed with wealth and possessions. We turn good gifts God gives others into something to envy. We turn the good gifts he's given to *us* into cause for discontent because they could be better.

I've got so far to go, but I've found a couple things to be helpful with this. One is keeping my eyes on the truths in God's Word and away from the stuff that skews my priorities (for me, home decorating shows, certain Instagram accounts or magazines, etc.). Another is admitting to God that I can't overcome this on my own, asking for his help with contentment, and resting in the peace that Jesus' perfection covers all my failures.

Save us from success!

Pastor Mike Novotny

What do you think of Gideon? In Judges chapters 6-8, we meet a nobody named Gideon whose faith seems remarkably flawed. When Jesus appears to Gideon, Gideon wants a sign to prove that his guest is actually God. Later in the chapter, Gideon doesn't believe God will keep his promise, so he asks for a second sign involving a fleece. Then, still afraid, he asks for a third sign. Then, in chapter 8, God still finds Gideon shaking in his sandals, so he gives him a fourth sign. Talk about testing God's patience!

But that's not Gideon's biggest problem. Read his story to the end, and you'll find that the real problem is not Gideon's four signs but rather the fact that he doesn't ask for a fifth. After a mighty victory in battle, successful Gideon doesn't need God anymore. And his life ends in catastrophic failure, a golden object used for idolatry. **"Gideon made the gold into an ephod . . . and it became a snare to Gideon and his family"** (Judges 8:27).

If God has given you great success—reaching retirement, the blessing of a new child, a dream job—learn from Gideon's mistake. Stay desperate. Pray continually. Begin each day in the Word, seeking trustworthy "signs" of God's presence and his plans for you. After all, we need Jesus just as much today as we did when our faith journey began. Thankfully, Jesus longs to be with you always, to the very end of your life on earth—and beyond!

Trash mouth
Pastor Mark Jeske

Think back to your younger years. Where did you learn the meaning of "street" words, i.e., cussing, swearing, body parts? Probably from your (slightly older) friends, who learned from their slightly older friends. Perhaps your parents and their friends had a salty vocabulary. Young people don't want to look weak, dumb, or naïve, and a trash mouth is a quick and cheap way to sound sophisticated and street-smart.

Grown-ups do it too, of course. Occasionally they will be aware of their bad manners. "Pardon my French," they'll say, thus insulting the French people too. One of the ways in which you can live your faith is to control your trash mouth: **"Do not let any unwholesome talk come out of your mouths, but only what is helpful for building others up according to their needs, that it may benefit those who listen"** (Ephesians 4:29).

Why does this matter? Swearing (i.e., using God's name to guarantee the truth of your words or to add emphasis) is unnecessary if you have a reputation for telling the truth. Cursing (i.e., calling on God to punish somebody or something for you) isn't your business. God will handle any damning that needs to be done. Body vulgarity is often used to ridicule somebody else. Sexual vulgarity is not mere talk—it may send everybody the message that you approve of committing adultery.

Here's God's filter for your mouth: Is what I'm saying helpful for building others up?

The spiritual-but-not-religious experiment

Pastor Mike Novotny

Do you know someone who is "spiritual but not religious"? After witnessing a thousand sex and/or stealing scandals and overhearing a million petty fights in their parents' churches, many young Americans are turning away from organized religion altogether. They still consider themselves spiritual people, but who needs the flawed institution of organized religion? Maybe you feel the same way.

We should sympathize with our loved ones who struggle with the necessity of church. It's hard to be committed to such an obviously imperfect institution. Yet we should also remind ourselves that another culture tried this experiment before. For nearly three hundred years, the people of Israel tried to give, pray, and worship without organized leadership. The story is summarized in the book of Judges where **"everyone did as they saw fit"** (Judges 21:25).

Spoiler Alert—It did not go well. The people added idols to their "worship" of the Lord. They gave in to short-term pleasures. The grandchildren of the very people whose feet walked through the Red Sea fell far from God fast. As the author repeats time and again, the people needed a king, someone to love them sincerely and protect them from themselves.

So let's deal with our church's flaws without running away from the church. If Israel's story is any indication, simply being spiritual does not lead us closer to Jesus.

april

With great power the apostles continued to testify
to the resurrection of the Lord Jesus.

Acts 4:33

A life-changing sentence

Pastor Mike Novotny

If you could pick any person—any friend, any family member, any celebrity, any pet, anyone alive or passed on—to walk through the door and be right here, who would that person be and what would that person make you feel? What would you feel if your husband was still here? Or your crush from work showed up? Or your daughter from California surprised you? Or your favorite musician walked into your coffee shop? Or your grandson came bumbling though the door? I bet you would feel a lot! Even if nothing else changed in your life, that person's presence would have the power to change you.

Okay, here's the big question, the question that's changing my life, the question that can change yours—Is God better than that person? Is your version, your view, of God as exciting, thrilling, and comforting as your view of that person? If I told you, "GOD is here!" what would you feel? More or less than before?

Jesus made us an amazing promise in Matthew 28:20: **"Surely I am with you always."** That promise will make you nod an emotionless "amen" unless you remember who Jesus is. More faithful than the best spouse. More creative than the best artists. More beautiful than a newborn child. More comforting than a lifelong friend. Jesus is better than them all. And, because he's full of grace and forgiveness, Jesus is with you always.

Lies: You can have it all
Pastor Mark Jeske

Henri Estienne, Parisian printer and bookseller, is credited with the wry life observation: "If youth only knew; if age only could." He must have been a senior citizen when he uttered those words—young people think they'll be strong and invincible forever. His words bear the wisdom and flavor of one who knows the fatigues and aches of age.

It is a law of human existence that you pass through seasons of life. Each season is a golden age for a different thing. It is a lie that you can have it all. Much better is the life attitude that celebrates the blessings of each season and patiently waits for God's timing to fill in the gaps: **"Wait for the Lord; be strong and take heart and wait for the Lord"** (Psalm 27:14).

You can't have both dating independence and a marriage commitment at the same time; you can't have a batch of young children without exhaustion; you won't have the financial security of a 70-year-old when you are 23. There is a season of financial self-denial; there is a season of financial happy exhaling when your debts are paid and you can travel. It's all good.

You don't have to have it all right now, and you don't have to torment yourself as a loser if you have unfulfilled dreams and longings. Wait cheerfully for the next season of life; wait confidently that God has new blessings tomorrow; wait serenely knowing that the unlimited joys of heaven await you.

Reflector

Pastor Matt Ewart

"The essence of being human is that one does not seek perfection."—George Orwell

The struggle of many artists, musicians, and authors is that perfection is unattainable. A painting can always be made better. A song can always be remixed. A book (or devotion) can always be worded *more* better.

At some point, you need to just consider your work good enough and let the world have it.

Perhaps you know how imprisoning it can feel never to be satisfied with what you're doing. So today, meditate on an important scriptural truth that will bring you some freedom.

It's not about settling for average. It's not about caring less about what you do.

It's about looking in a different direction.

You see, perfectionism draws you inward with the lie that you're capable of doing better and responsible for doing better. But Jesus did not call you to be perfect. He called you to reflect.

I doubt that the moon feels terrible for not being brighter than it is. Its job is simply to reflect light, and it does a perfect job of that.

So too your role is not to be perfect. Jesus Christ already attained that for you. Your job is simply to reflect the peace that comes from God's grace shining on you.

"The Lord bless you and keep you; the Lord make his face shine on you and be gracious to you; the Lord turn his face toward you and give you peace" (Numbers 6:24-26).

Change your thinking
Linda Buxa

We worked our way up the mountain. From the previous days' rain, the trail was muddy and slick but not too dangerous. Then we reached the last bit of ascent. There it was, rocky and narrow—and we needed sure footing on each step.

My friend and I worried about our kids the whole way, talking about how as moms we so easily fall into fatalistic thinking. We continued the chatter on the way down.

Finally, my husband asked us to change the topic. After all, it was doing us no good to talk about our fears. We were, in fact, probably making it worse for ourselves.

You can relate, can't you?

We walk around at home, school, and work and notice all the ways that everything has gone wrong and imagining all the things that might go wrong in the future. We make it worse for ourselves by dwelling on our fears. We all need a reminder to change our thinking and change the topic back to Jesus.

So here's your reminder for today and every day: **"Finally, brothers and sisters, whatever is true, whatever is noble, whatever is right, whatever is pure, whatever is lovely, whatever is admirable—if anything is excellent or praiseworthy—think about such things. Whatever you have learned or received or heard from me, or seen in me—put it into practice. And the God of peace will be with you"** (Philippians 4:8,9).

A proverb and a prayer
Jason Nelson

"Let love and faithfulness never leave you; bind them around your neck, write them on the tablet of your heart. Then you will win favor and a good name in the sight of God and man. Trust in the LORD with all your heart and lean not on your own understanding; in all your ways submit to him, and he will make your paths straight" (Proverbs 3:3-6).

Lord, how shall we live? What has happened to acting dignified in the public square? Is shamelessness here to stay? Vulgar and deceitful people ascend to the heights of power and flaunt their lack of decency. Are we learning to tolerate their schemes just so we won't be left out when it's pie-slicing time? Is this the new normal? It can't be. You say we should wear love and faithfulness like medallions around our necks because those values are etched so deeply in our hearts. Our love for you and faithfulness to you should be out front for all to see. They are the cornerstones of a good reputation. May we never sacrifice them on the puny altars of expediency. Anything we might gain today is not worth losing our good name over. We can't have it both ways. The straight path is not a journey for half-hearted pilgrims. Lord, we want to trust you wholeheartedly. Help us follow your ways of doing things without any reservations so others can have complete confidence in us. Amen.

God loves a cheerful giver

Pastor Mike Novotny

The other day my eight-year-old and I were playing driveway volleyball when we saw our elderly neighbor. She was standing in front of her garage, reaching up with a broom, trying to clean the leaves out of her gutter. I decided to stop our game and, before long, I was on a ladder sweeping out her stubborn leaves. While I pulled the leaves out of the gutter, my daughter swept them into a big pile. She was red cheeked and sweaty on this hot day. But not once did she whine. Not once did she mope. Not once did she give me a frustrated look. And I was so proud of her! So proud of the love she gave our neighbor. So proud of the joy she brought to an elderly sister in the faith. (So proud that I broke out the ice cream before Mommy got home to make dinner!)

That's how your Father feels too. When you decide in your heart to give generously, trusting in Jesus to provide for your every need, God loves it. You might not see his face like my daughter saw mine, but believe these words—God loves a cheerful giver.

Giving our time and money is one of the hardest parts of the Christian life. It requires every bit of God-given motivation. So take Paul's words to heart today as you consider your response to Jesus' forgiveness, grace, and salvation: **"Each of you should give what you have decided in your heart to give, not reluctantly or under compulsion, for God loves a cheerful giver"** (2 Corinthians 9:7).

Creation is in the rest of the Bible too
Pastor Mark Jeske

The Genesis accounts of God's creation describe his amazing power, wisdom, and love for his human creatures. But the creation accounts also show that all people, made by God *for his purposes*, are accountable to God for the way in which they live their lives.

To get out from under that obligation, skeptics for centuries have sniffed at the historicity of Genesis chapters 1-11. But God's creation is taught not only in those chapters but in the rest of Scripture too. In the days of Ezra and Nehemiah, a group of Levites, Israel's teachers, led the nation in this prayer to the Lord: **"Blessed be your glorious name, and may it be exalted above all blessing and praise. You alone are the LORD. You made the heavens, even the highest heavens, and all their starry host, the earth and all that is on it, the seas and all that is in them. You give life to everything, and the multitudes of heaven worship you"** (Nehemiah 9:5,6).

You can't have it both ways. Either the Bible and its creation account are true, or they are a gigantic fraud. The world arose and developed in its stunning complexity either by a string of incredible coincidences and random mutations, or it was crafted by intelligent design.

You can't embrace much of the Bible and just slice off a few chapters at the beginning. If you reject the authority of Genesis, you have rejected the authority of all of Scripture.

Devoted to the Word

Pastor Mike Novotny

In describing Christianity, the brand-new movement that was about to change the world, Dr. Luke tells us, **"They devoted themselves to the apostles' teaching"** (Acts 2:42). When those Christians did life together, they consistently talked about the apostles' teaching. And what did the apostles teach? Read Acts 2:1-41 and you'll find the answer—Jesus. Jesus' identity. Jesus' sacrifice. Jesus' cross. Jesus' resurrection. The early Christians devoted themselves to the Bible and the Jesus at the center of it.

And the best groups of Christians today devote themselves to the same thing. Try to read the Bible by yourself, and it will confuse you. But show up with other Christians and humbly admit, "I don't get it," and you will grow. In fact, despite what your pride might tell you, admission of ignorance is what makes your faith better! Because in your spiritual family, God has grouped together decades-old Christians and those still wet from their baptisms. He's gathered people who couldn't find Habakkuk with a gun to their heads and those who know Paul's Romans chapter 1 quote of Habakkuk chapter 2 helped the reformer Martin Luther grasp the gospel for the first time.

Here's the tough news: The Bible can be a hard book to understand. But here's the good news: Your Father has put people in your path who can help you understand it. And love the Jesus who's in it. So let's devote ourselves together to the teaching that changed the world.

Thorns protect the flowers
Jason Nelson

I never want to romanticize suffering. I take it very seriously. But I can't overlook what God has done through suffering people. Suffering made some people spiritual *tour de forces*. Thorns on a stem or a vine deter predators from destroying the plant. They prevent deer and rabbits from chewing it to death. Thorns in a person's life protect unseen flowers so flowers can transform into beautiful fruit.

Fannie Crosby had a minor eye inflammation when she was six weeks old. She was treated by a careless doctor and left blind for the rest of her life. It was a dark life that bloomed from the inside out. She wrote over eight thousand gospel songs including "Blessed Assurance" and "To God Be the Glory." She said, "I could not have written thousands of hymns if I had been hindered by the distractions of seeing all the interesting and beautiful objects presented to my notice."

Thorns have gotten a bad name because they are so difficult to remove. The apostle of great visions and revelations, Paul, wanted his gone. **"Three times I pleaded with the Lord to take it away from me"** (2 Corinthians 12:8). But he was stuck with it. Paul recognized the purpose of his thorn just like Fanny understood hers. They might be together right now, singing a chorus she wrote:

And I shall see him face to face,
And tell the story—Saved by grace.

(from "Saved by Grace" by Fanny Crosby)

Lies: If I avoid my problems, they'll go away

Pastor Mark Jeske

Most of us feel that we have about as much stress as we can handle. So it's understandable that we would postpone tough jobs, put off a face-to-face that's going to be difficult, and procrastinate on unpleasant chores. Understandable but dumb.

The little voice that whispers to you that maybe the unpleasantness will go away all by itself is lying to you. In fact, you may make the problem bigger by letting it slide. Clogged drains don't clear themselves, and a rotted window sash does not mysteriously generate sound wood. *Get after it today!*

It's even more urgent when it comes to people stress. Jesus thought this so important that he built antiprocrastination teaching into his famous Sermon on the Mount: **"Settle matters quickly with your adversary who is taking you to court. Do it while you are still together on the way, or your adversary may hand you over to the judge, and the judge may hand you over to the officer, and you may be thrown into prison"** (Matthew 5:25).

Have you done some damage to a relationship? Don't let the clock chime midnight without apologizing and seeing what you can do to make amends. The sooner you act, the smaller the job will be. Has someone done something hurtful to you? Explain politely how you feel, and you may restore a relationship by giving the other person the chance to say, "I'm sorry."

What important task have you been putting off?

Martha's mistake
Jason Nelson

I think it's time someone speaks up for Martha. For too long she's been maligned in Sunday school lessons and sermons for being some kind of infidel who wasn't interested in listening to Jesus. The takeaway is always, don't be like **"Martha, Martha"** (Luke 10:41). Don't be so busy with the routines of life that you don't have time for God. Yes, Jesus came to Mary's defense and reminded all of us that ignoring his Word would be ignoring something we need more than anything. But had Mary made the mistake of saying, "Lord, don't you think Martha should be sitting here as attentive to you as I am," Jesus probably would have said, "Yeah, but we still gotta eat."

Martha wasn't ignoring Jesus' teaching. That wasn't her mistake. It was a small house, and she would have heard everything from the cook's corner anyway. She made the classic mistake that "doers" of the Word make. She criticized her sister for being a "hearer" only and leaving the chores to someone else. Had she kept still and gone about her business, she likely would have avoided any rebuke from Jesus. But she just had to bring it up because she'd been in that situation before, and it irritated her. So, I'd like to cut her some slack. I know she was paying attention because when Lazarus died, it was Martha who said, **"Lord . . . if you had been here, my brother would not have died"** (John 11:21).

Live with confidence
Pastor Jeremy Mattek

Brittany was diagnosed with brain cancer and had 14 months to live. When the doctors told her that her death would be painful, Brittany and her husband moved to Oregon because of its Death with Dignity Act. The law allows you to take a medication that ends your life painlessly. And that's what she did.

Ashley was also diagnosed with cancer, but she chose not to start treatment because she was ten weeks pregnant. The doctors told her that in order for the treatment to be effective, the pregnancy would have to be terminated. "There's no way I could kill a healthy baby because I'm sick," Ashley said. When she was eight months pregnant, her cancer was terminal and the baby had to be delivered. The baby was healthy, but Ashley died.

Jesus could've avoided the pain of life and stayed in heaven, but he died. It wasn't suicide. It was loving someone else's existence so much more than he loved his own, believing it was better for him to die in pain than to live without you forgiven. Why?

Because he knit you together in your mother's womb, and he loves you. That's the real tragedy when people choose to "die with dignity." They could have lived with confidence that **"neither death nor life, neither angels nor demons, neither the present nor the future, nor any powers, neither height nor depth, nor anything else in all creation,"** will cause us to miss out on heaven (Romans 8:38,39). They could have lived knowing that no matter how unfair life is, it's going to be okay because God is holding them in his hands.

Your reputation
Pastor Matt Ewart

Mankind's first murder quickly made its way into history. And I'm not just talking about the fact that it's documented in the Bible.

It seems that after Cain killed Abel, word spread that killing another human being was actually a thing that people could do. And the potential for it to happen again was out there. A certain individual mentioned in Genesis chapter 4 built his entire reputation on the idea that he was ready and willing to kill if the need should arise.

That kind of reputation makes it pretty easy to control how other people behave around you.

But Jesus introduced a different type of reputation that is actually even more powerful, albeit more difficult to attain.

"Then Peter came to Jesus and asked, 'Lord, how many times shall I forgive my brother or sister who sins against me? Up to seven times?' Jesus answered, 'I tell you, not seven times, but seventy-seven times'" (Matthew 18:21,22).

The reputation Jesus taught would leave a person incredibly vulnerable to being used as a doormat. It would call for extraordinary love and patience. It would leave no promise of getting what you want.

But it's the reputation that Jesus has with you—a reputation that's founded on stubborn forgiveness.

How you live today will contribute to your reputation. Instilling fear in others will immediately change their behavior around you. But only a reputation based on forgiveness has the power to change hearts.

All the "feels"

Pastor Matt Ewart

One thing that stands out in the last week of Jesus' life is that Jesus went through all the "feels." If there was a human feeling to be had, Jesus experienced it to the fullest during this last week.

In fact, it was on Palm Sunday that you see Jesus doing something that he normally did not do.

He wept.

"As he approached Jerusalem and saw the city, he wept over it and said, 'If you, even you, had only known on this day what would bring you peace—but now it is hidden from your eyes'" (Luke 19:41,42).

Rather than ruminate on his own sorrow for what he was about to go through, he wept at the thought of the complete destruction that would eventually befall Jerusalem. He lamented how this was preventable but now unavoidable. The Prince of peace was among them, but they chose to defer his rule.

By extension, Jesus' weeping on Palm Sunday was for all mankind. A destruction that was preventable but now unavoidable was at hand. A destruction that would be absolutely complete.

But a destruction that is now absolutely finished. Disregarding the anguish that would go along with all the feels, Jesus endured the feel of the betrayal, the mocking, the thorns, the whip, the nails, and even the cross. He chose not to dull or escape all that he felt.

But Palm Sunday isn't about what he felt with his body. It's about what he cherished in his heart. You.

GOD is here

Pastor Mike Novotny

The other day I asked my friend Katie, "Who would be the most life-changing person to walk through that door and be here with us?" Katie leaned in and muttered, "I'm supposed to say Jesus, right? . . . Because I'm thinking about someone delivering sushi. . . . But I love dolphins too. Can a dolphin show up?" "You bet," I said. "How about a dolphin swims through that door with a rainbow roll on its dorsal fin?" And Katie beamed with excitement.

I have the same spiritual problem as Katie. I know the technical answer to my question—the greatest joy and peace and rest are found in Jesus. But what really gets my heart going is something else. In other words, I believe God is here, but I forget that *GOD* is here. I bet you forget that too.

Which is why we need to eavesdrop on the angels. In Isaiah 6:3, the angels shouted, **"Holy! Holy! Holy."** *Holy* means "set apart," "wonderfully different." The angels preached, "You think sunsets are good? and babies smiling? and puppy videos? and last-second field goals? and a new boat? You should see GOD! GOD is holy! He's even better! This is the GOD of love, of forgiveness, of mercy, the GOD who came into the world to show us grace. This is the GOD who created mountains and sunsets and water and waves. This is the GOD who invented colors and sound and taste buds. This is not some dusty God from a theological textbook. This is the GOD of glory! And, because of the cross of Jesus, this GOD is here with us!

I'm a Christian, but . . .
Linda Buxa

"I do believe; help me overcome my unbelief!" (Mark 9:24).

I never used to understand that passage. As I get older and see the war within me, the more I get it. In reality, I love Jesus, but I'm not always a big fan of some of the things he says, so I decide which part of his message I will promote and which part I will try to hide.

I believe, but I don't want to deny myself.

I believe, but I don't want to forgive as I have been forgiven.

I believe, but I don't want to talk humbly to you about your sin.

I believe, but I don't want to stop worrying.

I believe, but I'm not willing to confess my sins.

This is why the good news of Jesus is so important. Because we hear that **"God demonstrates his own love for us in this: While we were still sinners, Christ died for us"** (Romans 5:8). Even while we were against him (not even believing), God was for us. He sent Jesus to live and die for us, buying us back from Satan, who owned us. Now the Holy Spirit works in us, reminding us that there are no "buts."

Now, like every high school fan base, we get to cheer, "I believe. . . . I believe that. . . . . I believe that we. . . . . I believe that we will win."

Forever.

Jesus' forgiving grace

Pastor Mike Novotny

I once heard of a pastor who had the best/most unsuccessful counseling idea. When couples brought their conflicts into his office, he would say to the husband, "Draw me a pie chart that divides up the blame in your marriage. What's your fault? What's hers?" Of course, it was never 50/50. It was always a majority her fault. But the pastor wouldn't argue that. Instead, he would say, "Okay, I'll believe you. But let's just talk today about this little slice that you admit is your fault. Let's repent of that, ask for Jesus' forgiveness, and apologize to your bride. Let's pray for God to change that about you."

But do you know what the pastor found? No one wanted to do it. Instead, the husbands would excuse their sin or justify it or want to change the subject to her sins. (Want to guess what happened when the pastor started the exercise with the wife?)

Which is why we so desperately need to start with the forgiving grace of Jesus. In Ephesians chapter 5, Paul talks about the unconditional love and respect that make relationships work. But before those famous verses, he says, **"Forgive each other, just as in Christ God forgave you"** (Ephesians 4:32). Once the grace of God settles deep in our hearts and the Spirit assures us of our forgiveness in Jesus, we are able to walk into our relational conflicts and own our sin. No excuses. No accusations. Just apologies. And, as God would have it, that humility is often the first step in healing what sin has broken.

The names of God: Redeemer

Pastor Mark Jeske

During the American Civil War, President Lincoln and the U.S. Congress had a desperate need for military manpower, so they instituted a military draft in 1863. It was hated, of course, and hated even more because well-to-do families could either bear the cost of sending a substitute or paying the expensive commutation fee to redeem a son or grandson from going into what they feared would be the infantry meat grinder.

Does it surprise you to know that God allows personal redemptions? His Son, Jesus, volunteered to do battle with Satan on behalf of a sinful human race, bear the world's condemnation, suffer the punishment, go to hell for us, and then die. Through faith in him and his extraordinary work, *he allows you to claim his righteousness as your own*! You've been redeemed! **"You know that it was not with perishable things such as silver or gold that you were redeemed from the empty way of life handed down to you from your ancestors, but with the precious blood of Christ, a lamb without blemish or defect"** (1 Peter 1:18,19).

In 1863 plenty of people were able to afford the redemption fee to stay out of combat. You and I could never afford the cost of going it alone in God's holy and severe court—his nonnegotiable demand is a sinless life, completely pure in thought, word, and deed. You have one chance—put all your hopes, faith, and trust in your Redeemer, Jesus Christ, and live.

It's in the Word
Pastor Mark Jeske

People do know a few things about God all on their own. They know he exists—every culture on earth involves stories about a power greater than man. All of nature sings of intelligent design, of order, of brilliant engineering. People sense that God (whoever he/she/it may be) is good, and their consciences make them nervously aware of a certain accountability.

But God's rescue plan through Jesus Christ is revealed knowledge, not inherent knowledge. And God absolutely insists that people acquire this knowledge through other people. Those who know share what they know. **"How, then, can they call on the one they have not believed in? And how can they believe in the one of whom they have not heard?"** (Romans 10:14).

The amazing stories of Israel's Old Testament history demonstrate that God will spare no effort to do what he alone can do. But he absolutely refuses to do for us what he has enabled us and empowered us and commissioned us to do, and that is to share Jesus with one another.

Share what you know. Share whom you know.

The names of God: Messiah/Christ
Pastor Mark Jeske

In Old Testament times, God had a unique ceremony by which he would show his choice of a spiritual leader and then invest that leader with special gifts of the Spirit to fit him for his work. Prophets like Elisha, the kings, and a new high priest were to be *anointed*. A specially mixed ceremonial oil was splashed on their heads in front of an audience so that all would know the Lord's choice.

All those leader types, however, were only placeholders for the great Anointed One (in Old Testament Hebrew: *Meshiach* or *Messiah,* in New Testament Greek: *Christós*) who was to come. This future hero would bring security, prosperity, and righteousness to the nation and to the whole world. It would be the Israelites' great gift to all people, the very fulfillment of their national identity.

A woman drawing water at a well in the town of Sychar was stunned one day to realize that she was speaking with none other than this long-awaited Prophet-Priest-King: **"The woman said, 'I know that Messiah' (called Christ) 'is coming. When he comes, he will explain everything to us.' Then Jesus declared, 'I, the one speaking to you—I am he'"** (John 4:25,26).

Jesus' anointing was not with oil but with the water of the Jordan River (see Matthew chapter 3). His anointer, John the Baptist, identified his holy mission: to take away the sin of the world.

Christ, have mercy!

Less me, more Jesus
Pastor Mark Jeske

His conception and birth were swathed in drama and miracles. He burst onto the scene at age 30, just like his famous relative Jesus, and attracted huge crowds to hear him speak. He brilliantly fulfilled his God-given mission to prepare the way for the public revelation of the world's Savior. And then, after a ministry of maybe a year and a half, he was arrested and thrown into a dungeon.

"When John, who was in prison, heard about the deeds of the Messiah, he sent his disciples to ask him, 'Are you the one who is to come, or should we expect someone else?'" Does that question sound as though John's faith was collapsing? Jesus didn't think him weak or unworthy. He replied, **"Truly I tell you, among those born of women there has not risen anyone greater than John the Baptist"** (Matthew 11:2,3,11).

John is a hero to me because he humbly accepted God's verdict that a ministry of a mere 18 months was enough. How he must have groaned in his prison cell. How shocked he must have been on the death walk to the place of his beheading.

John was content to fade out. "I must decrease," he said. "He must increase. Look—the Lamb of God, who takes away the sin of the world."

My temper
Pastor Mark Jeske

I can sure tell when other people are losing their tempers. I hear the pitch of their voices rise. I note the sharpness of tone. I see the flashes in their eyes, the scrunch of their brows, the hard line of their mouths. They have stopped listening because they have so many *important* things to say. I can tell that their emotions are clouding their logic. So why can't I see those same things when I'm doing them?

In the midst of an argument, why do I feel so righteous? so defensive? so bitter? Has God done nothing for me? Have I not been spoiled rotten with blessings I don't deserve? Has he not called me to be a peacemaker, not a warmonger? When you see me going off like this, call a time-out and whisper this Scripture passage in my ear: **"A gentle answer turns away wrath, but a harsh word stirs up anger"** (Proverbs 15:1).

I function best as God's ambassador in a fallen world, not so much when I show everybody that I'm right but when I help to de-escalate a conflict and reconcile two enemies into being friends again. Here's what I'm going to work on this week: keep my voice soft, ask a lot of questions before pontificating, assume kind and good motives in others rather than assuming the worst, listen twice or three times before speaking, and double-check my agenda to make sure it's God's.

Say it with me: "Gentle."

Not until you bless me

Pastor Mike Novotny

It's not insulting to be demanding with God. Some Christians, in a desire to be humble, turn all of their prayers into question marks, into soul-numbing, expecting-little "God willings." But there are times when your prayers should be much bolder. There are times when you should be demanding with God.

Think of the strange night when Jacob wrestled with God, who was disguised as a man: **"Then the man said, 'Let me go, for it is daybreak.' But Jacob replied, 'I will not let you go unless you bless me'"** (Genesis 32:26). Jacob wouldn't let God race off to his morning appointment. Instead, his fingers clamped onto God's arms. With a dislocated hip, Jacob had to be clinging desperately to him. Yet in that desperation, Jacob demanded, "Don't you even think about walking away until you do something good for me." And God did. Instead of being insulted, he was honored. Jacob was clinging to God's promise, believing that God could not lie like his mother, Rebekah, or his Uncle Laban. Jacob believed God was faithful.

God is faithful to you too. What God said about being with you right now has to be true (Matthew 28:20). What he said about working out all things for your good, even that painful thing, has to be true (Romans 8:28). What he said about forgiving all of your sins, not just the ones people talk about at Bible study, has to be true (1 John 1:9). So cling to God. Insist on his character. Refuse to let him go until he blesses you.

Quantity and quality
Pastor Matt Ewart

They say that money won't make you happy. But if I had the resources, I wouldn't mind experimenting.

The prophet Jeremiah snuck in a cheeky comment about wealth that caught my attention. He was addressing a king who was building an excessive palace at the expense of his people, and he said, **"Does it make you a king to have more and more cedar?"** (Jeremiah 22:15).

No, it doesn't make you a king to have more and more cedar. Nor does it make you a better king. It just makes you a king . . . with a lot of cedar.

What was obvious in Jeremiah's eyes might be less obvious in your life, but the same principle must be applied:

The quantity of what you have does not improve the quality of who you are.

In fact, the quantity of what you have merely amplifies the quality of who you are. Money doesn't give you happiness—at best it distracts you from unhappiness. Great wealth doesn't give you security—it only gives you something new to worry about.

Maybe what you need to hear today is that neither your purpose nor your value is determined by what you have. Your value was determined at Christ's cross, and your purpose was unleashed in his empty tomb. It doesn't really matter whether you are assigned poverty or riches. Who you are in Christ is what enables you to reflect Christ-like love in this world.

A gallery and a treasure chest
Jason Nelson

The human mind is a picture gallery, and the human heart is a treasure chest. God did not install a border wall in our gray matter that isolates what we see from what we remember. If you want to create lasting impressions on people, hang pictures in their minds. That's what sticks. The people who watched President Obama's State of the Union address in 2013 may not remember a thing from Marco Rubio's response, but they will never forget the image of Senator Rubio awkwardly reaching for a bottle of water in the middle of his remarks.

Sweet Mary took in every scene of her son's short life. She saw it all from the nativity to the crucifixion. She watched her son deal with people and saw their reaction to him. It all made an impression on her faith because she also needed to understand who he was. What she saw was as important as what she heard. Her nights must have been filled at times with pleasant dreams and at other times with horrible nightmares because she **"treasured up all these things and pondered them in her heart"** (Luke 2:19). Her faith developed in the heart of her mind as she interpreted the pictures in her mind. The Bible and life itself hang pictures in our minds. They are exhibitions of God's power and God's love. When we reflect on them, they warm our hearts and we treasure who he is.

Stop a quarrel before it starts
Pastor Mark Jeske

I bet you know how to accelerate a disagreement into a full-blown fight. I bet you know the buttons that you can push on a spouse, parent, or child to jack up emotion and "get into it." Are you aware of *your* buttons, the ones others can push to get you upset? Do you have insecurity buttons? Can people get you going by referring to your lack of educational attainments? Referring to your weight? Hair loss? Prison record? Financial struggles? Driving skills?

Do you have enough self-awareness to feel the rush of anger in your belly, blood to your cheeks, and lack of oxygen in your brain? Are you able to stop an argument before it starts? **"A gentle answer turns away wrath, but a harsh word stirs up anger"** (Proverbs 15:1).

It starts with deciding to like yourself. Why? Because you're so fabulous? No. Rather, because Jesus likes you. If you allow the gospel to affirm your identity, if you allow the Word of God to assure you of your eternal worth to God, you won't be so insecure and vulnerable to the slights, slings, and arrows that come at you each day. The gospel of Christ also helps you to decide to like other people *even when they say potentially hurtful things*.

You can cut other people some slack because God has been so patient with you. You can decide that saving a relationship is a bigger win than venting anger in an argument.

No lie
Linda Buxa

A fact-checker report from the *Washington Post* says that in President Trump's first year, he made 2,140 false or misleading claims. By day 558 in office, that had risen to 4,229 claims.

Now, I have no idea if they were really false and misleading or whether the *Washington Post* made false or misleading claims about those false or misleading claims. All I know is I was filled with gratitude that no human puts a fact-checker on me, publishes it in a newspaper, and posts it on a website.

See, I know that I mislead and lie to others; I skew the truth to make myself look better. I know that I even lie to myself, rationalizing why my sin wasn't really sin or that it wasn't destructive.

I could easily beat myself up about this, which is why I love the two reminders in Colossians 3:9,10: **"Do not lie to each other, since you have taken off your old self with its practices and have put on the new self, which is being renewed in knowledge in the image of its Creator."**

Reminder one: Do not lie. Because I still lie, I need to hear the command.

Reminder two: I have a new self. "Liar" is not my identity.

When Jesus died on a cross, he took the punishment for all the times I lied (and still lie) and gave me his record of having never lied.

I'm thankful that God's fact-checker—the Bible—tells me this truth.

Where two or three gather

Pastor Mike Novotny

One of the Bible's most beautiful passages just might be one of its most misquoted. Ever heard Jesus' famous words: **"For where two or three gather in my name, there am I with them"** (Matthew 18:20)? Normally pastors quote this verse so they don't feel bad when only two people come to Bible study. At least Jesus showed up!

That's true, but that's not the context. The context of Matthew chapter 18 is the agonizing conversation with a sinner who doesn't seem to care at all about sin. When you are waiting at the coffee shop to talk to your sister about her affair. When you and a guy from church are driving to your friend's house to discuss why he thinks he can be close to Jesus without a regular connection to Jesus' Word or Jesus' people. When you try to speak the truth in the most loving way you can to your daughter, but her arms are crossed and she's not listening.

Those are brutally hard moments. But in the midst of it, where two or three gather in Jesus' name to reach out, to share the Word, to beg for repentance, guess where Jesus is? With you. Right in that moment, God is with you. No matter how they react. No matter what they decide. No matter if they love you or hate you for caring, remember Jesus' promise: "There am I with them."

Crocus watch
Jason Nelson

My favorite tree is a towering white pine because it's majestic, soft, and always green. My favorite bird is the red cardinal because he jumps out at you and his call is very certain. My favorite fish are walleyes because their early spring bite is very subtle and they are delicious if you catch some. And my favorite flower is the crocus because it's the most courageous blooming thing in the ground. Against the odds, it punches its little round head through the last snow of winter and announces to the world, "Tada! Spring is here." You have to love a flower with an attitude like that.

When **"flowers appear on the earth; the season of singing has come"** (Song of Songs 2:12). So let's all be on crocus watch. Let's keep our eyes peeled for the earliest signs that we're heading out of the rough seasons of our lives. Better days are coming. Let's all sing, "Tada!"

Let's not just be on crocus watch for ourselves. Let's be on crocus watch for one another. That's how polio was cured and measles were eradicated and why more people are surviving cancer. People were on crocus watch for one another. Some saw that titanium and plastic could blossom into new hips and knees. Some had a hunch the power of sun and wind could become power we can plug into. In every season, wide-eyed people are on crocus watch. And "Tada!" God makes our lives better through them.

Thank God for detours

Pastor Mike Novotny

You're late to the company party. Your hot dish is getting lukewarm on the backseat as you zip through yellow lights (well, orangish, to be precise). But then you see the sign—Detour. You try not to take God's name in vain as you hear the lovely voice of your GPS navigator, "Recalculating . . ."

Life is like that, right? You have a simple plan to get from A to B. Graduate, get a good job, and then start a family. Invest for a few more years, retire, and enjoy the last decades of your life. Move, find a reasonable apartment, and get connected to a good church. But then you get detoured. Roadblocked. And you try not to take God's name in vain as you recalculate.

Which is why you need to remember Mary and Joseph. Pledged to be married. Expecting a child. Ready to settle down. But then Caesar's decree came and life got detoured. **"So Joseph also went up from the town of Nazareth in Galilee to Judea, to Bethlehem the town of David, because he belonged to the house and line of David"** (Luke 2:4). From home to Bethlehem was almost 90 miles and over 1,000 feet in elevation to climb with a very pregnant Mary. I would call that a detour! But God was up to something. Getting the pregnant virgin (Isaiah 7:14) to the promised birthplace of the Savior (Micah 5:2).

That puts our detours in perspective. God is up to something—getting the right people to the right places to accomplish his purposes. So take a deep breath, trust his plan, and thank God for detours!

may

Come near to God and he will come near to you.

James 4:8

Lies: Life should be getting easier

Pastor Mark Jeske

Christians love, love, *love* the passages in Scripture that promise God's blessings on a believing life. We love to pray that God will take our problems away and expect that those prayers will be answered with a Yes. We love the assurance of angelic protection, material prosperity, security, and good health. Indeed, sometimes it furthers God's agenda to send us treats.

But not always. Sometimes he allows us to suffer setbacks and defeats, to taste pain and sadness, to lose rather than gain financially. What?! Isn't God all-powerful? Aren't we his dear children, the apple of his divine eye? Why are there so many psalms like this one: **"Have mercy on me, Lord, for I am faint; heal me, Lord, for my bones are in agony. My soul is in deep anguish. How long, Lord, how long?"** (Psalm 6:2,3). Aren't our lives supposed to be getting easier? Here's the lie: that the hardships in your life prove that there's something really wrong with you, or worse—that there's something really wrong with God.

The truth is that we live in a permanently broken world. In spite of all the romantic dreams of social planners and their optimistic utopian communities, we have to make do in a world still groaning under the curse of human sin. No one escapes its consequences. Illness, crime, injury, and war afflict believers as well as unbelievers.

Here's the difference: God sets limits to the sufferings his children must endure, and he makes all things work out for their good in the end.

Keep struggling
Pastor Jeremy Mattek

A few years ago, there was horrible flooding in Louisiana. A man named Josh got in a boat when the waters started rising in order to stay safe. As he made his way through the deep waters of the city, he saw a dog trapped under a bush with its eyes and nose barely above water. When Josh pulled it into the boat, it collapsed from exhaustion.

Now if that dog had *stopped* struggling in the water, it would've meant that it had given up hope. So in that sense, a struggle is a good thing, a sign of hope.

Just like your faith struggles. In Luke 13:24, Jesus said, **"Make every effort to enter through the narrow door."** "Make every effort" literally means to "struggle." Jesus wants and expects you to struggle because your faith struggles mean you have hope that heaven is in the future.

And hope is exactly what we have because Jesus chose to struggle for his life on a cross so that we, who fail in our faith so easily, could be forgiven of all the struggles that make us ashamed to stand in front of him.

When you start to feel down about your struggles, the best way to calm your fears is to shine the spotlight on Jesus, on who he is and what he did. Then you'll always see yourself as someone God has already chosen to love here on earth and forever in heaven.

That hope will always give you a reason to keep struggling.

Paying the price for being incomplete

Jason Nelson

We are underperforming in many important arenas because the teams on the field are incomplete. Too many things are still under the thumbs of old white men like me. Men bring something to the table. But when women aren't seated around the table, we miss half of humanity's brainpower. We miss more than half of humanity's compassion and almost all of humanity's intuition about solving problems. And we miss the point of how God completed the team at the very beginning. **"It is not good for the man to be alone."** No kidding! **"I will make a helper suitable for him"** (Genesis 2:18).

An incomplete team would have meant disaster for God's people during the chaotic time of the judges. A warrior named Barak had the good sense to stand down and team up with Deborah the prophet, who held court under a palm tree. She ordered him into battle against the enemy. He was supposed to be the tough guy. But he had cold feet. He wasn't going into battle without her. **"If you go with me, I will go; but if you don't go with me, I won't go"** (Judges 4:8). Deborah took it in stride and made an adjustment on the fly: **"Certainly I will go with you"** (verse 9). She wasn't afraid and didn't care who got credit for the victory. But it wouldn't be Barak. She just wanted to make sure everyone was following the Lord.

Entry requirement
Pastor Matt Ewart

Someone once asked me why God would make the entry requirement for heaven so high. If he loved the world, why not drop the expectations down a bit? Perfection is kind of impossible.

Well, here's the thing. God did not just arbitrarily pick a standard that nobody could attain. *Perfection* was as low as he could go, and here is an illustration to show why.

If nobody else is watching you right now, go ahead and cup your hands together so that there is a dark, empty space inside of them. Make it nice and dark. Good.

Now take that darkness and throw it toward the nearest light source.

How far did your darkness get? I literally just tried it, and mine didn't make it very far at all. Darkness cannot exist in the presence of light. Darkness is consumed by the light.

You already knew that, but here's the point: **"God is light; in him there is no darkness at all"** (1 John 1:5).

In order to exist with God, there can be no sin, no evil, no darkness at all. Anything less than holiness cannot exist in his presence. But here's where the good news kicks in.

"The blood of Jesus, his Son, purifies us from all sin" (1 John 1:7).

Through faith in Christ, God looks at you right now and sees you as his holy one. You meet the requirement. You are fit for heaven. Now live this day in light of that good news.

Living with loss: A child
Pastor Mark Jeske

Of all the types of human loss to have to endure, I think for me losing a child would be the bitterest. My mother-in-law's sister died as a child in her father's arms on Christmas Day. I don't know how the dear man bore his grief.

King David's infant child was seriously ill: **"David pleaded with God for the child. He fasted and spent the nights lying in sackcloth on the ground. The elders of his household stood beside him to get him up from the ground, but he refused, and he would not eat any food with them"** (2 Samuel 12:16,17). We know all the reasons why death has invaded our world and sometimes claims victims we think are far too young to die. We know about the wages of sin. It still hurts terribly.

David and Bathsheba probably thought about their dead child every day for the rest of their lives. But they had two important gifts from God to sustain them and keep them going: One is that those who die in the Lord will live in the Lord. Our loved ones, including children, are believers through the power of Word and sacrament, and connected to Christ by the power of Christ they are immortal. We will see them again. Second, God gave the grieving parents urgent and important work to do so that their lives wouldn't just grind to a halt, paralyzed by their crushed hearts.

I think the best way to deal with emotional pain is to serve others.

Devoted to prayer
Pastor Mike Novotny

Okay, confession time. I stink at prayer. *Stink* might be a strong verb, but it's the right one. I've tried prayer apps, repeating calendar reminders, journaling, and a dozen other systems over the years, but prayer feels way harder than reading my Bible or going to church. Recently, I started keeping track of my blocks of dedicated, personal prayer time. After two months, I tallied up all the minutes and ended up with . . . 15. Not 15 *hours* of prayer, but 15 *minutes*. In 2 months. Yikes.

But I'm not giving up. I'm re-devoting myself to the kind of prayer the apostles embraced. **"They devoted themselves . . . to prayer"** (Acts 2:42). Why try prayer again? Because prayer works. The devil fears people who persist in prayer. And I've seen the power of prayer among my church family. When a small group of Christians starts a texting thread that is always open for prayer, God does amazing stuff in their hearts and at their church. When we pray the gospel over each other, God does amazing stuff, breaking chains of guilt and erasing years of shame. When we don't see prayer as the token starter pistol for dinner or the closing requirement before bed but as a privilege and a power source, God does amazing stuff. So, even if the new habit is hard, prayer is worth it. God is listening. And he can't wait to hear the sound of your voice. Would you join me in prayer today?

Givers get!

Pastor Mike Novotny

Every farmer agrees with Paul's famous words: **"Remember this: Whoever sows sparingly will also reap sparingly, and whoever sows generously will also reap generously"** (2 Corinthians 9:6). You reap what you sow. You get out of the ground what you first put into it.

Every generous giver agrees. While the world might assume givers give away their happiness, God promises otherwise. And some of you have experienced it. You've been there when the church you supported baptized a woman in Jesus' name. You've seen the preschoolers with their oversized backpacks singing "Jesus Loves Me" at the school you supported generously. You've heard stories of missionaries you supported bringing the gospel, bringing hope, bringing the forgiveness of sins. You've reaped a harvest of joy!

And most of the stories you haven't heard. When the pastor you paid to serve full time helped that family hang on after the affair. When the staff you supported was there at the hospital or in the funeral home to give the hope of heaven in Jesus. When the teenager who felt such shame over his sin texted your pastor, desperately needing grace, and he gave it. You were a part of that. Do you believe that? You were there. Your gifts made that possible.

To quote Paul, "Remember." Remember the impact of your generosity, and soon you will find Jesus' words ringing true: It is more blessed to give than to receive.

A little respect, please
Pastor Mark Jeske

Baseball fans sitting in the stands, even way up in the nosebleed sections, are not shy about pointing out what they believe to be bad calls by the ump and suggesting deficiencies in his vision. Football fans will howl when they think a penalty flag on the home team is unjustified, especially when they can watch the replay on the big screen. Voters in our country also are not bashful about pointing out shortcomings in their elected officials.

Thus it's probably not surprising that people feel entitled also to criticize the way God is managing the universe. Even faithful believers sometimes groan in their struggles and wish God would do things in different ways. Our problem: we can't see what God sees; we haven't been all the places God has been; we have existed for only a tiny snapshot in earth's history and often lack the big, I mean really big, picture. God is patient with our complaints, but he would like a little respect: **"Where were you when I laid the earth's foundation? Tell me, if you understand. . . . On what were its footings set, or who laid its cornerstone— while the morning stars sang together and all the angels shouted for joy?"** (Job 38:4,6,7).

All the things that God does in human history, and all the things he allows to happen, are woven together in a strategic plan that works out for the benefit of the believers. When you are confused or disappointed in your spiritual life, cut God some slack, okay?

Forgiveness sagas
Jason Nelson

The story of civilization is a forgiveness saga. Unfold a big world map on a table and drop a dime on any modern population center. Drill down into the history of that place, and you'll discover that before citizens enjoyed peace and progress, a lot of forgiving had to occur. Weaker aborigines had to forgive stronger invaders before they could forge a society together. The tawdry subplot in almost every instance is that conquerors used their religion as cover for brutally mistreating people. "Since God gave me the victory, it is his will that I lord it over you." Then the oppressed had to forgive God himself, like he was behind it all.

Find your big family photo album and open to the last reunion picture. Drop a dime on the face of anyone in the picture and delve into his or her memory. You will discover that in order for any relatives of yours to smile for the camera, a lot of forgiving had to occur. People could easily hold grudges against other smiling faces standing nearby. But, we moved on. "Since my God has forgiven me, I am letting go of any memory that would make me feel bitter toward you."

People's lives are sagas, and forgiving others is the only way forward. **"Lord, how many times shall I forgive my brother or sister who sins against me? Up to seven times?"** Jesus answers with a multiplier: **"I tell you, not seven times, but seventy-seven times"** (Matthew 18:21,22).

Reaching out in love
Pastor Mike Novotny

Not long ago, a church in Texas followed the four agonizing but necessary stages of Jesus' teaching on dealing with sin (Matthew 18:15-17). Sadly, the story didn't have a Hallmark ending. Instead of repenting, the former church member posted the church's written call to repentance on Facebook and accused the church of being hateful. "Jesus was angry with people just like you," he posted for the internet world to read.

When I read the story, I was moved by the love, gentleness, and commitment of this church. They started by quietly addressing their brother's sin. Then some members of this man's small group Bible study got involved. Eventually, the concerned group told the church. They talked, prayed, wept together, and offered to help. They studied Scripture. But when the man refused to change after over a year of dialogue, they sent the letter he later posted. On it were the signatures of every brother and every sister involved at every stage, the bleeding ink of a community of broken hearts.

Is your heart broken by someone who seems to be walking away from Jesus? If so, let this church's example be a wonderful guide to speaking the truth in love. Even more, remember the example of Jesus, who not only taught these words but lived them when he reached out to us all: **"If a man owns a hundred sheep, and one of them wanders away, will he not leave the ninety-nine on the hills and go to look for the one that wandered off?"** (Matthew 18:12).

Dealing with sin

Pastor Mike Novotny

Why would any Christian in his or her right mind listen to Jesus' teaching in Matthew 18:15-17? Why would any of us even dare to discuss our concerns about a friend's marriage, a brother's divorce, a sister's posts, or the personal life of someone from church? Why not let God judge sinners himself?

The answers to those questions are clear to anyone who has lost something they love. Why do you leave the comfort of your couch to drive 12 mph through the neighborhood after your dog has escaped the yard? And why do you stay up, lose sleep, or drive to the police station when your daughter doesn't come home after practice? And why does a good shepherd leave the comfort of the 99 found sheep and spend a sleepless night searching for the lost 1?

Answer—Because of love. Because true, deep, Christian love always protects. If you love your brother in Christ, you protect him from the punishment of sin. If you love your church family, you protect them from the penalty of sin. If you love your community, you protect them from the offense of not dealing with abuse, adultery, or any other sin that hurts the people Jesus loves.

Why go through these stages, as difficult as they can be? Why have a hard conversation this week? Jesus' answer to you could be summarized in Paul's famous words from 1 Corinthians 13:7. Because love **"always protects."**

A beautiful woman. A beautiful friend.

Pastor Jeremy Mattek

There's a woman in Scripture named Tabitha. Her funeral gives us one of the most touching scenes in the entire Bible. Tabitha made clothes for widows, and when those widows heard that Tabitha had died, they grabbed the clothes she had made for them, went to the funeral, and held on to them the whole time, showing anyone who came what they loved so much about this woman. But it wasn't the clothes they loved so much.

There's a story about a nurse who volunteered to help wounded soldiers during the Civil War. When she was younger, her face was horribly disfigured in a fire. When she was asked why she volunteered to work among so much death and pain, she replied, "The wounded soldiers don't notice my scars as much as the others. To them, I'm beautiful."

The reason these widows showed up at Tabitha's funeral is because Tabitha made them feel beautiful. She made them feel important and loved, just like so many moms do for so many of us.

And just like God did for all of us when he sent a Savior to show us just how beautiful and valuable we've always been to him. **"Greater love has no one than this,"** Jesus said, **"to lay down one's life for one's friends"** (John 15:13).

When your body hurts
Linda Buxa

My back had been mildly hurting for a few days, but by the fourth day, it was *killing* me! (I'm not exaggerating.) I couldn't think about anything else except how much pain I was in and how desperately I needed relief. Finally—*finally!*—I drove to the chiropractor and got my rib put back in place. (This has been an issue since I fell through our garage ceiling a few years ago.)

As soon as I was adjusted, my whole body relaxed and I could think clearly once again. That's because mild pains are usually easy to handle, but when one part of the body is *suffering*, the rest of the body is consumed with helping and healing.

Paul, who lived about two thousand years ago, said the same thing happens with a different kind of body—the body of Christ. **"If one part suffers, every part suffers with it; if one part is honored, every part rejoices with it"** (1 Corinthians 12:26).

The people who call themselves Christians are part of the body of Christ, and when one person in that body is suffering, the rest of the body feels that pain. As Jesus' family, we mourn with him when a loved one dies; our hearts break when she loses yet another child to miscarriage; we support him when he loses a job; we sit with her when she gets the diagnosis. We help carry his or her burden when the burden is too heavy to bear alone, all because the rest of the body is consumed with helping and healing.

Then they came for me
Jason Nelson

Martin Niemöller was a Lutheran pastor in Nazi Germany. He eventually found the courage to publicly oppose Adolph Hitler. As a result, he spent seven years in a concentration camp. He left us with this haunting poem about social responsibility.

First they came for the socialists, and I did not speak out—Because I was not a socialist. Then they came for the trade unionists, and I did not speak out—Because I was not a trade unionist. Then they came for the Jews, and I did not speak out—Because I was not a Jew. Then they came for me—and there was no one left to speak for me (https://en.wikipedia.org/wiki/First_they_came_...).

So, who is my neighbor?

"A man was going down from Jerusalem to Jericho, when he was attacked by robbers. They stripped him of his clothes, beat him and went away, leaving him half dead. A priest happened to be going down the same road, and when he saw the man, he passed by on the other side. So too, a Levite, when he came to the place and saw him, passed by on the other side. But a Samaritan, as he traveled, came where the man was; and when he saw him, he took pity on him. He went to him and bandaged his wounds, pouring on oil and wine. Then he put the man on his own donkey, brought him to an inn and took care of him" (Luke 10:30-34).

So, who is my neighbor?

Worship with heart and mind
Pastor Mark Jeske

If you travel across our land and visit churches at worship from various denominations and religious tribes, you will encounter vast differences in worship styles. You may see Christians reading earnestly from printed prayer books a century old but in other places worship leaders exuberantly improvising their prayers. You may find some congregations singing historical liturgical chant and others with a gospel band playing in the style of a boisterous blues revue. Some congregations hear their pastor's messages with intense concentration and reverent silence, while other audiences shout affirmations and encouragements to their preacher.

Is worship for the head or for the heart? Yes. **"So what shall I do? I will pray with my spirit, but I will also pray with my understanding; I will sing with my spirit, but I will also sing with my understanding"** (1 Corinthians 14:15). God made us with heads and hearts, minds and emotions. If we neglect one or the other, we will not be giving God our whole selves when we worship him.

Worship needs content. The gospel of Christ is history. God did things in space and time, and these mighty acts need to be related in a convincing and coherent way and their implications laid out logically for people to grasp. But worship is not only understanding and believing God but *loving him back* for his great love to us. Worship leaders who are designing congregational experiences need to be mindful that people have hearts too.

It's okay to clap in church.

Guilt by association
Pastor Matt Ewart

Have you ever felt like you should distance yourself from certain people to make it clear that you do not associate yourself with their behavior? You've probably felt that way.

But Jesus certainly didn't act that way.

One of the criticisms aimed at Jesus was **"this man welcomes sinners and eats with them"** (Luke 15:2). He was so close to sinful people that he was accused of condoning the behavior that earned them the "sinner" label.

But that's not the whole picture. Thanks to our first parents, this entire world was labeled "sinful." All of creation was under penalty of death. But Jesus chose to dwell among us anyway—not to communicate that sin is okay but to take the sin away.

He so closely associated with sinners that our label actually transferred onto him. He suffered and died as the result. And now out of his resurrection, there is a new label affixed to every repentant heart that gets filled up with forgiveness: *Child of God.*

As God's child, think about all the people you'll encounter this next day. You will stumble upon some people who have earned labels because of their past behavior. Most people have labels that you don't even know about.

Would Jesus associate himself with them? Absolutely. His presence does not mean he approves of sin. It means he is present to administer grace that leads to repentance, forgiveness, and life to the full.

The cure for conflict

Pastor Mike Novotny

Have you ever seen a Newton's Cradle? A Newton's Cradle is the famous office accessory with the five metal spheres that hang in a row. Pull the first one back and it crashes into the other four, sending the final sphere flying. Then, the final sphere swings back, crashes into the other four, and sends the first one flying once more. And on and on the back-and-forth goes.

Lots of relationships are like that. Someone hurts us with their words (or lack of them when we were in need). They text or email something harsh and unfair, crashing into our hearts and wounding us deeply. In reply, our sinful nature swings back, proving that "hurt people hurt people." Yet, as you know all too well, no one considers the score settled after one round of sin. In a broken world, we all count the score differently, which is why instead of settling the score, we go into another "overtime" of hurting each other in an exhausting match that can last for years.

Tired of all that? Jesus wants to help. If your relationship with your dad or your sister or someone from work or a grouchy neighbor resembles Newton's Cradle, can I encourage you to read Philippians chapter 2 today? There you will find a strong call to humility and forgiveness. Even better, you will find the humble heart of Jesus who **"humbled himself by becoming obedient to death—even death on a cross!"** (verse 8). When our sins came crashing into Jesus, he absorbed the pain and forgave us. Thank God for his immense mercy! Thank God for his amazing grace! And may the grace we have received now be given to others in Jesus' name.

God is faithful

Pastor Mike Novotny

Ed's wife struggled with anxiety. Often her fear of what might happen the next day would keep her up at night. Sometimes the anxiety was so intense she would wake her husband up and ask him to pray. One night, Ed started to pray for his bride when some words popped into his mind, words about the God of angel armies, the friend who goes before us and goes behind, the God who is always by our side.

Soon after, Ed called up his friend Chris with an idea for a song, a song Chris Tomlin would later bring into churches around the world. In their hit "Whom Shall I Fear?" Ed and Chris wrote about God being their sword and shield and that even when troubles are around, they have nothing to fear.

Sounds like King David. In Psalm 27, he sang, **"The LORD is the stronghold of my life—of whom shall I be afraid?"** (verse 1). If God is protecting me with his faithfulness and his unbreakable promises, of whom shall I be afraid?

Christian, sing with that same boldness. The devil would love a dozen "what ifs" to keep you up this night. But he fails to mention the presence and power of your God. Jesus is not only the God of angel armies but also the faithful friend who will never leave your side. He is your sword and shield, no matter how many enemies threaten your joy. So sleep well, and do not be afraid.

Above the crowd

Jason Nelson

"Jesus entered Jericho and was passing through. A man was there by the name of Zacchaeus. . . . He wanted to see who Jesus was, but because he was short he could not see over the crowd" (Luke 19:1-3).

This is my favorite Bible story. One reason is that Jesus concludes it by stating his mission in no uncertain terms: **"The Son of Man came to seek and to save the lost"** (verse 10). That's concise enough to pass the T-shirt test. We could all wear tie-dyed T-shirts imprinted with *Seek and Save.*

Another reason is that Zacchaeus had the same problem every child has: trying to see Jesus over bigger people who are obstructing a clear view of Jesus and his mission. It illustrates our job as parents. To always raise our children to see above the crowd. To always lift them up and elevate their thoughts to the ways of the Lord.

How do we do that? Set the devices aside. Let them climb up in your lap with a big Bible story book that takes two hands to hold. Show them beautiful pictures that almost look real but still leave room for imagination. Point to the sycamore tree, Zacchaeus, and Jesus. Let them repeat the names as you tell them the story until they can tell it to you. Ask a few really important questions. Who did Zacchaeus want to see? *Jesus.* Why did he climb a tree? *So he could see Jesus above the crowd.*

Lies: I won't be happy unless I get my way

Pastor Mark Jeske

Ask a DJ—one of the most popular karaoke bar songs has to be Frank Sinatra's signature "My Way." Can't you just see a guy with a flushed face after three beers crooning into a borrowed mic about how he did it his way? It's a bit of a cliché, but the fact is that people will fight and claw to get what they want. They love Frank's song because they want to live life their way too. But their dream of happiness that way is a lie.

Our Savior Jesus shows us a better way. His life's mission on earth was to make the lives of other people better, not to seek his own power, comforts, attention, or pleasures. In the Garden of Gethsemane, in his earnest prayer gathering up strength for the final struggle with Satan, he expressed his dread of what lay ahead for him, but he humbly and lovingly yielded to his Father's will and agenda.

Jesus expects no less of us. Embedded in the prayer that Christians all over the world recite in private and public worship are his matchless words: **"Your kingdom come, your will be done, on earth as it is in heaven"** (Matthew 6:10). You've said this a hundred, a thousand times. Do you mean it?

God's *agenda* brings satisfaction and long-lasting contentment; God's *value system* is more reliable than ours; God's *power* is behind his way.

There's a discrepancy
Pastor Matt Ewart

Have you ever had buyer's remorse over fast food? It can happen. I've seen it.

Three friends and I were each ordering separately at a certain establishment. Although all four of us paid the same amount of money, what one friend got for his money was far less than what the rest of us received. Let's just say he was a little salty for the rest of the afternoon.

And a little hungry.

When you put in good money, you want a good return. You should get what you pay for. That's how this world works.

But that's not how God works. Trust me; you wouldn't like the result if you got what you deserved. It doesn't matter how good you think you are. You would not get a good return.

Thankfully God is not fair. Every sin should be punished on the spot, but in God's mercy he carries that sin to the cross where it can be settled. If anyone has any reason to complain about fairness, it isn't humanity.

There's a time and a place to keep people honest in this world for the sake of peace and civility. There might even be a time to ask for a refund if the order isn't what you expected. But for today, remember this:

There's a discrepancy between what you have and what you deserve. And in Christ, the discrepancy falls in your favor.

"Give thanks to the Lᴏʀᴅ, for he is good" (Psalm 107:1).

Ambition in the church

Pastor Mark Jeske

These are hard days to be in authority in the church. We live in an age of severe antiauthoritarianism. It seems as if nobody trusts institutions any longer. Some of that skepticism is deserved—stories abound of pastors who sexually abused their young parishioners and of supervisors who protected the abusers and covered up the crimes. Some church leaders have disgraced their ministries with adulterous affairs and embezzlement.

Still—God's church needs leaders, needs structure, needs overseers. In spite of our many human failings, the soul-saving work of the church must go on, for God doesn't have a Plan B. The church will always be the most effective place to learn, receive the sacraments, worship publicly, pray en masse, and be mentored in your serving. That means that Christians still need to recruit, train, and encourage leaders for tomorrow. For all the obvious weaknesses in the organized church, the only alternatives are a disorganized church or no church at all.

Humility in church workers is a good thing. But, you know, we need *ambitious* people too. Ambition can be selfish, but in a godly way it can just mean that a person wants to use God-given gifts. St. Paul agreed—he told his young trainee Timothy, **"Here is a trustworthy saying: Whoever aspires to be an overseer desires a noble task"** (1 Timothy 3:1). Whom do you know that you can encourage to go into full-time ministry? Whom do you know who is serving well and whom you are convinced could serve at a higher level?

Called to love others
Linda Buxa

"Nobody's in the mood to heal divisions; everybody's in the mood to exacerbate them." That's what the political analyst said on the radio the other day.

"If it is possible, as far as it depends on you, live at peace with everyone" (Romans 12:18). That's what God said in a letter written by the apostle Paul to people who lived in Rome about two thousand years ago.

If we're honest, we know how true the first statement is, right? We wish for calm and reasonable people to prevail, but really we wish other people would simply change their opinions and beliefs to match ours. This doesn't only happen in politics. We feel this way about football teams, homeowners association rules, fashion, parenting.

If we're honest, we know how hard the second statement is. It calls for sacrifice from people who call themselves Christians. We're called to love others deeply and serve them at our own expense. It might seem like too much. Yet God isn't asking for anything he didn't do first. He sent his Son to come to earth and sacrifice his life—all so we could live at peace with the Father now and forever. Now with the same comfort this peace gives us, we comfort others. With the same love we've been shown, we love others. With the same grace we've been given, we pass it along freely to others.

How do you expect to tell others about Jesus if you're hard to get along with?

Abusive talk
Pastor Mark Jeske

One of my children patiently explained to me once why he would ridicule and belittle his younger sibling. "Dad," he said, "I'm just getting him ready for the real world. It's a jungle out there." Hahaha. Call it "family Darwinism." I still asked him to knock it off.

I know that game. In my college dorm, the ridicule was constant. I guess the guys justified it as a way to keep anybody from getting too arrogant. We anointed ourselves as God's agents for creating a humble spirit in other people. I fear that we just perpetuated a culture of abuse.

Abusing other people is a sport. It's how the pecking order is established—the most aggressive mockers rule the roost. Spouses do it to each other to establish dominance and control. Athletes do it to spread fear and self-doubt. There is no excuse for it—it's just bad: **"Do not let any unwholesome talk come out of your mouths, but only what is helpful for building others up according to their needs, that it may benefit those who listen. Get rid of all bitterness, rage and anger, brawling and slander, along with every form of malice. Be kind and compassionate to one another, forgiving each other, just as in Christ God forgave you"** (Ephesians 4:29,31,32).

You know, the trash-talkers were maybe feared, but they were never loved. I think you will have a lot more friends if you develop a reputation for building up other people.

More roots, more fruit

Pastor Mike Novotny

The other day I read an article called "Tree Roots: Facts & Fallacies." (Sounds interesting, I know.) The author wrote, "If a large portion of the root system is destroyed, a corresponding portion of the leaves and branches will die." Catch that? If some of a tree's roots are destroyed, the entire tree won't die. Just a corresponding portion of the leaves. In other words, fewer roots, less fruit. Or, to put it positively, more roots, more fruit.

Makes me think of our spiritual lives. The apostle Paul famously wrote, **"But the fruit of the Spirit is love, joy, peace, forbearance, kindness, goodness, faithfulness, gentleness and self-control"** (Galatians 5:22,23). The Holy Spirit produces amazing fruit when we have roots in Jesus. Think of joy, for example. Joy is that untouchable source of spiritual happiness that we tap into through faith. You can have joy even in hard times because you are forgiven, loved, and put through this "pruning" for a purpose.

Which is why your roots are so important. If you stopped reading these devotions and just went to church, your "tree of faith" might not die. If you never connected with a supporting community of fellow Christians, you'd probably make it to heaven. But you would have less fruit.

On the flip side, if you would gather for worship *and* grow through home devotions *and* invest your life in a small group of Christians, those "roots" would produce more fruit. More joy. More peace. More love.

So which root could you plant today that would produce more fruit tomorrow?

Love God more than anything

Pastor Jeremy Mattek

Peter Marshall was a pastor whose wife got tuberculosis and was bedridden for 18 months. To encourage her, he told her about a missionary friend who had been bedridden for eight years. The friend couldn't understand why God would put her in bed while there was mission work to be done. She prayed to get well, but feeling like that prayer wasn't working, she prayed something different: "If I'm to be sick for the rest of my life, your will be done. I want *you* even more than I want health." Within two weeks, she was well.

Hearing the story made Peter's wife realize that she had loved the feeling of being healthy more than she loved God.

Now it's not wrong to love being healthy. We can love that as long as we remember to love God even more. Why? Because he first loved us more than anything. In the Garden of Gethsemane, knowing full well the people he would lose and the coming pain, Jesus said to his disciples, **"'My soul is overwhelmed with sorrow to the point of death . . .' Going a little farther, he fell with his face to the ground and prayed, 'My Father, if it is possible, may this cup be taken from me. Yet not as I will, but as you will'"** (Matthew 26:38,39).

The Father's will was to put Jesus on that cross, to love us more than anything, to forgive us when we've loved anything more than him, and to let us walk through life confident that he will always answer our prayers with the greatest love.

Walk with the wise
Diana Kerr

You've probably heard the saying that goes something like this: "You are the sum total of the five people you spend the most time with." It's basically a modern version of Proverbs 13:20: **"Walk with the wise and become wise, for a companion of fools suffers harm."**

You will become like the people you hang out with, for better or worse. Yeah, you can blame your friends for your screwups, but maybe you need to blame yourself for hanging around those friends in the first place.

Remember when you were a kid and your parents had strong opinions about the friends who were "bad news"? Well, now you're an adult—you get to choose your friends on your own, no parental opinions involved. Just remember that there are consequences to those choices. Do you want friends who will cause you to compromise your values or friends who will strengthen your values? Do you want friends who will make you timid about bringing faith into a conversation or friends who challenge your faith and its presence in your life? Do you want friends who will make it easy for you to stray from God or friends who won't allow you to stray?

Don't be shy in asking God for help in surrounding yourself with friends who will make you wise in his ways. And a little hint about the five people you spend the majority of your time with: Make Jesus one of those five people.

Make it better
Pastor Mike Novotny

I know a guy who's living in exile. He's in a jail cell right now, far away from his family and friends and the comfort of his own bed. But whenever I talk to him, I hear hope in his voice. "Pastor, I started a Bible study in here," he grins. He shares the names of the guys in his cellblock, their personalities, and their views about God. He prays for open doors for the gospel and is ready to baptize people in the shower!

Of course he wishes his exile was over. Of course he wishes he could rewind his life and do it differently. But until God changes his situation, he's not going to be bitter. He's going to make that place better.

Sounds like God's message to the exiles in Babylon. He said, **"Seek the peace and prosperity of the city to which I have carried you into exile. Pray to the LORD for it, because if it prospers, you too will prosper"** (Jeremiah 29:7).

That's a good message if your life has taken you into "exile," into a place you never would have chosen. Your nursing home, your apartment after the divorce, your not-so-dream job might feel like an exile, a foreign place, but God has put you there for a reason. Not only has God forgiven you of your sins through his Son, Jesus, he is working also to bless and prosper the place he has put you.

Remember—Life is not over. God still has plans. Plans to give you hope and a future.

Im-pul-sive

Jason Nelson

Sometimes we make decisions and ask, "What was I thinking?" after the fact. *Ready. Fire. Aim.* That can leave us filled with regret or having buyer's remorse. It's not that God can't make good use of passionate people with itchy trigger fingers. He just has to get them to a point where they steady their own impulses. If you like to strike while the iron is hot, you are in good company. The Bible tells us King David and St. Peter had those tendencies too.

"Then Simon Peter, who had a sword, drew it and struck the high priest's servant, cutting off his right ear" (John 18:10). That was a big oops. **"One evening David got up from his bed and walked around on the roof of the palace. From the roof he saw a woman bathing. The woman was very beautiful. Then David sent messengers to get her. She came to him, and he slept with her"** (2 Samuel 11:2,4). That was a very big oops.

It helps to live long enough to become wiser and fatigued. Maybe that's why Peter and David were able to give this advice later in life: **"Therefore, with minds that are alert and fully sober, set your hope on the grace to be brought to you when Jesus Christ is revealed at his coming"** (1 Peter 1:13). That's a good idea. **"Let the one who is wise heed these things and ponder the loving deeds of the LORD"** (Psalm 107:43). That's a very good idea.

GOD is there

Pastor Mike Novotny

I still remember her heartbreaking words: "I keep jumping to reach God, but I feel like I'll never get there." The woman from my church knew she fell short of Jesus' high standard of love every day. And she felt that GOD, a glorious and good God, was so far away that she'd never get to him.

Ever felt that? When we mess up spiritually, especially when we know better, the most natural thing in the world is to feel what that woman felt. After all, Isaiah said, **"Your iniquities have separated you from your God"** (59:2). Maybe you feel that today. Maybe something from way back—your abortion, your divorce, the words that came out of your mouth to your dad or about someone of another race or toward your ex. Or maybe it's something from just now. Some default setting to control or get the last word or make a big deal out of nothing or keep score instead of showing grace. You know you have issues, and you assume God is taking a step back, just like everyone else would.

If that's you, listen to Jesus' friend Peter: **"Christ also suffered once for sins, the righteous for the unrighteous, to bring you to God"** (1 Peter 3:18). To bring you to God. Not just to bring him or her or them to God. You. Your sins separated you, but Jesus suffered for your sins. Jesus took them out of the picture. He didn't make you crawl up the morality ladder to get up to him. He came down to get to you. Because of Jesus, GOD is here!

Who controls your microphone?
Linda Buxa

The other day I heard the phrase, "Whoever controls the microphone controls the narrative." The people were discussing media and politics, but I think it is just as true when it comes to faith and our relationship with God. Who controls your microphone?

Is it your own voice saying you are not good enough? Maybe the church of your childhood made you feel only guilt, instead of telling you about freedom in Jesus. Maybe it's the names your parents called you, or possibly the voices of the internet make you feel less valuable because there's no Photoshop in real life. Perhaps the voices come from a wife who belittles you or a husband who undermines you. Maybe your adult children have pushed you out of their lives. Or your boss berates you in front of everyone.

All those microphones are lying to you. Only the One who made you and chose you before the creation of the world has the right to control the narrative. Only the One who sent his Son for you and punished him in your place gets to assign you value.

God calls you a redeemed child and heir of the kingdom of heaven. He calls you precious and gives you the right to approach him boldly. He gives you a spirit of power, not timidity.

Because God controls the microphone, **"we demolish arguments and every pretension that sets itself up against the knowledge of God, and we take captive every thought** [and every microphone] **to make it obedient to Christ"** (2 Corinthians 10:5).

june

I sought the Lord, and he answered me;
he delivered me from all my fears.

Psalm 34:4

GOD will be here

Pastor Mike Novotny

I cringed slightly as I listened to the teenagers from our church answer this question: "What does your faith mean to you?" Because nearly every one of them said, "My faith means . . . that when I die, I will go to heaven."

Ahh . . . that's true, but faith is so much more than that. Faith is not just a golden ticket you keep in your pocket in case you die today. Faith is trust in God's present presence. Jesus died and rose so that every Christian could smile and say, "GOD is here." He is. Not he will be. GOD is here!

This view of faith is the key to confidence, to peace, to contentment, to joy. **"Do not be afraid, for I am with you"** (Isaiah 43:5). GOD, the holy, glorious, incredible, thrilling, peace-giving GOD is here with you by the blood of Jesus. That's the good news. Even though you walk through the valley of the shadow of death, you will fear no evil, for GOD is with you. Even though there are a dozen messed-up things in your life and a dozen more coming tomorrow, nothing can touch the promise of God—"I am with you." Those are the words that have changed the world. And those are the words that can change your life. So smile, brothers and sisters— GOD is here!

Why don't they ask me for help?

Pastor Mark Jeske

All parents at one time or another have had the heartbreak of watching one of their kids struggle, muddle around, and make a mess of things. We sit in the principal's office, in the hospital, at the police station wondering why? And how? We hurt for them, but we hurt for ourselves too. What are we? Chopped liver? Why didn't they come to us for help? Why did they keep us out of their lives, avoiding and evading?

God knows that sad feeling—he's been going through it with his children for millennia: **"They do not cry out to me from their hearts but wail on their beds. They slash themselves, appealing to their gods for grain and new wine, but they turn away from me"** (Hosea 7:14). Why would anybody pass up God's help? Perhaps people want to control the situation by creating a scenario in which it is *their* actions that solve the problem. Perhaps they don't want to feel obligated to a divine rescuer. Perhaps Satan's temptations have confused their perceptions of how things happen in the world. Perhaps the seductive lure of other gods just seemed so much cooler.

Maybe that's why God so often allows suffering into our lives. Suffering has a way of breaking down stubborn hearts, clearing mental fog, and creating an opportunity for prodigal sons and daughters to despair of the false promises of idols and give their heavenly Father a chance again.

It's not too late. God is waiting to hear their voices. And yours.

Worship is remembering
Pastor Mark Jeske

The Deists in England and colonial America in the 1700s believed in a God who created the world, but they had no confidence that he was still engaged, that he actually intervened and acted in human history.

Scripture tells the stories of a God *intensely* interested in everything going on here. Though he dwells in heaven's resplendent light, his fingerprints are all over the human story as it has unfolded. Read the Word! Hear the stories! **"Remember the wonders he has done, his miracles, and the judgments he pronounced"** (1 Chronicles 16:12). Imagine the crash of Jericho's walls coming down. Listen for Goliath's grunt as David's stone crashed into his forehead. See the Israelites cross the Jordan River on dry ground, the waters on the north end piling up as they waited for God's invisible hand to let the flow resume.

Worship is *remembering*. Remember how ferocious the power of the angel armies must be as they swiftly and silently slew 185,000 Assyrians besieging Jerusalem. Imagine how good miraculous bread and fish tasted on a Galilean hillside after you had missed several meals. Pretend that you were the parents of a demon-possessed boy who was liberated from his tormentor. Imagine the stunning joy when the early visitors to Jesus' empty grave were told by angel messengers that he was alive.

Remember what God has done for you personally—prayers answered, gifts given, spirits lifted, sins forgiven. Remember what it cost Jesus to do these things for you as you worship him.

Scared to give?

Pastor Mike Novotny

If you're scared to give generously, whether your time to serve others or your money to spread the gospel, Paul's words are exactly what you need. **"God is able to bless you abundantly, so that in all things at all times, having all that you need, you will abound in every good work"** (2 Corinthians 9:8). Paul is all about the fear-erasing "alls."

"In all things at all times." Good times, bad times. Tuition times, tax times. Got a raise times, lost my job times. That time and this time. God will bless you through it all.

"Having all that you need." All the promises you need—the presence of God, the power of God, the mercy of God, the grace of God, the Spirit of God, the Son of God. All your heart really needs to be happy, to have hope, to breathe, to be blessed is God, and you have him because Jesus brought you back to him.

So "you will abound in every good work." With God, you're not scraping by in life. No bare minimums. No, you are abounding! Doing the exact works God lined up for you to do. This church to support. This poor family member to feed. This neighbor in need.

If you're scared to give, remember that giving is like farming. A generous life is like a seed. And the God who created the sun and rain will provide it *all* to make that seed grow.

Uncontainable
Pastor Matt Ewart

If God would just show up in a real, measurable way, a lot more people would take him seriously. I know I would benefit if I could look up into the sky and literally see God right there smiling at me. Ever wonder why he doesn't do that?

My mind wanders to a movie with Chris Farley (a really big guy) and David Spade (a really small guy). In one scene Farley puts on one of Spade's suit coats that is obviously ten sizes too small for him. After a few moments of taunting, Farley swings both of his arms toward his body and rips the suit in half.

You haven't lived until you see a really big guy rip a suit coat in half.

As much as that suit coat was not designed to contain a big person, so much more this universe cannot possibly contain the God who made it.

When Solomon completed a temple for the Lord, he made this observation: **"But will God really dwell on earth? The heavens, even the highest heaven, cannot contain you"** (1 Kings 8:27).

It would take a miracle for God to fit inside this universe. But miracles happen when they need to.

Jesus, the Son of God, who by nature would have destroyed this universe if he had simply stepped into it, took on actual flesh and blood so he could enter it.

God didn't just show up in a measurable way. He showed up in the only way that we could see him and know him.

It's hard to love, but it's worth it

Pastor Jeremy Mattek

Recently in Springfield, Missouri, people on the street noticed a man pacing on top of a downtown building. It became evident that he was thinking about jumping, so they shouted words of encouragement to convince him to come down. Then they wondered if the man could hear them. So they made large signs that said things like, "Let us help." "You're valuable." "You're not alone." And it worked. The man came down.

What a great thing those strangers did. But that can also be exhausting—being there for people who are needy, people who suck energy out of you as their needs demand your attention. Sometimes they don't give any indication that your investment in their lives is even working. It can be hard to keep going.

Jesus knows that better than anyone. He promised to always be there for us. It was hard to keep that promise. It was hard to be patient with his disciples, to be whipped and crucified and beaten. But no matter how hard it was to love us, he did. Simply because he promised he would. And he wanted you to know that if God makes a promise, he'll keep it. So today, as you think of those who demand your time and energy, hear this promise from 1 Corinthians 15:58 to remind you that your hard work will always be worth it.

"Therefore, my dear brothers and sisters, stand firm. Let nothing move you. Always give yourselves fully to the work of the Lord, because you know that your labor in the Lord is not in vain."

Light becomes hope
Jason Nelson

When darkness was so thick you could wear it, God had an idea. **"Let there be light"** (Genesis 1:3). In a flash, he knew he could get photons excited enough to glow. He made them glow in the direction of his magnetism. He dialed in different intensities so he could create day and night, dusk and dawn. He sourced light in suns, moons, stars, and on his own face. He figured out that light across a spectrum would make for a very colorful existence. He put all the physics in place in the blink of an eye. There it was. Light. And he wanted others to enjoy the beauty of light as much as he did. He willed for people to see the light and reflect the light. To be the image of light.

Darkness didn't surrender. It never does. It's powerful too. It always threatens to snuff out any little bit of light. But God is light. He will not let evil take us back to only darkness. God is there in every ray of hope for a happy ending. His face lit up with pleasure in his one and only Son who is the Light of the world. Christ's love for us brightens our mood.

When you feel darkness creeping in, may the light of the Lord bless you and keep you. May his face shine on you and show you his grace. May he look you right in the eye and give you peace. Amen.

june 8

The power of "all y'all"
Pastor Mike Novotny

Unless you read Greek, you might have missed the powerful principle Paul shared with the Corinthians: **"But when you are tempted, [God] will also provide a way out so that you can endure it"** (1 Corinthians 10:13). What's easy to miss in modern English is the number of *you*s contained in Paul's "you."

Up where I live in Wisconsin, we use the same word for talking to one person or lots of people: *you* singular and *you* plural. But Greek is more like the American South. Greeks had a special word for *y'all* when speaking to more than one person, which Paul uses here multiple times. In this passage, Paul is literally saying, "But when *y'all* are tempted, God will also provide a way out so that *y'all* can endure it."

What's the difference? Paul knows little of a "personal relationship with Jesus" that can handle the crushing weight of temptation. He knows everything of a community in relationship with Jesus that battles temptation together. And that is how you say no to sin, whether gossiping about relatives or self-medicating with food or alcohol. By myself the weight of this temptation is too much. But not with y'all. With all y'all's wisdom and prayers and accountability and forgiveness, this is not more than I can handle. This is not more than I can bear.

So leverage Paul's powerful method of resisting temptation. Reach out and involve others. Tell them your struggles and ask for their prayers. Harness the power of "all y'all"!

Wouldn't you rather be serving God?

Pastor Mark Jeske

When people repent of their sins and come to faith in God, their capacity for spiritual judgment and action changes. Scripture tells us that unbelievers are spiritually dead. But the corollary is that believers *can* discern good from evil, *can* understand consequences, and *can* make good choices. And so God expects that of us. When spiritual amnesia sets in and God's people start to forget who they are and for whom they are working, God will sometimes allow hardships to come upon them—not to punish or destroy, but as an exercise in refreshing their memories.

The prophet Shemaiah once spoke to the Israelites to help them understand that God still loved them but was going to use the Egyptian Pharaoh Shishak as a schoolmaster for an important lesson: **"When the Lord saw that they humbled themselves, this word of the Lord came to Shemaiah: 'Since they have humbled themselves, I will not destroy them but will soon give them deliverance. My wrath will not be poured out on Jerusalem through Shishak. They will, however, become subject to him, so that they may learn the difference between serving me and serving the kings of other lands'"** (2 Chronicles 12:7,8).

This is a big deal. As Bob Dylan once said, "You gotta serve somebody." Other masters are cruel, unloving, abusive, expensive, and destructive. They promise everything and deliver nothing.

Wouldn't you rather be serving God?

Communicating clearly

Linda Buxa

Our daughter was coming up the driveway when my husband made the universal signal for "roll down your window." (You know, the crank-your-arm-in-a-circular-motion signal.) Because she has never literally had to roll down a window, she didn't know he wanted to talk to her. She kept on driving. As we all do when someone misunderstands, he made the motion more fervently. Still, she drove on.

Later, we laughed about the miscommunication.

It's easy to think we are communicating clearly when—in reality—we aren't. It's funny when it comes to a car window. It's not funny when we're talking about Jesus, because there is much more at stake.

If you believe in Jesus, you have the job of communicating clearly to people who don't yet know about Jesus. They will not know some of your big, fancy church words, because they haven't learned them. Don't say, "We all know the story of Noah." (They might not.) Tell them the story of a man who built an ark and how God saved him and his family. Don't expect them to have the same standards of morality, because they haven't yet learned about God's good plan for his people. Don't assume they've heard the story of salvation. Tell them exactly what Jesus did and how eternities are changed because of him.

Instead of expecting them to learn your ways, take a great lesson from 1 Corinthians 9:22: **"I have become all things to all people so that by all possible means I might save some."**

I carry a lot of anger
Pastor Mark Jeske

I know why people carry anger for a long time because I've done it myself. It doesn't make us happy, but it does offer some powerful advantages: we have moral high ground and can "righteously" despise the one we think hurt us, and anger helps us justify ourselves and blame others. Letting go would just let the other person off the hook. And angrily bringing up old hurts is a weapon in our arsenal that we can bring out when it's helpful to win an argument or fight.

But anger is toxic, poisoning mind and belly. Anger is prison, and only we have the key, because it is a self-imposed imprisonment. You and I are not destined or forced to stay angry. It is a sick choice we make. The gospel of Christ calls us to a different way, a better way: **"If it is possible, as far as it depends on you, live at peace with everyone. Do not take revenge, my dear friends, but leave room for God's wrath, for it is written: 'It is mine to avenge; I will repay,' says the Lord"** (Romans 12:18,19).

Those who have been forgiven much by the Savior can demonstrate that their gratitude is real by showing mercy to the other fools and sinners around them. Furthermore, you don't have to fear that someone who has hurt you is going to get away with it. God saw everything and will take care of the punishing in his own way.

Give it all to him. Right now.

Do not be afraid

Pastor Mike Novotny

My grandma Novotny used to love wearing angel sweatshirts. Standard-issue gray with long sleeves and an angel stitched onto the chest. I can still remember the details of those angels—winged, diapered, and chunky enough to be a future diabetic risk.

But I have a hunch the Christmas angels didn't look like that. **"An angel of the Lord appeared to** [the shepherds]**, and the glory of the Lord shone around them, and they were terrified"** (Luke 2:9). Those grown men were "terrified" by a single angel. I have a hunch he wasn't wearing a diaper . . .

That detail reminds me of what happens when God's glory and human sinfulness meet. When God pulls back the curtain and we humans experience holiness, it is terrifying. We fall on our faces. We hide our eyes in the dirt. Somehow, instinctively, we know we are not worthy to stand, to look, to laugh.

But listen to the angel's message: **"Do not be afraid. I bring you good news that will cause great joy for all the people. Today in the town of David a Savior has been born to you"** (Luke 2:10,11). Because of the Savior born to us, we do not have to be afraid. Despite our sins, we do not have to fear that God will punish us, exclude us, or condemn us. Instead, we can stand up and see his glorious face. And we can worship with the angels.

God's kingdom work starts so small

Pastor Mark Jeske

I love reading the history of congregations and church bodies, especially the stories of their founding and early days. How tiny the groups were at first! How scraggly and forlorn and poor they were. What huge obstacles they had to overcome to make it into their second decade. How devastating their early setbacks. And yet they made it and grew and flourished.

That's how God works. His Word is powerful. Like a tiny seed, it has the power to bring about explosive growth when it is planted into fertile and ready soil: **"The kingdom of heaven is like a mustard seed, which a man took and planted in his field. Though it is the smallest of all seeds, yet when it grows, it is the largest of garden plants and becomes a tree, so that the birds come and perch in its branches"** (Matthew 13:31,32).

God is not scared of really small beginnings, and you shouldn't be either. If you are thinking of starting a ministry, as long as it is based on God's Word and God's Great Commission agenda, as long as it serves people's needs and has Christ at its center, you don't have to feel overwhelmed by the size of your task. Just plant those seeds, throw your energy and prayers into it, and expect the mustard seed to grow into a tree where a lot of people can find shelter.

The Word works!

Whose world is ending?

Jason Nelson

I knew some wannabe prophets who predicted the end of the world would come in their lifetimes. But they're gone now. They saw things they didn't like and assumed that must be it. They pressed Cold War era events through the book of Revelation like it was a prophetic strainer. Evil nations with nukes came out as the beasts God warned about. A swath of Christians still thinks that way and has influenced American foreign policy, especially relating to Israel because it figures in the apocalyptic story line.

It's tempting to call for the end of all things when some things aren't going your way. But I think it's a selfish prophet who says, "Since my world is coming to an end, yours should too." Jesus said, **"You know how to interpret the appearance of the sky, but you cannot interpret the signs of the times"** (Matthew 16:3).

I'm sorry if you feel like your world is coming to an end. Some worlds are already gone. My grandfather's is gone. But, despite his predictions, mine is still here. I accept that my world is coming to an end and that I will never get a '72 Malibu SS. But I don't want my children's world or my grandchildren's world to come to an end. If I last that long, I won't want my great-grandchildren's world to end either, because I believe God is still **"reconciling the world to himself in Christ"** (2 Corinthians 5:19).

It's hard to keep a promise

Pastor Jeremy Mattek

Carl Lewis won his first gold medal in the 1984 Summer Olympics. His father died one year before the next Olympics. At the funeral, Lewis took his gold medal and placed it in his father's casket. His mom wasn't sure that was a good idea, but he said, "Don't worry, Mom; I'll win another."

The 1988 Olympic 100m dash meant a lot to Lewis. He ran the fastest 100m of his life but finished second to a Canadian, Ben Johnson. Three days later, Johnson tested positive for steroids. His gold medal was given to Lewis, who then kept the promise he had made to his mom. However, he was reminded that no matter how great the promises are, no matter how hard you work to keep them, challenges will sometimes make it hard or even impossible for you to do it.

It's why marriages fail, hearts are full of guilt, and relationships break. Because we're up against Satan and his temptations. We're proof that it's hard to keep a promise.

It was hard for Jesus too—to hang on a cross, to suffer, to keep his promise to love and forgive us. But he did. And because he kept that promise, you can be confident that he'll also keep this one: **"No temptation has overtaken you except what is common to mankind. And God is faithful; he will not let you be tempted beyond what you can bear. But when you are tempted, he will also provide a way out so that you can endure it"** (1 Corinthians 10:13).

A godly choice

Pastor Matt Ewart

One of the fathers in the Bible whom I admire the most is Joseph. He was engaged to Mary, and he was in the process of preparing a household for his soon-to-be wife and, God-willing, family.

But his plans and his dreams changed the moment he discovered that his fiancée, whom he had not been with yet, was pregnant. He planned to quietly break off the engagement rather than destroy Mary's reputation. He made what would have been a good decision that he could have peace with.

But sometimes there's a difference between a good decision and a godly decision.

It took angelic intervention for Joseph to abandon his good choice in exchange for a godly one. Rather than the quiet divorce, he **"took Mary home as his wife"** (Matthew 1:24).

This single act would cost Joseph so much. There would be suspicious neighbors, financial burdens, and even physical danger that would accompany this godly choice to be a father.

But that was nothing compared to what his Child would face.

Nobody would have blamed Jesus for making *good* choices, like saving his own reputation by disassociating himself from those labeled "sinners." Yet Jesus opted for the godly, sacrificial choices every day, culminating with the cross.

You have a Father in heaven who is better than good. He chose the path of sacrifice so that you could have peace with him. Be thankful for that peace today.

But God said

Pastor Mike Novotny

I once made the mistake of promising my kids more than I could deliver. At the start of a lazy Saturday, I said, "Girls, today we are going to eat lunch and take naps and do the Slip and Slide and make dinner and read the Bible and watch a movie and play some board games." But, as I should have guessed, we couldn't fit in everything that Daddy planned. When bedtime arrived, before the board games were out, want to guess what my kids whined? "But, Dad! You said!"

It's hard to admit, but we are all less than faithful to our promises. Most of the time we don't intend it, but it still happens. We make a promise, but then something comes up that we didn't know about. Or we run out of time or energy and have to change the plans.

But this is one more reason I love God. Psalm 33:4 praises, "[The Lord] **is faithful in all he does.**" Because God knows everything (nothing surprises him) and because God can do anything (he never runs out of energy), he keeps every promise he makes. He is faithful. So when he promises that your prayers are more than token religious habits, he means it. When he assures you that your time in his Word will never come back empty, he means it. A faithful God couldn't mean anything less.

So hold your Father to his Word. Insist, with the faith of a child, "But, God, you said!"

He is the artist; we are his canvas
Pastor Mark Jeske

Of all the aspects of human life that we crave for ourselves, near the top of the list has to be getting control. We want control of our work situation, we jockey for control in our relationships, and we try to control our children long after they become adults. We would control even the weather if we could.

What usually happens is that we come crashing up against things over which we have little or no control. If we are going to be in God's cast for his play, we want starring roles. We want to be the mighty hero or the princess. We don't want to be the sick girl or the boy in a wheelchair. Jesus' disciples were having trouble processing why God allowed a man to be born with a major disability. They assumed it must have been a punishment: **"'Rabbi, who sinned, this man or his parents, that he was born blind?' 'Neither this man nor his parents sinned,' said Jesus, 'but this happened so that the works of God might be displayed in him'"** (John 9:2,3).

Jesus' answer is full of grace. No, the blindness was not a punishment. The man was chosen to be a canvas on which God intended to paint something beautiful. People were going to be led to faith and saved for eternity *after seeing what God did in his life.* As St. Paul once said, God's strength was made perfect in his weakness.

Are you willing to let God use your life as a platform for his works of grace?

Summer storm
Jason Nelson

Have you been on a big lake when a storm rolls in? Dark clouds gather in the distance, and the distance creeps closer and closer. The air is still in a threatening way. The time lapse between lightning you see and thunder you hear is a gauge for how much time you have to get off the water. Don't take any chances. One more fish just isn't worth it, is it?

"The voice of the Lord is over the waters; the God of glory thunders, the Lord thunders over the mighty waters. The voice of the Lord is powerful; the voice of the Lord is majestic" (Psalm 29:3,4).

In 2011 a tornado ripped through our property. Twenty acres of red oaks and jack pines were uprooted and twisted into a tangled mess and dropped all around our house. Our woods were gone, but our house was spared. It really was. We had the land clear-cut because it was such a mess. For quite a while we looked out the windows at bare soil. But now the trees are coming back.

"The voice of the Lord strikes with flashes of lightning. The voice of the Lord shakes the desert. . . . The voice of the Lord twists the oaks and strips the forests bare" (Psalm 29:7-9).

When the next storm rolls in, listen for the voice of the Lord. In this Psalm, King David says watch from someplace sturdy, like God's temple. Everyone with you will have the same reaction: **"Glory!"** (verse 9).

Lies: I need everyone's approval
Pastor Mark Jeske

To some degree everybody needs to be liked. Mainly that's a good thing. Friends can make our lives a lot better—they can bring encouragement, insights, comfort, smackdown when needed, and a sense of belonging. In his time of suffering, grieving the loss of family members, livestock, and health, Job ached for some compassion and support from his friends. But he got none: **"Have pity on me, my friends, have pity, for the hand of God has struck me. . . . Will you never get enough of my flesh?"** (Job 19:21,22). Understandable.

But you can overdo the need for other people's approval. It's a false dream to think that you need everyone to like you—it's a lie. Not possible. Some people may resent you because they covet your gifts or blessings. Some may be so caught up in their own struggle that they have no energy left for you. Some may be so insecure and needy that they interpret any resources flowing toward you as just that much less flowing toward them. Some pretend to like you just to see what they can get out of it.

If your emotional well-being is dependent on pleasing everybody, you will be miserable all the time. Get your priorities straight: Serve God first. His Word will inform you how to do that. Serve your family and take care of their needs as best you can. Take care of your job obligations and care for your own mental and physical health.

When you get those priorities straight, there will be friends enough.

Self-control
Pastor Matt Ewart

"Like a city whose walls are broken through is a person who lacks self-control" (Proverbs 25:28).

From my personal experience, the attribute that every Christian wishes they had more of is self-control. And the proverb quoted above shows why.

A person who lacks self-control is extremely vulnerable. Temptations scream through the heart unabated. No roadblocks are in place to deter the sinful nature. Anything goes.

And you know this. You feel so guilty when your self-control has failed you. You let your tongue loose *again*. You drank too much *again*. You let anger control you *again*. Why can't you fix this?

Read the proverb above one more time because there's part of it that you skipped over.

What you have isn't just a self-control problem. It's a *brokenness* problem.

Sin has broken through your heart and left you weak, vulnerable, and prone to further attacks. The first step forward is to heal the brokenness, and brokenness is something that only Jesus can fix. So here's what you need to do today.

When your defenses are being tested, remember that you do not have the power to withstand the attack. This is not a self-discipline thing. This is a Jesus thing. You need his forgiveness and power. And regardless of your past performance, he is your strength. He has forgiven what got you to this point, and you can hold him to his promise that his Spirit is what produces the fruit of self-control.

Not my God
Linda Buxa

When President Obama was elected, a number of people said, "Not my president!" Then, when President Trump was elected, people from the other end of the political spectrum said the same thing. This is the adult equivalent of children putting their fingers in their ears, closing their eyes, and saying, "La-la-la-la-la. I can't hear you!" This is simply avoiding reality. The fact is, for American citizens, both men actually have the title of president.

Many people do the same thing with God. Maybe they're afraid they'd have to change their lives or don't want to face the truth; maybe they plan to deal with faith later and prefer their own god for now. So, for now, they put their fingers in their ears, close their eyes, and say, "La la la la la. Not my God!" This is simply avoiding reality. The fact is, for all people of the world, God really is their God—and denying that will have eternal consequences.

The truth is that one day, **"at the name of Jesus every knee should bow, in heaven and on earth and under the earth, and *every* tongue acknowledge that Jesus Christ is Lord, to the glory of God the Father"** (Philippians 2:10,11).

That's why you are vital to God's plan—*now!* You have been called to tell people the good news of Jesus. As you speak his Word, the Holy Spirit will work to unplug their ears and open their eyes to the truth.

What does this mean?

Pastor Mike Novotny

I grew up constantly answering the question—What does this mean? My pastor forced me to think through that question whenever I memorized something from the Bible. But what does this mean? He didn't let me get away with reciting truths that I had yet to truly understand.

Which is why I want to ask you the same question about Christmas. Two thousand years ago, an angel announced to a group of shepherds, **"Today in the town of David a Savior has been born to you"** (Luke 2:11). That sounds nice, but what does that mean? Could you define the name *Savior* in your own words? Would your definition seem like good news to a seven-year-old or someone clueless about Christianity?

Here is how I define it—A Savior is someone who rescues you from danger. A firefighter is a savior if he runs into a burning building and carries out an unconscious child. A doctor is a savior if her split-second decision delivers a person from certain death.

And Jesus is a Savior too. He rescues us from the danger of sin. Sin just once and you face the eternal danger of being separated from God's presence (and all the joy, peace, happiness, safety, comfort, love, friendship, etc. that come with it). But since sin is humanly unerasable, we need someone to save us.

Thank God that Jesus did. Back in Bethlehem, a Savior was born. Not a teacher. Not a coach. But a Savior to rescue you from the danger of sin. That is what the angel's beautiful words mean.

Correctness isn't political

Jason Nelson

We should be able to speak our truth in a free society. So should other people. But it's a rotten lie to suggest belittling people is allowed in order to push back against some social bogeyman called "political correctness." What kind of emptiness has infected our culture that some people are willing to display really bad manners because they think it's called for. Some self-proclaimed Christians have engaged in this subterfuge and disgraced the gospel. Being sensitive to others' concerns is not wimping out. There are things that are correct, and politics has nothing to do with it. Nowhere in the Sermon on the Mount does Jesus suggest it's okay to insult others under certain circumstances.

Take a warning from Isaiah about topsy-turvy morality: **"Woe to those who call evil good and good evil, who put darkness for light and light for darkness, who put bitter for sweet and sweet for bitter"** (Isaiah 5:20).

There are people in the big basket that's all of God's children whose beliefs I don't agree with or whose lifestyle I can't condone. I am willing to say so and explain myself. But I can't *dis-love* them because of it. I can't disrespect them to make my point. I can't abuse them with epithets to show them who's boss. Name-calling is not evangelism or speaking the truth. One of the least correct things I can think of is dishing out evil and calling it good.

The end of anxiety

Pastor Mike Novotny

I should have been anxious. I was about to speak to the biggest audience of my entire life, a crowd of over one thousand people. I should have been terrified of what they would think of me, but that day I wasn't. Because the Holy Spirit helped me remember, "GOD is here. The GOD who loves me, accepts me, and delights in me is here. And he will be here no matter what happens today."

Does anxiety ever get the best of you? Do you freak out trying to impress your boss or your colleagues or your classmates or the guys on the team or the women at church? Do you worry about how you'll perform or how they'll react? Do you drive home with those crazy thoughts, hoping that you didn't sound stupid or look dumb?

Let the apostle Paul free you from all that. He wrote, **"Do not be anxious about anything"** (Philippians 4:6). How? **"The Lord is near"** (verse 5). The Lord GOD, the glorious and good and more than enough GOD is near. If the boss is mad or not, GOD is here. If you do a great job or fall short of your potential, GOD is here. If they applaud you or boo you or are bored by you, GOD is here. What could she do? What could he say? What could they decide that would change that sentence? Nothing. So don't be anxious. The GOD you need to be okay is not way over there. Because of Jesus, he is right here.

You are loved forever

Pastor Jeremy Mattek

When Martin Pistorius was 12 years old, he became sick with cryptococcal meningitis and fell into a coma. He couldn't move, speak, or do anything. But after 12 years of being in that coma, Martin woke up and got his life back. He eventually got married and is now a motivational speaker.

After he woke up, he told everyone that while he was in the coma, he could hear them and feel everything, which is significant because he stayed in a care center for many hours most days. He was often plopped in front of a TV, which was a much better experience than the ones he had when he was with certain staff members who yanked him by the hair to move him, slammed a metal spoon into his teeth while feeding him, yelled at him, poured hot tea into his mouth when he was sick, and even abused him. He heard and felt everything, but he couldn't choose to walk away.

God could choose to walk away from us. He didn't have to send his Son into a world that would one day kill him. God had a choice, and he chose to send Jesus. Jesus chose to go through pain because he wanted you to know that you will always be able to rely on something—on the promise of God's love for you. Jeremiah 31:3 says, **"The LORD appeared to us in the past, saying: 'I have loved you with an everlasting love.'"**

He has. And he promises that he always will.

I'm afraid I'm too far gone

Pastor Mark Jeske

One of the most powerful features of the Star Wars movies is that they retell the greatest of all human stories, the conflict of good and evil. Luke Skywalker's father, Anakin, had thrown in his lot with evil and had become the sinister Darth Vader. Luke pleaded with his father to come back, but Vader believed he was too far gone. "You don't know the power of the Dark Side. . . . It is too late for me."

Perhaps you know someone who has tasted that kind of despair, or maybe you've felt it yourself. It is a serious thing to push God out of your life, and the longer you've done it, the heavier the blanket of inertia that weighs down your shoulders. As long as you think you must generate the goodness and positive energy to change yourself, you will remain stuck.

Let God talk to you: **"'Come now, let us settle the matter,' says the Lord. 'Though your sins are like scarlet, they shall be as white as snow; though they are red as crimson, they shall be like wool'"** (Isaiah 1:18). He knows your sins and loves you anyway. He knows how long it's been and wants you back still. Let his gracious words of forgiveness wash your sins away through the precious blood of Jesus. Let the power of his Spirit jump-start your drooping willpower.

Let the kindness of his tone convince your fearful heart that it's not too late.

Let's talk eagles
Jason Nelson

The inspiring symbol of so many things was on the verge of extinction. In 1963 there were just four hundred nesting pairs of bald eagles in the U.S. Over the years, their numbers were decimated by people who hunted them for their feathers and talons and by the widespread use of pesticides that poisoned their innards. The shells of their eggs became too thin to allow baby eagles to survive to the hatching point. But because we all agreed we didn't want to lose the eagles, they made a comeback. Federal government, state governments, private landowners, and others cooperated to save them. There are now tens of thousands of eagles around America. We can add this to the list of all the things they stand for. They represent what we can accomplish when we work together.

In late winter, I regularly go down to the open water of the big river near my home. I watch the eagles. Ten years ago there were just a couple of them. Today there are dozens. I would have much less appreciation for truths like these had I never seen eagles soar in person: **"I carried you on eagles' wings and brought you to myself"** (Exodus 19:4). **"Those who hope in the LORD will renew their strength. They will soar on wings like eagles; they will run and not grow weary, they will walk and not be faint"** (Isaiah 40:31).

What else should we save so future generations will have a better understanding of God?

Child champion: Little Samuel

Pastor Mark Jeske

A woman named Hannah, living in the tribal territory of Ephraim in the 11th century B.C., had a tough life. Not only was she unable to have a child; she was part of a polygamous marriage, and her rival wife had many sons and daughters and taunted poor Hannah cruelly because of it. Hannah prayed repeatedly for a child and nothing happened.

But then—her miracle. She bore a son, a gift from God, and she named him *"Sh'mu-El,"* Samuel, which means "heard by God." Whereupon she decided to do the most amazing thing, so great was her overwhelming gratitude to God: **"When her husband Elkanah went up with all his family to offer the annual sacrifice to the LORD and to fulfill his vow, Hannah did not go. She said to her husband, 'After the boy is weaned, I will take him and present him before the LORD, and he will live there always'"** (1 Samuel 1:21,22).

Astonishing! She took her little miracle boy to the town of Shiloh, the location of the ark of the covenant and altar of sacrifice to the Lord, and placed him into the care of Eli, the high priest. What a sacrifice! Even more amazing is the child champion who made the best of his new home. What a brave little man! Do you suppose he ever cried, "I want my mom!"?

Samuel grew up to be one of the greatest prophets in Israel's history.

june 30

How to tackle temptation
Pastor Mike Novotny

When author Bill Frey was 11 years old, he tried to get a big stump out of his front yard. For hours he dug and chopped and crowbarred, but the stump wouldn't budge. In the middle of the project, Bill's dad came home and watched his son sweating up a storm. The father commented, "You're not using all your strength." The exhausted kid screamed back in frustration, but his father just smiled, "You're not using all your strength. You haven't asked me to help."

Your heavenly Father is saying the same thing about the temptation you're facing. That same-old sin might feel like a stump stuck in the ground that won't budge despite all your best efforts. But listen to Paul's words: **"No temptation has overtaken you except what is common to mankind. And God is faithful"** (1 Corinthians 10:13).

The temptation you're facing is not new, even if it's new to you. Your Father has seen his kids tempted by that very sin a billion times just this year, and he has helped millions of them overcome. God wants to help you too. God is faithful, meaning he's committed to his promise to be with you as you face temptation, to give you his Spirit when you feel weaker than your temptation, to forgive you of your sins when you fall into temptation, and to raise up fellow Christians who can help encourage you in the face of that temptation.

So, child of God, ask your Father to help!

july

Here is a trustworthy saying that deserves full acceptance: Christ Jesus came into the world to save sinners—of whom I am the worst.

1 Timothy 1:15

God rescues wretches

Pastor Mike Novotny

In the mid 1700s, English writer Samuel Johnson made a resolution to get up in the morning to pray. In 1738 he wrote, "Oh, Lord, enable me to redeem the time which I have spent in sloth." Twenty-one years later, he was praying the same prayer: "Enable me to shake off idleness and sloth." Two years later he admitted, "I have resolved until I have resolved that I am afraid to resolve again." Just a few years before his death, he wrote, "When I look back upon resolution of improvement and amendments which have, year after year, been made and broken, why do I yet try to resolve again?"

Ever been there? Making the same promises to God as you did 30 years ago? The apostle Paul knew that feeling: **"For I do not do the good I want to do, but the evil I do not want to do—this I keep on doing"** (Romans 7:19). Paul didn't just do bad stuff. He *kept on* doing it! His struggle was exhaustingly persistent.

But Paul knew where to turn in the midst of feeling spiritually stuck—**"What a wretched man I am! Who will rescue me from this body that is subject to death? Thanks be to God, who delivers me through Jesus Christ our Lord!"** (Romans 7:24,25). I adore those words. God rescues wretches. Wretched men. Pathetic women. Actual sinners. Me and you.

That's why, like Samuel Johnson, we keep trying. Christ's love compels us. His grace motivates us to get up and take on sin once again. And, no matter what happens, grace will have the final word. Thanks be to God!

Using God's measurement
Pastor David Scharf

Oliver Smoot was a freshman sorority pledge at MIT. He and his friends were tasked with measuring the Harvard Bridge with a new unit of measurement, so they developed the "smoot." A smoot is 5′ 7″ in length, which is also the height of Oliver Smoot. He measured the bridge by laying end over end—it was 364.4 smoots plus or minus an ear. Apparently, to this day, you can turn in math homework in smoots to your professor at MIT and he or she is obligated to make the conversion. But try that anywhere else and you'll fail. Because you can't make up your own unit of measurement.

Do you ever try to make up your own units of measurement with life? We try to invent the "Bob," who justifies being angry with his wife but who would never drink too much. We invent the "Alice," who justifies drinking too much but who would never cheat on her husband. We invent the "Louis," who justifies cheating on his wife with porn but would never cheat on his taxes. Do you see my point? We can't make up our own units of measurement. We fail.

But where we've failed, Jesus did not. He came to live under God's perfect law perfectly. God now measures our lives according to Jesus. And when that happens, the measurement comes out true every time. You and I are free. **"Great peace have those who love your law"** (Psalm 119:165).

Not so simple

Pastor Mike Novotny

My wife and I set a crazy goal this year—not to go out to eat for six straight months. That's why I bought us a cookbook entitled *Simple.* The quick-and-easy meals were, even for a kitchen novice like me, pretty simple. And I am proud to report that after seven weeks, we have only gone out to eat a few times. So far, so good!

I wish achieving my spiritual goals was simple. I'd love it if expanding my compassion for the needy or letting small annoyances go was simple, a few steps I could complete in a few minutes. But the apostle Peter knows better—**"Make every effort to add to your faith"** (2 Peter 1:5). Adding compassion and patience takes more than a dash of effort. It requires "every effort."

Like mine, your sin is stubborn. And, like mine, your tempter is unrelenting. He will not let you honor God without a fight. So prepare your heart for the battle. Don't expect a quick prayer to change your character. Make every effort—memorize Scripture, pray continually, confess frequently, set wise boundaries. You can change, but it will not be simple.

Does the challenge scare you? Then don't forget Peter's words: **"His divine power has given us everything we need for a godly life through our knowledge of him who called us by his own glory and goodness"** (2 Peter 1:3). Divine power. Everything we need. Our knowledge of God. Our calling as his forgiven, loved, and empowered sons and daughters.

No, it won't be simple. But with God all things are possible!

Commitment to freedom
Independence Day
Pastor David Scharf

Today the U.S. celebrates the freedom that our country's soldiers have won and fought to preserve for over 240 years. Thank you to all of those in the military, and thank God for committed soldiers! What do you suppose would happen if on the front lines of a battle, half of the soldiers decided not to participate in the fight? The outcome is easy to predict. It would be a disaster!

The Christian life is the same. There's a battle to fight for freedom. There's no room to slack and say, "I'll get to learning and practicing my faith later . . . but, I'm still a Christian!" No, a Christian's life calls for total commitment. Thankfully, we have a Savior who did not flee when facing the cross in our battle against sin and Satan. He was totally committed to our freedom. He sacrificed everything for us on that cross and died on the battlefield . . . so that we would be free. He was bound by death so that we might be free from it eternally! As Jesus himself said, **"So if the Son sets you free, you will be free indeed"** (John 8:36). You are free!

Let that motivate you to live in that freedom and strive every day to defend it with the Holy Spirit's power! Let that move you to answer the Christian's call to duty from our Savior with total commitment!

"Fight the good fight of the faith" (1 Timothy 6:12).

A nation of laws
Jason Nelson

God decreed that good governments should be built upon the right kinds of laws. Not just any old laws, but the right kinds of laws like the ten he gave us. The more righteous and fair its laws are, the nearer that nation is to God. Our obligation as Christians is to . . .

"Observe them carefully, for this will show your wisdom and understanding to the nations, who will hear about all these decrees and say, 'Surely this great nation is a wise and understanding people.' What other nation is so great as to have their gods near them the way the Lord our God is near us whenever we pray to him? And what other nation is so great as to have such righteous decrees and laws as this body of laws I am setting before you today?" (Deuteronomy 4:6-8).

Laws of justice and mercy help a nation honor God. Righteous laws protect every citizen from evildoers who lie, cheat, steal, kill, or want to rewrite laws for selfish reasons. Our founding fathers were a little rough around the edges, but they got this right. In a government ordained by God, no man or woman can ever be above the law.

"There is danger from all men. The only maxim of a free government ought to be to trust no man living with power to endanger the public liberty. But a Constitution of Government once changed from Freedom, can never be restored. Liberty, once lost, is lost forever."

—John Adams

America is an idea

Jason Nelson

"So the land had peace" (Judges 3:11).

America is an idea that can be traced back to England and John Locke's "Second Treatise on Civil Government." Locke assumed there was a God who created people to be free. That freedom would be expressed as people pursued life, liberty, and owning property. Our founding fathers picked up on that idea and declared, *"We hold these truths to be self-evident, that all men are created equal, that they are endowed by their Creator with certain unalienable Rights, that among these are Life, Liberty and the pursuit of Happiness."* It is our shared commitment to this idea that holds us together as a nation—nothing else.

People from around the world come to America to enjoy the blessings of this idea. I could move to France, but I could never become French. A Frenchman could move here and become an American if he was committed to the idea. Our history is the story of clarifying the idea, and our Constitution and amendments codify how we carry it out. Social unrest forces us to reset the balance between asserting individual rights or suppressing them for the common good. This amazing idea is difficult to maintain. Sometimes it seems that we are too big and too diverse to remain the *United* States of America. But we can be one nation under God if we are all committed to that idea.

America! America! God shed his grace on thee
And crown thy good with brotherhood
From sea to shining sea!

Lasting treasure
Pastor Mike Novotny

In early 2018, a couple from Colorado sold everything they owned and bought a boat in pursuit of their dream to sail the open seas. And they did. For one day. But on day two, their boat struck something under the water. Water flooded in, and they had to abandon ship. The boat capsized, and they lost everything. The woman cried, "Everything I've worked for, everything I've owned since I was a child, I brought with me. It's just floating away, and there's nothing I can do."

Can you relate? You might not have lost your net worth in a tragic boat accident, but I bet you have experienced the painful reality of temporary things. Your health doesn't last. Your romantic connection fades. Your finances dip into the red. Your friends lose touch. Your sight, hearing, and memory slowly decline. And you join that poor woman in lamenting, "It's just floating away, and there's nothing I can do."

Actually, there's something you can do—look to Jesus. He promised, **"But store up for yourselves treasures in heaven, where moths and vermin do not destroy, and where thieves do not break in and steal"** (Matthew 6:20). Jesus promised us lasting treasure in heaven, where there is no theft or loss or decay. Even better, Jesus went to a cross so that heaven itself would be our eternal treasure, a gift that no bankruptcy, divorce papers, or cancer cell could take from us.

So, when life reminds you that everything is temporary, fix your eyes on Jesus, your lasting and eternal treasure.

Salt makes everything better
Pastor Daron Lindemann

I'm eating more vegetables these days. Honestly, they can taste kinda bland. I like to sprinkle a little salt on them to make them taste better.

We're most familiar with salt on the kitchen table. But did you know that salt can whiten your teeth, drive away ants, and historically it was used as currency? Salt rations were given to Roman soldiers as pay for their work, giving us our English word *salary*.

In the good old days, doctors would rub salt in wounds to prevent infection. Yowza!

Leviticus 2:13 says, **"Do not leave the salt of the covenant of your God out of your grain offerings; add salt to all your offerings."** God's covenant promise needed some salt. Why?

In ancient times, traders carried pouches containing valuable salt. When two traders came into agreement on a deal, they'd seal the agreement with an exchange of salt. I give you a pinch of mine; you give me a pinch of yours, and we both place that salt in our pouches.

It implies that for either of us to break the agreement, we'd have to find the salt that we exchanged and take back our agreement—but that's impossible.

Jesus is the ultimate offering of God's covenant. When he suffered and died, he was making you a promise. He deposited the salt of his suffering into your pouch, never able to take it back. He's fully committed to you.

Give him a pinch of your salt too.

Think different
Sarah Habben

In 1997 Steve Jobs returned to a struggling Apple with all the force of his abrasive genius. "Think different" became Apple's iconic slogan for the next half-dozen years. Jobs was convinced he could change the world with his products. And he was unapologetic about the people he trampled along the way.

The apostle Paul urges believers to *think different.* **"Do not conform to the pattern of this world"** (Romans 12:2). That "pattern" is the trail ruts made by Satan and followed by Steve Jobs and me and every other sinner: me first; you last. Those ruts are so deep that it seems normal to fight to be first—in family decisions or for dessert, in line for the bathroom or a Big Mac. Paul says, *"Think different.* Not *me* first, but *God* first": **"God helping you: Take your everyday, ordinary life—your sleeping, eating, going-to-work, and walking-around life—and place it before God as an offering. Don't become so well-adjusted to your culture that you fit into it without even thinking. Instead, fix your attention on God. You'll be changed from the inside out"** (Romans 12:1,2 MSG).

When believers *think different,* we think of the cross. Before God demanded our loyalty, he gave us his life. On the cross, Christ chose pain and death and paid our debt. Such a radical act of love reshapes us from the inside out! We don't just think different, we *are* different: newly created to serve our God and neighbor—to change the world—with every breath of our ordinary, everyday lives.

Consider him

Sarah Habben

Christian hearts can get awfully weary in a sinful world. A friend of mine endured four long years of harassment in a corrupt workplace. Teachers are dissed by students they are called to serve. Students are alienated by classmates for being "different." Weariness follows the gloom and guns on the evening news. It settles over you with the word *cancer* and after the argument at your family table. Weariness waylays you whenever temptation wins. Weariness can erode a Christian's resolve on the race marked out for us.

The author to the Hebrews knew how weary a Christian heart can get. He gives this encouragement: **"Consider him who endured such opposition from sinners, so that you will not grow weary and lose heart"** (12:3).

Consider Jesus. He left heaven to rescue sinners. And how was he received? With *opposition* from those he had come to save! Not just our indifference. Not just harassment. But also with derision, with whip, with spit, with thorn, with nails, with sword, with death. Consider him!

But don't end at his grave. Consider him who rose from death. Who sent his Spirit. Who feeds your faith. Who surrounds you with a great cloud of witnesses. Who puts his promises on their lips and into his Word and sacraments. Consider him!

When weariness pulls your soul back when it should push forward, when God seems too silent or too slow to answer prayer—when you wonder if he really loves you . . . consider Jesus.

And don't lose heart.

Worship is rejoicing
Pastor Mark Jeske

There's a lot of logical content to our worship life. There are stories to be told, analyzed, and digested. There are doctrinal truths to be learned and applied. There are internal scriptural connections to be noted, prophecies fulfilled, Old Testament passages quoted in the New, and careful distinctions made. There is biblical geography to be studied; as well as linguistics, cultural, military, and political history.

But there is also emotional content to our worship life. There is also "Yee-haw!"

How can you not get excited about the thrilling triumph of good over evil, Christ over Satan? How can you not want to dance at the stupendous promise of the grand resurrection and reunion of believers? How can you not want to shout for joy to see the exciting progress of the Great Commission to spread the gospel to the ends of the earth? Think of it—a couple hundred believers have become a couple billion. Whoa! **"Glory in his holy name; let the hearts of those who seek the Lord rejoice"** (1 Chronicles 16:10).

Rejoice indeed! Although there are solemn warnings in Scripture that we must heed, although there are terribly sad stories of human failure, and although we bring our own brokenness and weaknesses, the dominant emotion in our worship life is *joy*. The gospel triumphs over human sin. Mercy triumphs over judgment. Satan has lost. Jesus has won! Won big!

Say it with me—"Yee-haw!"

Should Christians diet?

Pastor Mike Novotny

If the Bible says our bodies are temporary and our souls are eternal, should we think much about calories and sodium and sugar? Or should we focus our efforts on faith, hope, and love? Good questions. To be honest, the Bible doesn't have many answers. Even that passage about honoring God with your body (1 Corinthians 6:20) is in the context of prostitution, not portion size!

However, there is one passage that grabs my attention: **"Do not join those who drink too much wine or gorge themselves on meat, for drunkards and gluttons become poor, and drowsiness clothes them in rags"** (Proverbs 23:20,21). Why not gorge yourself at the buffet or have one glass of wine too many? Because you end up drowsy. God didn't create your body to be full of energy while processing that amount of meat.

That's why food matters so much to God. He wants us to have the energy needed to do good works in his name. Two hours after lunch, he has an opportunity lined up for us to serve our boss or listen to our kids or lend a hand to a neighbor in need. Those acts of love, like most good works, will require energy and focus. This is why God wants you to be wise when packing your lunch.

I bring a small black notebook to the gym to keep track of my workouts. Inside the front cover, I wrote these words: *Do this work, so you can do his work!* So, fellow Christian, take care of the only body God has given you. Your ability to love others just might depend on it.

Bloom where you're transplanted

Jason Nelson

"Seek the peace and prosperity of the city to which I have carried you into exile. Pray to the Lord for it, because if it prospers, you too will prosper" (Jeremiah 29:7).

Every once in a while, Jeremiah surprises us. He wasn't enthusiastic about his call to proclaim God's judgment on Israel. He didn't enjoy living through events he predicted, and he made his feelings known. He was tough on the remnant of believers left in Jerusalem and on the exiles living in Babylon. But we can cherry-pick some words of encouragement from the "weeping prophet." No matter where you take up residence, work hard to make it a better place. If it prospers, you will too.

Followers of Jesus should be contributors to the peace and prosperity of the communities we live in. Many small towns and city neighborhoods are rebuilding their economies and seeking a healthy way of life for their residents. Participating in local efforts can make a difference for everyone. For instance, the annual penny war sponsored by merchants in my town funds a food pantry that poor people depend on. A grass roots environmental group I joined is mobilizing farmers, industry leaders, resort owners, and outdoor types to fight toxic algae blooms in a waterway we all depend on. My church cleans up the fairgrounds after the tractor pull because someone needs to do it. The potential for fostering peace and prosperity is limitless. Let's make our presence felt.

Grumbling

Pastor Mark Jeske

With all the evil in the world, you might wonder why we would waste time focusing on a sin of talk. "Talk is cheap," you know. Shouldn't we put the spotlight on real evils like murder, terrorism, cyber hacking, drug cartels, and sex trafficking?

Those things are terrible indeed, but they can be endured. The believers over the centuries have weathered all that and more. Scripture wants us to pay attention, not just to evil in other people but the acids that corrode our own souls. One of the worst is a spirit of bitterness and thanklessness: **"Don't grumble against one another, brothers and sisters, or you will be judged. The Judge is standing at the door!"** (James 5:9). Grumbling sends a message to God that you feel cheated in life, that all his lavish blessings to you are not enough.

Allowing yourself to grumble against other people, especially out loud and in public, makes you think that you're the supreme judge of morality. It's gratifying to a sulking spirit to think you deserve better. In fact, we deserve nothing but condemnation ourselves because of our many sins; all we have and enjoy now are blessings from a generous God. If we intentionally harbor a bitter and complaining spirit, we risk putting ourselves again under his judgment.

That all stops right now. This very minute, resolve with me that no grumbling will come out of your mouth today.

Hiding with Jesus

Pastor Mike Novotny

I get tons of compliments on my phone case. For years now, I have used a phone case that has a hidden space for a few business cards, my license, etc. Whenever I flip open that case and pull out a card, people are impressed.

I thought of my phone case when I recently read Paul's stunning words: **"And your life is now hidden with Christ in God"** (Colossians 3:3). I thought of my life like a paper business card—easily bendable, instantly creaseable. Then I thought of Jesus' life like my license: tougher, stronger, and as close as can be. Then I thought about God like the phone case. Thick plastic hiding the cards stored inside. The result? My life is "with Christ in God." My spiritual and eternal life is safe, because I am not exposed but hidden by the love and power of my Savior.

By the grace of God, Christian, your life is in the same place. Your salvation is not a flimsy business card waiting to be bent or creased or destroyed. Your peace and joy are not one rip or one spill away from being ruined. No, you are safe in God. Protected by his power. United to his Son. Wherever Jesus is, you are with him. And since Jesus is always with God, in a place of acceptance and approval, guess who gets to spend today in the light of God's beaming face, his smile of approval, and his unfathomable delight? You!

You think my phone case is impressive? You should consider your place in the presence of God!

When church is a pain
Pastor Daron Lindemann

Sometimes church is a pain. Then there's the church sign with good intentions, inviting everyone to learn what the Bible teaches about hell. The sign reads, "Do you know what hell is? Come hear our preacher."

The apostle Paul opens his second letter to the Corinthians like this: **"For I wrote you out of great distress and anguish of heart and with many tears, not to grieve you but to let you know the depth of my love for you"** (2:4).

In the first five verses of this letter, Paul uses the Greek word for "pain" seven times. Quite a way to set the tone! Throughout all of his New Testament letters, Paul uses a form of the "pain" word 24 times, and 18 of them are in this letter.

"Want to know what pain is? Come hear Paul." But the problem wasn't Paul's preaching. The problem was this church. It was, well, a pain.

Paul's previous letter to them lists these pains. They were symptoms of sin. So Paul dealt with sin as the problem and forgave it.

If your church is willing to deal with its sins, God promises to forgive in the depth of his love for you. Faithful spiritual leaders will also be quick to forgive repentant churches with a depth of love.

Not all church problems are sin. When they are, don't be afraid to address them. Or the pain will only get worse.

Follow God's example
Pastor David Scharf

"Follow God's example, therefore, as dearly loved children . . . just as Christ loved us" (Ephesians 5:1,2). Did you see that? You can follow God's example, not so that God will love you but *because* God loves you. Just consider how dearly loved you are! God chose you before the creation of the world; he sent Jesus to die on a cross to wash away your sins and then found you with the sweet message of your salvation. In another spot in Ephesians, the apostle Paul prays that you might **"know the hope to which he has called you, the riches of his glorious inheritance in the saints"** (1:18). Do you see what that's saying? We all have things in life that when we look at them, they make us feel rich. Maybe it's a car or a family heirloom or a child. But do you know what makes God feel rich? God feels rich when he looks at you! You are dearly loved!

Suddenly, I want to please the One who loves me like that. I want to imitate God. Have you ever noticed that? You start to imitate those you love. It's almost imperceptible to you, but it's obvious to everyone else. Husbands and wives have tons of inside jokes. Friends start to imitate each other's style in clothes and music. Kids are chips off the old block—there's truth to the phrase, "the apple doesn't fall far from the tree."

So what will I do for the One who suffered hell in my place? I want to be just like him!

Rock-star parents

Pastor Mike Novotny

The other day a dad thanked me for commanding him to be mediocre. During a recent sermon, I had asked him and all the other fathers in church to stand up for the congregation to see. Then I ordered them, in Jesus' name, to be mediocre at their careers/jobs.

Does that seem like a weird thing to say during worship? I didn't think so. Because I wanted to give those fathers the time needed to be rock stars at home. Paul wrote, **"Husbands, love your wives,"** and a chapter later, **"Fathers . . . bring** [your children] **up in the training and instruction of the Lord"** (Ephesians 5:25; 6:4).

If there's one thing I've learned about being a husband and a father is that you cannot microwave relationships. As much as I love phone-free quality time, I know that quantity time is necessary too. Some of the best moments with my wife and daughters come unplanned, as we talk during family dinner or make impromptu plans on a task-free Sabbath day. But those moments never happen unless I say no to the endless stream of emails, invitations, and opportunities at work.

What I love about our Father in heaven is that he always has time for me. Time to listen. Time to speak. Time to love. Don't you love that about him too? I pray that every father could give a little glimpse of our Father's heart with the quantity time he invests at home.

I learned this lesson from a garage sale

Pastor Daron Lindemann

It was the end of my second garage sale, and I still possessed a bunch of junk. Just like my first garage sale. What went wrong?

My neighbor came over. We surveyed the 1980s vinyl LP records, the rusty yard tools, the unwanted clothing items, a pair of in-line skates, and everything else.

"Looks like I still own all this stuff," I complained.

"Actually, it looks like this stuff owns you," he corrected. Ouch. He was right. The goal of my garage sale was to make money, not get rid of stuff. I was holding on too tightly. In order to give it up, I wanted unreasonable prices. Nobody else agreed about how valuable my stuff was!?

Jesus once said, **"Life does not consist in an abundance of possessions"** (Luke 12:15).

But our possessions disagree. They want to be our master. Our possessions want to possess us.

Don't let that happen. Don't give in to the urge to upgrade everything. Stop expanding storage space for more of the same stuff. Admit this: Holding privileges or having things you never use (because you're too busy earning the money to pay for them) demonstrates that your stuff owns you.

Repent and reverse that trend before it's too late. Live with contentment. Stop giving unreasonable value to your stuff. Discover more about God's riches and how he wants to own you and bless you. Be more generous and willing to share.

Money magnet

Pastor Mike Novotny

At first glance, Jesus got it backward: **"For where your treasure is, there your heart will be also"** (Matthew 6:21). Wouldn't it be better to say that where your heart is (your passions, your causes, etc.), your treasure (your money, donations, etc.) will be also? Perhaps, but that's not Jesus' point. His point is, as a fellow pastor once said, that your money is a "heart magnet." Spend money there, and your heart will suddenly care.

You've experienced this. You put five bucks into the office March Madness pool and picked North Carolina to win it all. Even if you couldn't name a single player from UNC, you start to care about their scores. Or think of the stock market. When you're 12, you couldn't care less about the S&P 500 or the Dow Jones. But put a lifetime of investments into the market and the about-to-retire couple has strong emotions connected to this year's dips and gains. Why? Because money is a magnet for your heart.

But Jesus' words aren't just a warning about foolish spending. They are an opportunity to increase our passion for the things of God. When we invest in Jesus-exalting ministries and God-approved causes like the poor in our communities, our hearts start to care. We care about the things of God, the things that last, the things that cause Jesus to get excited.

No, money can't buy you a place in heaven. But it can get you passionate about the things of heaven. So, spend wisely. For where your treasure is, there your heart will be also.

Hosanna youth choir

Pastor Mark Jeske

Jesus' disciples had a problem with Jesus' child fol-lowers, and ironically so did his enemies. The crowds of people who welcomed King Jesus to Jerusalem, his royal capital, on Palm Sunday with their palms and psalms had set up a rhythmic Hebrew chant: *ba-RUCH ha-BA' b'SHEM adoNAI.* **"Hosanna to the Son of David! Blessed is he who comes in the name of the Lord!"** (Matthew 21:9). *Hosanna* means "Save us now!" The kids loved it. All the rest of that day and into Monday they played with the leftover palms and kept the "Ho-sanna" chant going.

Jesus' enemies hated it: **"When the chief priests and the teachers of the law saw the wonderful things he did and the children shouting in the temple courts, 'Hosanna to the Son of David,' they were indignant. 'Do you hear what these children are saying?' they asked him. 'Yes,' replied Jesus, 'have you never read, "From the lips of children and infants you, Lord, have called forth your praise"?'"** (Matthew 21:15,16).

Isn't it ironic that these kids figured out deep spir-itual truths that the religious professionals could not see? They were applying Psalm 118's messianic proph-ecy to the humble man riding on his little donkey and giving him worship and praise that belonged only to Israel's King. This Hosanna choir, these child champi-ons, were giving the Lord the praise he deserved.

I hope that you can hear children's voices praying and singing in your church.

Grudges are stubborn things

Jason Nelson

Pastor asked us in Bible class, "Which is easier for you—forgiving other people or forgiving yourself?" I held back this time and was surprised that nearly everyone said they had more trouble forgiving themselves. Apparently, those humble people found it easier to give others a pass but struggle with letting themselves off the hook for mistakes or problems in relationships. I felt embarrassed. I was the only one who admitted to holding grudges. It's not that I don't regret things I have done. I do. It's just that I still grit my teeth over things people have done to me.

Grudges are stubborn things because they are necessary in the autobiographies of people who see themselves as innocent victims. We settle in to that narrative. I can readily defend my resentments over the injustices I have suffered at the hands of others, but God won't have it. **"Do not seek revenge or bear a grudge against anyone among your people, but love your neighbor as yourself. I am the Lord"** (Leviticus 19:18).

So, to all the people out there who said things about me that weren't true, broke promises I believed, cheated me out of money, or hurt my feelings, I still think about you now and then. It would seem condescending if I just announced into the ether, "That's okay. I forgive you." But I'm working on it because God will not have it any other way. And he is the Lord.

Leave the mess
Sarah Habben

My youngest child is a pack rat. She saves lunch napkin notes from Mom. She saves feathers and stones, empty Tic Tac boxes, and stale ChapStick. Her filing system includes the floor. Her closets don't close.

Every so often, I put on my hazmat suit and come to the rescue. And when I present her with an organized room, she is delighted and filled with new resolve. Mom graciously cleaned her room . . . why would she choose to live in a mess any longer? (At least for that first week.)

Now consider our spiritual mess. Because he knows we cannot clean ourselves, Jesus absorbed the entire hazardous mess of our sins on the cross. He suffered hell in our place. We should shudder to think, "Christ paid my bill, so it doesn't matter if I sin." It should shame us to treat Jesus' forgiveness as a reloadable gift card. We are saved *from* sin, not *for* sin!

The apostle Paul writes, **"Shall we go on sinning so that grace may increase? By no means! We are those who have died to sin; how can we live in it any longer?"** (Romans 6:1,2).

When temptation comes knocking, the Spirit enables us to say, "The part of me that wants to come out and play has died." Christ drowned that evil desire in our baptisms and scrubbed clean the room of our hearts. His grace does not lead us to plot more sin but fills us with delight and a new resolve that asks, "How can we live in sin any longer?"

No mirrors in church

Pastor Mike Novotny

Is it just me or are mirrors made to rob us of happiness? I remember being at a dance party once, having a good time, when I noticed the mirrors to one side of the dance floor. Suddenly, I found myself glancing in their direction, curious as to how goofy I looked as I attempted not to embarrass myself on the dance floor.

Mirrors make us me-centered. When we step into the bathroom, we notice the fit of our clothes, the bags under our eyes, the tuft of hair that cannot be controlled, and a million other things we were ignorant of before stepping in front of our own reflections.

This is why I am so glad that we don't have mirrors in our church. Step into the space where we gather to worship, and you'll find a cross and a baptismal font and a screen for Bible passages, but you won't find a single mirror. Why? Because, while self-reflection and honest confession are good, fixing our eyes on Jesus is even better. **"And let us run with perseverance the race marked out for us, fixing our eyes on Jesus, the pioneer and perfecter of faith"** (Hebrews 12:1,2). We fix our eyes on Jesus. Through songs and sermons and readings and art, we take a break from our mirror-covered, me-centric world of self and we think about Jesus. His love. His mercy. His grace.

Unlike that day on the dance floor, moments of true worship don't make us self-conscious and embarrassed. Rather, they make us Christ-conscious and excited about his promises. Thank God for mirror-less spaces. Thank God for Jesus-focused churches!

The confession of sleep

Pastor Mike Novotny

Author David Murray says, "Show me your sleep pattern, and I'll show you your theology." I like that. I grew up reciting, "I believe in God the Father Almighty, the Maker of heaven and earth." But the real test of your faith might not be what you confess on Sunday morning. It might just be the time you went to bed on Saturday night.

In the beginning, **"God created mankind in his own image, in the image of God he created them; male and female he created them"** (Genesis 1:27). The triple use of "created" reminds us of something crucial—God set the rules for our bodies. Just like tanks weren't created to float, our bodies weren't created to thrive on little sleep and lots of coffee. Break the rules at your own risk. Keep them for great reward.

The older I get, the more I have come to appreciate my Creator. He made me human, with boundaries, limits, and a certain capacity for work. I'm not God. Therefore, I need to sleep. Therefore, every time I put my phone down and get the quantity time I need, I am confessing my faith.

The same is true for you. Thankfully, you are not alone. The Holy Spirit, even right now, is opening your eyes to the truth of God and his created order. Even now, Jesus is with you, erasing any shame you might feel for past sins that you cannot change. Even now, your Father is ready to continue his third-shift work so that you can close your eyes and rest. So sleep well, child of God. That's what faith does!

Evidence of the Spirit: Joy

Pastor Mark Jeske

I must admit that I am drawn to joyful people. By that I don't necessarily mean joke tellers (although I like them too). Humor and joy are different things. Humor can encourage us to laugh at the absurdities of life, but humor can also be abusive and cruel, enjoying other people's pain. Why do you think slipping on banana peels and Punch and Judy puppets clobbering each other (and their many variations) are such timeless material for comedy acts?

Joy is different. Joy is a chosen spirit of optimism and self-confidence. And it's not just because you feel rich, fit, and smart. Inner joy is produced by the Spirit of the Lord who lives in us. It is the quiet conviction that we are God's masterful creation, holy through the blood of Christ and dearly loved, protected by ten thousand angels, and given important work to do. Joy is built on the confidence that we can endure any disaster because we're on our way to heaven.

"The fruit of the Spirit is . . . joy," said St. Paul (Galatians 5:22). By that he didn't mean that Christians should be known for their slapstick routines. He meant that Christians are optimists, knowing that they have a great future and thus are able to be kind and patient even with difficult people. They can also like themselves.

The enemies of a joyful spirit are jealousy, bitterness, resentment, fear, and self-hatred. Banish them from your heart right now! Choose joy!

Arresting anger
Jason Nelson

If God said to me, "Jason, I will give you one chance to change the world. I will answer one prayer immediately. Make it a good one. This is your only opportunity, so you better get it right. I gave Solomon this chance, and he asked for wisdom. What do you want?" Without hesitation, I would say, "Lord, please make people less angry because anger is killing us."

The words I most regret saying, I said when I was angry. The things I most regret doing, I did when I was angry. Anger is the universal symptom of underlying pain. Anger is what we express when we don't know how to deal with our grievances. Anger is killing us because it triggers abuse and violence. Anger is never a sign of strength. It is always a sign of stress and weakness. If we can't reduce the heat under simmering unhappiness, it will eventually boil over into some kind of angry outburst.

Solomon said, **"For as churning cream produces butter, and as twisting the nose produces blood, so stirring up anger produces strife"** (Proverbs 30:33). Some people stir up anger on purpose. They want to divide us so they can pit one "energized" faction against another. Then may the angriest party win. What will escalation of anger ultimately lead to? God answered Solomon's once-in-a-lifetime prayer. I hope he will answer mine. **"Don't be quick to get angry, because anger is typical of fools"** (Ecclesiastes 7:9 GW).

The Prince of peace

Pastor David Scharf

Peace. Peace is knowing that everything is the way it should be between you and God.

Orsvr. Do you know what that word is? Obviously it's not a word, but these are the letters that show on-screen when typing the word *peace* if your fingers are just one letter off of home row on a computer keypad. My fingers made all the right motions; they just weren't grounded in the right spot. So close, yet so far away from *peace.*

Have you ever noticed that the world offers us its opinions on where to find peace? A great job, a strong marriage, being close to family, loving what you do for a living . . . Those are wonderful things and gifts from God to be thankful for, but if we're not grounded in the right spot, peace is always going to sound more like "Orsvr." So close, yet so far away from true peace.

Make no mistake. You *can* have true peace. But it's not something that you need to do or something that you need to hope still happens. Two thousand years ago, a child was born who changed everything. **"And he will be called . . . Prince of Peace"** (Isaiah 9:6).

This child's name is Jesus, and he is God Almighty. But for you he became human. And why? So that the palm that held the universe could take the nail of a soldier one day. Jesus is your home row. Only by starting with him can you spell *peace* in your life.

Meeting the real you
Pastor Mike Novotny

I can't wait to meet my wife. I've been dating her for nearly 20 years now, which makes me ache for the day when we will actually meet each other. The same is true with my kids. After a decade of being their dad, few things get me more excited than the day when we will see each other face-to-face. In fact, I'm personally pretty excited to meet myself!

Huh? Are you worried about my mental health? Don't be. I'm just meditating on Paul's words: **"When Christ, who is your life, appears, then *you also will appear* with him in glory"** (Colossians 3:4). Catch that? You will appear with Christ in glory. In other words, the real you, the glorious you, the you that God always wanted hasn't appeared just yet. The brilliant you, the shockingly impressive you, the sinless you is about to make its grand entrance on the day that Jesus appears in the skies.

I can't wait for that day! Imagine not just seeing the people you love but meeting the glorious versions of them. The versions that are bursting with joy and hope and love, the versions that have zero aches or pains or complaints or sins to spoil good days. Imagine meeting friends and family and heroes of the faith whose entrance into the room always increases your joy. Always. Just imagine . . .

No wonder the Bible ends with the cry of every Christian heart: **"Come, Lord Jesus"** (Revelation 22:20). When the Lord Jesus comes, we will finally see his glorious face. And we will finally see your glory too.

Think like Jesus

Pastor Mike Novotny

I'm not an artist. But—can I brag a bit?—my drawing was really good. I'm talking about the picture of Jesus' thought bubble. I drew a stick figure Jesus and a big thought bubble emerging from his brain. Then I added another stick figure—you—to the right of the thought bubble and, with a few small circles from your brain, connected your thoughts to Jesus' thought bubble. Can you picture it? Okay, maybe my art wasn't that great after all . . .

But the passage that inspired the art is the greatest: **"Since, then, you have been raised with Christ, set your hearts on things above, where Christ is, seated at the right hand of God. Set your minds on things above, not on earthly things"** (Colossians 3:1,2). Paul wants you to set your heart and your mind on the things above. Put on your God glasses every morning and see the world like God sees it. Join Jesus' thought bubble!

This won't make your problems go away, but it will give you a divine way of approaching life. Past sins turn into thoughts of amazing grace. Present challenges turn into thoughts of being pruned, refined, shaped into God's image. Future worries turn into thoughts of Jesus' place at the right hand of God, so you don't have to be afraid.

Joining your thought bubble to Jesus' is the key to letting go of your fears and anxieties and finding joy in the unbreakable promises of God. So, please join Jesus today! There's enough room in his picture to include you!

july 31

Only sleeping
Pastor Mark Jeske

Near the top of the most miserable of all human experiences is to suffer the death of a child. Every parent I know would trade places in a minute. All family deaths hurt, but to see a young life cut short just tears your heart out. Have you ever attended a funeral with a little casket?

Jesus Christ alone can give assurance to bereaved parents that there can be a second act. Children can be believers too—in fact, Jesus told his hearers on several occasions that children were not only *capable* of saving faith; they were *models* of saving faith whom grown-ups should emulate. Through Word and Baptism, God's grace can touch even very tiny lives and wash them clean enough for heaven.

The blessed biographer St. Luke recorded a story from the life of Christ that will forever encourage believing parents who are grieving this worst of life's tragedies. A 12-year-old girl had died in her home, and her lifeless body was laid out in shock and sadness. People gathered to help grieve, and they set up a supportive racket: **"All the people were wailing and mourning for her. 'Stop wailing,' Jesus said. 'She is not dead but asleep'"** (Luke 8:52).

If I said that, you could be skeptical. Since Jesus said that, we can lay our children's bodies to rest in the confident expectation of resurrection to life eternal. He spoke words of life, and the girl sat up.

He will do it again on a grand scale.

august

Look to the LORD and his strength;
seek his face always.

1 Chronicles 16:11

It's never all or nothing
Jason Nelson

I never want to insult you. I hope you trust me on that. But I do like to challenge you because I know you can handle it. So, I have a word for the gullible: **"If any of you needs wisdom to know what you should do, you should ask God, and he will give it to you. God is generous to everyone and doesn't find fault with them"** (James 1:5 GW).

I'm not finding fault either. But gullible people fall for *all-or-nothing* propositions. Falling for them on a regular basis amounts to a cognitive disorder because it plays to chronic anxiety in us. Salespeople exploit it to get us to stop reading the fine print and act fast. What happens in your head when you hear, "This offer is for a limited time only"? All-or-nothing marriages end in divorce. All-or-nothing friendships—aren't. Framing a policy position as all or nothing is fearmongering. "If we restrict access to assault weapons, *they* will take all your guns away and you will never go duck hunting again." Beware of anyone who tells you it is all or nothing.

Life is not a zero-sum game. One side of an argument doesn't always cancel out the other. Rational people are willing to dicker with each other to close the deal. They explore alternatives and compromise to find common ground. It is the art of the deal and the art of democracy. If anyone tells you to "take it or leave it," be prepared to get up and walk away.

A generous tax collector
Pastor Mike Novotny

I was nervous before talking to my church family about Jesus' bold teaching on money from Matthew chapter 6. Given the bad experiences many people have had with pastors, churches, and finances, I always tread carefully and pray passionately for the message and my motives to be clearly understood.

But then a small detail took away my fear. It dawned on me that Matthew chapter 6 was written by . . . Matthew. And do you know what he was famous for before he met Jesus? Taking people's money! But then Someone changed his heart. **"As Jesus went on from there, he saw a man named Matthew sitting at the tax collector's booth. 'Follow me,' he told him, and Matthew got up and followed him"** (Matthew 9:9). Matthew followed Jesus back to Matthew's house, where Jesus ate with him, drank with him, and honored him. Then Matthew followed Jesus to a cross, where the Savior gave him a priceless treasure—eternal life through the forgiveness of sins. In Jesus, Matthew got eternally rich. Whatever he gave up to follow Jesus was nothing compared to what he gained.

This is why we don't have to be afraid to talk about faith and finances. Because the very passages we read and preach are from the guys who found something better than all the money in the world. They saw Jesus face-to-face and realized he was worth everything they had to give.

So please don't be afraid of Jesus' radical teaching of generosity. Remember the One who speaks such bold words and believe your Savior is in the business of giving to you, not taking from you. Just ask Matthew.

Degrees of punishment
Pastor Mark Jeske

Not everyone believes that there will be a judgment day. Their disbelief will not make it disappear, of course. That day will come without warning, like a thief in the night. When they experience it, they will be in shock.

Those who do believe are usually intensely curious about how the divine decisions will be made. It pleases some people to construct a mental picture of the judgment process that conforms to *their* idea of justice. Far better to humble ourselves before the Word and just let God explain to us what he is going to do. Only faith in Christ and the shedding of his blood will make us clean enough to approach him. Only faith in Christ will open the gates for us.

Another misconception of judgment day is that the experience of hell is the same for all the condemned. Not so, according to Christ himself. The Judge will tailor a judgment that exactly fits each situation. Does that mean that there will be different degrees of torment, depending on how much people knew and on how strenuously they rebelled against God's will?

"Woe to you, Chorazin! Woe to you, Bethsaida! For if the miracles that were performed in you had been performed in Tyre and Sidon, they would have repented long ago, sitting in sackcloth and ashes. But it will be more bearable for Tyre and Sidon at the judgment than for you" (Luke 10:13,14).

Yes.

Called Out

Pastor Mike Novotny

The other day, a Christian called me out. I had said something foolish in one of my sermons that caused some real damage to some fellow Christians. My intention was never to hurt anyone, but I did. That's why he emailed me. And he didn't pull any punches. He called out my sin and bluntly told me how much of his respect I had lost. Honestly, it was hard to read.

But I'm so glad he did. After all, he was just obeying Jesus: **"If your brother or sister sins, go and point out their fault, just between the two of you. If they listen to you, you have won them over"** (Matthew 18:15). He pointed out my fault. Not with a dozen friends carbon copied, but with an email just between the two of us.

Do you know what happened? I was able to own it, to apologize, to ask for his forgiveness. I was able to share the steps I had taken to reconcile with the people I sinned against. Even better, I was able to express my faith in the grace God still has for a sinner like me.

And do you know what happened then? He forgave me too! He graciously put my sin in the past. He expressed his desire to move on and love one another well. That's the power of Jesus' teaching about sin in the family of God.

So, can I encourage you to imitate this dear brother in the faith and be gracious with those who repent? I know sin stings, and it is so tempting to hold on to another's wrong. But sorry sinners need grace. Sin carries such embarrassment and shame. Trust me, I know. But the grace of Jesus gives such hope and peace. Trust me, I know that too.

Protesting too much

Jason Nelson

In psychoanalysis, a "reaction formation" is a defense mechanism. Shakespeare used it in a play within a play. Gertrude recognized it in the character playing her in *The Murder of Gonzago.* "The Lady doth protest too much methinks." That was the tell to Hamlet that his mother was complicit in the death of his father because she protested her innocence too much when confronted with her guilt. The disciple Peter insisted that under no circumstances would he ever forsake Jesus and later went over the top in denying Jesus when a servant girl busted him as one of Jesus' disciples. Cookie thieves tearfully insist they never put one little finger in the jar despite the crumbs on their faces.

God watches us and must say to himself, "All these sinners do protest too much methinks." Our denials in the face of evidence of guilt are sound bites of history. *I never had sexual relations with that woman.* Really? *No collusion. No collusion whatsoever.* Oh, yeah? *Honey, I swear on a stack of Bibles I would never ever lie to you.* Ever?

These are red flags. That's why Jesus said, **"Don't say anything you don't mean. . . . You only make things worse when you lay down a smoke screen of pious talk. . . . You don't make your words true by embellishing them with religious lace. In making your speech sound more religious, it becomes less true. Just say 'yes' and 'no.' When you manipulate words to get your own way, you go wrong"** (Matthew 5:33-37 MSG).

Breakfast with Jesus

Pastor David Scharf

We've all heard it before: Breakfast is the most important meal of the day. Whether or not you agree, I'm sure that Jesus' disciple Peter would concur. In fact, he would probably tell you that one particular breakfast was the most important meal of his life, because it was during a breakfast with Jesus on the shores of Galilee that Peter vividly saw the forgiving heart of his Savior.

Three times during the breakfast, Jesus asked Peter if he loved him, each time a little more directly. Then three times Jesus commissioned Peter to go about his task as a gospel worker for Jesus. **"Again Jesus said, 'Simon son of John, do you love me?'** [Peter] **answered, 'Yes, Lord, you know that I love you.' Jesus said, 'Take care of my sheep'"** (John 21:16).

For a disciple who had recently denied knowing his Savior three times, Jesus' patience and forgiveness was humbling. How amazing that Jesus still wanted this denying disciple to be his spokesman! The amazing love and mercy of Jesus!

That's exactly the point. No matter how big your sins from yesterday, no matter how long you've stayed away from him, no matter how much you've denied him with your thoughts and actions, he welcomes you back and invites you to "have breakfast" with him. Whether you like to eat your Frosted Flakes for breakfast or not, start every day with Jesus and the day promises to be great!

The gift of rest

Pastor Mike Novotny

A retired pastor mentored younger ministers who were exhausted and ready to quit their jobs. "Here's your problem," the older pastor would say. "You're trying to live like an angel instead of a flesh-and-blood human. Here's your solution: First, exercise three times a week. Second, take one full day off. Third, spend at least one evening a week with your [family]." But the young pastors objected. They didn't have the time to do that. They were behind enough as it was. But the veteran preacher wouldn't budge. "Do those three things and call me back in a month if they don't work." No one ever called him back.

It takes faith to admit your limits, to decline the next heartfelt request of your time, to have margin in your schedule to work out and sleep enough and do the good works God has lined up for you at home. This is why Jesus' invitation is so beautiful and necessary: **"Come to me, all you who are weary and burdened, and I will give you rest"** (Matthew 11:28). What a promise! In the frantic rush of trying to make everyone happy, Jesus simply invites us to "come" to him, no matter how weary or burdened.

So often we live for the approval of others. Sadly, you can work 80 hours a week and still disappoint someone. Thankfully, God is offering his approval as a free gift, which is all ours through faith in Jesus. Can I encourage you to picture your Father's face today? His face is shining upon you. He is looking on you with favor. That's what happens when your heart is resting in Jesus!

Evidence of the Spirit: Forbearance

Pastor Mark Jeske

What a blessing it is to live so deep into the 21st century! The internet, search engines, apps, and the cloud all make it possible to retrieve, organize, and store boundless bundles of information. Copper lines are nice but not needed—everything's going wireless. And the data is not just text—images and videos fly around the world in a second or two.

What a curse it is to live so deep into the 21st century! You can get all the information you want really, really fast. Through a myriad of online shopping portals, you can get any goods you want really, really fast, and somebody will deliver the stuff anywhere you want. The curse is that we have all become really, really impatient. Nobody wants to wait for *anything*!

People develop slowly. You did. Somebody was patient with you, giving you the space to work out your skills and personality. Being willing to wait for people is learned behavior—guess where it comes from? Yep— **"The fruit of the Spirit is . . . forbearance"** (Galatians 5:22), which is another word for *patience*. The Spirit has been working on me a long time—I am such a work in progress. How dare I get snippy and judgmental because somebody else isn't up to my standards?

Shock somebody today with your patience. Be three times as likely to praise as to criticize. Look for signs of progress in people *and you will find them.* Find more joy in clapping and cheering for other people than in preening for attention for yourself.

WWJT?

Pastor Mike Novotny

Many years ago, I went to see a counselor for a sin I was struggling with. Some of his best advice was this—Focus on one thing, and you'll quickly forget about the other. Our brains can multitask but only singularly focus. So, instead of just thinking of all the ways to fight this sin, just think about something else. Because if I'd think about this, I'd stop thinking about that.

Maybe Paul would give us the same counsel when it comes to our challenges, our fears, our guilt, our worst-case scenarios, and our sins. **"Since, then, you have been raised with Christ, set your hearts on things above, where Christ is, seated at the right hand of God. Set your minds on things above, not on earthly things"** (Colossians 3:1,2). Set your mind on the things above, on the God who is all-loving, all-knowing, all-powerful, always with us, and always for us. Figure out, through a study of God's Word, if Jesus is nervous about this situation. Have a pow-wow with the crucified, risen, and ruling-at-the-right-hand-of-God Savior.

To put it simply, Paul wants us to ask, "WWJT?" What would Jesus think? What would the Son of God think about this, the same Son who loved you enough to hang on a cross, the same Son who is at God's right hand ruling the universe for your good, the same Son who promised that he would be with you always? Keep peppering your problems with that same question—WWJT?

Focus on those answers—focus on your Savior—and your fears don't stand a chance.

Jesus looked for you

Pastor Mike Novotny

Imagine this: The sun is going down. The sheep are in the pen. The exhausted shepherd can't wait to put down his staff. But first he has to count the flock. 97, 98, 99 . . . wait. He only has 99. He squints out at the field, looking for a patch of white wool. Nothing. So he tightens the straps of his sandals and grips his staff with resolve. He knows it will be work. He will go down into the valley, climb up the mountain, plunge into the shadows ready to fight any wolf who took away his one. That's what love does. Love leaves. Love looks.

This is what Jesus did for us. By nature, we wandered from the flock of God's family. Even after becoming one of God's faithful, we still are prone to wander. But Jesus loved us enough to look. **"Will he not leave the ninety-nine on the hills and go to look for the one that wandered off?"** (Matthew 18:12).

Jesus could have just stayed and prayed in heaven, but he didn't. He left the comfort of that place to look for us. His love compelled him to go and get us. And when he did, he didn't drag us home with a lecture about being a stupid sheep. No, he was so happy to have us back that he called every angel he knew and told them to get ready to party. **"Truly I tell you, he is happier about that one sheep than about the ninety-nine that did not wander off"** (Matthew 18:13).

What a Shepherd! What a Savior!

Perfect!
Sarah Habben

My daughters' math teacher demands that margins are drawn and homework is done in pen. But if your pen wobbles or a mistake is made on problem #13, you can't cross it out. Correction fluid and erasable pens are forbidden. You must simply pull out a fresh piece of paper and start all over again with problem #1.

More than once, I've had a daughter in late-night despair over a smudge or mistake that required a complete redo. The teacher would never collect that less-than-perfect paper and say, "It's good enough." He certainly wouldn't offer to rewrite it for her.

When God says, **"Be perfect, therefore, as your heavenly Father is perfect"** (Matthew 5:48), we sometimes delude ourselves into thinking he means, "Be good enough." But when it comes to our sins, even a crooked margin is grounds for condemnation—our selfish prayers, our fair-weather praise, our good works prompted by warped intentions. Our best attempts at doing good are **"like filthy rags"** (Isaiah 64:6).

God's demand for perfection shouldn't leave us congratulating ourselves or comparing our grades to someone else's. It can only leave us in tears, tired, frustrated at our shortcomings, and begging for rescue. Amazingly, God delights in our prayers for mercy. And, unlike certain math teachers, our Father is compassionate and gracious, abounding in love. God himself covers our messes and mistakes with the snow-white record of his Son's life and innocent death.

When God looks at us, he sees Jesus. And he says, "Perfect."

I'm afraid

Pastor Mark Jeske

You know, it's one thing to say you're not afraid of death when you're feeling perfectly healthy, when you actually fully expect to live another 40 years, when things are working out for you in life, when you feel loved and surrounded by great friends and family.

It's a whole different thing when you are aware that you are probably dying. It is humiliating to watch your physical abilities diminish. One by one things you used to be able to do for yourself are taken away. You don't feel quite so tough when you're wearing a catheter and have to use a bedpan. The devil will bring back memories of moral failings from long ago, and you may start wondering if those were really forgiven or are still notes outstanding with the divine Auditor.

You're supposed to be glad you're going to heaven, but the leap into the dark is so foreign, so unknown, that you grasp for the here and now, the familiar. Panic gnaws: **"My heart is in anguish within me; the terrors of death have fallen on me. Fear and trembling have beset me; horror has overwhelmed me"** (Psalm 55:4,5). There is only one antidote for that fear—the certain knowledge that your Savior Jesus has already gone through the entire experience and removed all the ugliness. When your spirit parts from your body, you will experience only the greatest thrill of your life—the healing, joy, relief, and celebration of finally being home.

Don't be afraid to put your hand in his.

Too strong for God?

Pastor Daron Lindemann

Have you ever heard the conundrum: "Is it possible for God to create a rock so heavy that he can't lift it?" *Umm.*

A simple yes or no won't do. God is more complex than that. So complex that he's bigger than our brains. If we think our brains will ever totally understand God, we don't understand him at all.

But our brains aren't the only problem. There's also our brawn. We think we're so strong that we don't need God's help.

The Bible says, **"Humble yourselves, therefore, under God's mighty hand, that he may lift you up"** (1 Peter 5:6).

If God's hand is so mighty, why does he need me to humble myself? Can't he lift me up without needing me to get lower?

That's another conundrum. A simple yes or no won't do.

If we think our strength is what we need, however, we're not that strong at all. Being too strong for God actually removes us from the strength of God. He can't lovingly lift us up if we're self-reliant, self-made, and self-righteous. But he might lovingly knock us down.

It's when we are weak, emptied, and not able to handle everything on our own that God's mighty hand can lift us up. **"Cast all your anxiety on him because he cares for you"** (1 Peter 5:7).

Why would you love a lord?

Pastor Mike Novotny

There is a confusing part of the Christmas story. When the angel speaks to the shepherds, he says, **"I bring you good news that will cause great joy for all the people. Today in the town of David a Savior has been born to you; he is the Messiah, the Lord"** (Luke 2:10,11). That last word confuses me. How can the "Lord" cause great joy for all people?

After all, a lord is someone who gets the last word. The one with authority over you. Your boss is your lord. The cop with the radar gun. The politicians who pass the laws you have to obey. Growing up, your parents were your lords. Be honest, did living under all that authority cause you "great joy"? I bet not.

So how is Jesus any different? Answer—He is the Lord of love. He is the King who used all his royal authority to fight for you. Instead of some power trip and pampering (think servants feeding him grapes), Jesus came in shocking humility (think servant Jesus washing feet). The reason we trust, even love, Jesus' authority is because we know his final word is always meant to bless us.

This is why we're not foolish to sing, "Joy to the world! *The Lord* is come." There is incredible joy knowing the One who gets the final word over death and over anything that would threaten our future is the Lord of everlasting love.

Jesus feeds your problems

Pastor Daron Lindemann

Where you see problems, Jesus sees opportunities.

A huge crowd wanted Jesus' attention in a remote location. He taught them and healed them all day into the evening. By then his disciples were tired. **"Send the crowds away,"** they told Jesus, telling him that the multitudes should disperse to the nearby villages for dinner.

"They do not need to go away," Jesus rebuked. **"You give them something to eat"** (Matthew 14:15,16).

It wasn't a crowd problem as much as it was a disciple problem. The Bible says that Jesus looked at the crowd with compassion. He saw people to serve and even save. The disciples, however, looked at the crowd with human calculations. They saw a problem that needed to be solved (by someone else).

The disciples said, "Not my problem."

Jesus said, "I'll help."

That's the first step in problem-solving. Define your problem. Then own it. Don't pretend it isn't real, don't ignore it, and don't blame others. Jesus stepped into the problem and owned it. With compassion. Not much different than when he stepped into our world—into our problems, sins, and mistakes—with a compassion that owned our sin problems to death.

Jesus isn't confused by your problems. He isn't scared. He has compassion. He will listen. He will love. And Jesus will involve you. In his forgiving grace, Jesus makes your problems opportunities for you to serve and grow.

Rediscovering virtue

Jason Nelson

Virtue is having high moral standards. Like yeast, it can work its way into everything. Virtue is also elusive. Goodness isn't picked like seashells on the beach. Goodness is from God because God is good. In Philippians 4:8, the apostle Paul takes virtue apart so we can actively pursue it as we **"think about such things."**

"Whatever is true." There is truth, and we can know it. God's Word is truth. Jesus is the Way, the Truth, and the Life. We should tell the truth to each other.

"Whatever is noble." We have tarnished it badly. But the image of God, in which we were made, left us capable of showing something no other creature can. Human dignity.

"Whatever is right." People can have different values about many things and even debate them. Values are good. But virtue it better. It lifts us above divisions because whatever is right is undeniable.

"Whatever is pure." We all want clean air to breathe and clear water to drink. Why would we consume anything else that is contaminated with something dirty?

"Whatever is lovely." The free market can help us rediscover virtue. If we stop paying for ugliness and subscribe to more that is beautiful, we will get what we pay for.

"Whatever is admirable." Respect isn't doled out willy-nilly. Respect is drawn out of us by people who are worthy of it. We can admire people for their virtue.

Watch for it. When **"anything is excellent or praiseworthy,"** we have rediscovered virtue.

Carry each other's burdens
Pastor David Scharf

Many hands make light the work. That is so true! Even for simple projects, another set of hands can be very helpful. I grew up in a big family, and we all pitched in to clean the house at the same time. It was amazing how much we could get done in a short period of time.

Carrying each other's burdens is one of the blessings we receive by being part of a group of believers like a congregation. Through the relationships that we form, we get shoulders to cry on and words of encouragement through life's ups and downs. But just what are the burdens that we help each other carry? The obvious ones may be when there is a death in the family, emotional or financial struggles, etc. But have you ever considered the role you play in helping someone deal with his or her sin?

"Brothers and sisters, if someone is caught in a sin, you who live by the Spirit should restore that person gently. . . . Carry each other's burdens" (Galatians 6:1,2).

As sinners ourselves, it's difficult to step in and address somebody else who is caught in a sin. But if we fail to, it may be his or her spiritual life on the line. Jesus wants us to carry those burdens as well, not hypocritically or in a superior way. Jesus wants us to point out what is taking someone away from him so that we can point that person to him and the forgiveness we all find in his cross.

Flee!

Sarah Habben

If you're curious about what determination looks like—bathing cats is a good way to find out. They do everything in their power to stay out of the water. As soon as they get wet, they go into panic mode. They writhe. They claw. They arch away from the water. They squirt from your grasp.

A baptized believer should be as eager to sin as a cat is to swim. The apostle Paul says that when it comes to the common (but lethal) sins of idolatry, sexual immorality, testing God, or grumbling, we should *flee*. **"God is faithful; he will not let you be tempted beyond what you can bear. . . . Therefore, my dear friends, flee from idolatry"** (1 Corinthians 10:13,14).

How often do we instead find ourselves running *to* those sins? Any sin, in the end, makes us idolaters. It doesn't matter whether we willfully ignore God's design for marriage or grumble about our pastors' sermons. Whenever we say, "*My* will be done" instead of "*Thy* will be done," we seat ourselves on God's throne. God will not bear such idolatry forever. His just judgment will come, as it did for the Israelites. But God does not want to scare us into proper worship. Rather, he draws us with his faithfulness. He gives us his Word as a shield. He presents his sinless Son who was tempted in every way and understands our struggle. He transforms us by his Spirit so that we become no more eager to sin than a cat is to swim.

Everything's somebody else's fault

Pastor Mark Jeske

Perhaps you've heard of conspiracy theorists. There are networks of suspicious people who believe, for instance, that a secret cabal of world masters is actually pulling the strings of all governments, that all elections are total shams. Others believe that the AIDS crisis in Africa is a deliberate American/European biological attack to keep the continent down or that the Kennedy assassination was a CIA plot or that the 9/11 air attack on New York and Washington was planned by secret government operatives.

All conspiracy theorists have this in common—they believe that all the bad things they see around them are somebody else's fault. You may not think of yourself as a conspiracy theorist, but you do know the alluring temptation of blaming other people for your troubles. But when your blaming finger is quick to point, you are unlikely to see clearly that your own attitudes, words, and actions have a lot to do with your problems. **"Who can discern their own errors? Forgive my hidden faults"** (Psalm 19:12).

Taking spiritual inventory and being willing to recognize and repent of your own sins will go a long way toward explaining what's going wrong in your life. It's also productive—blaming others never brings about change, because you can't change other people. But you can change yourself.

Has God sent you a friend or family member who will lovingly tell you the truth about yourself? Can you stand hearing your own faults called out?

Don't worry!

Pastor David Scharf

I read that an average person's anxiety is focused like this: 40 percent on things that will never happen; 30 percent on things about the past that can't be changed; 12 percent on things about criticism from others, mostly untrue; 10 percent on health, which only gets worse with stress; and 8 percent on real problems to be faced.

Wow! According to that, only 8 percent of worry is "legitimate." Jesus offers you something even better: Zero worry! Worry is the opposite of trust. Worried about not having what you need? Should you be? God promises to make all things work for our good, he promises to provide, and he promises to take us to heaven. What do you have to worry about? Literally, nothing!

"Do not worry about your life. . . . But seek first his kingdom and his righteousness, and all these things will be given to you as well" (Matthew 6:25,33).

God paid the ultimate price for you! He bought you with the priceless blood of Jesus! Look at what you already have. You've been given a gift that's more precious than all the gold in the world: faith in God's Son. You've been given the rock-solid assurance from the mouth of God that he will care for you during the speck of time you spend here in this life. You have been given the kingdom of heaven for all eternity.

Worried? Neither am I!

Sandcastles

Jason Nelson

"Everyone who hears these words of mine and does not put them into practice is like a foolish man who built his house on sand" (Matthew 7:26).

It's possible to build on sand, but you need to dig for very deep footings. Which means you aren't building on sand at all. So, Jesus' point is still valid. Wise people always build on something solid like Jesus' words. Sandcastles are temporary flights of fantasy. The next big wave washes them away. We know that. But generation after generation, we are drawn to sandcastles because they intrigue us.

In the wise man/foolish man parable, Jesus challenges us to be intellectually honest. He wants us to distinguish truth from things that sound like truth. This is the information challenge of our time. Things that sound like truth seem to find us. They come at us wave on wave in click bait that pops up on our devices to lure us to the shifting sands of someone's false claims and ulterior motives. We find truth by digging for it ourselves. Divine truth is revealed in the Bible. Current truth is reported by ethical journalists. Documented truth is recorded by good historians. It is all corroborated by credible evidence. Truth proves itself over time.

We need intellectual fortitude to be informed citizens and discerning consumers of information. It's hard work. Many things we hold dear depend on it because there is no foundation under a sandcastle.

I know I'm right

Pastor Mark Jeske

I hope you and I never get into an argument. I'm pretty stubborn, and even when seeming to yield, I'm probably just pretending to accept your ideas. Inside my brain I know I'm right.

Well, isn't it true that we all love to be right? We love to say, "I told you so." We love to win arguments. There is something of an adrenaline rush to outgunning somebody else's line of thought and points. And it's way more fun to blame other people for what went wrong than to take any responsibility. It's probably a good idea, though, to remember who is listening in on our conversations. It's good to remember who can hear even our thoughts: **"A person may think their own ways are right, but the Lord weighs the heart"** (Proverbs 21:2).

If that's true (and it is), we need to work on our hearts. So how do we change? 1) We can choose to act more humbly, inspired by our humble Savior Jesus. We can assume that we don't know everything and suppress our own egos. 2) We can listen first before flapping our own gums. We might learn something that way instead of revealing our own limits. 3) We can choose to find joy in praising someone else's words instead of letting our insecurities demand all the attention.

I will if you will.

Tattoos & Jesus in your heart

Pastor Mike Novotny

My friend Tony has a sweet tattoo of Galatians 2:20 inked over his ribs. Tony came to trust in Jesus in his mid-20s, which makes the words so powerful. **"I have been crucified with Christ and I no longer live, but Christ lives in me."** If you knew Tony, you would know how true that is. The old Tony didn't pray to Jesus, didn't gather to worship Jesus, didn't tell his children about Jesus, and didn't trust in Jesus to make him right with God. But that version of Tony is dead, crucified with Christ. Now a new Tony is alive, where Jesus is living in his heart and directing his steps.

You might never get that passage put under your skin, but I hope, like Tony, you savor the beauty of those words. Jesus lives in us. We fear God, love God, and trust in God because Jesus lives in us. We hate our sin, even as we struggle against it, because Jesus lives in us. We long to see the face of our Father a billion times more than we want to win a billion dollars, because Jesus lives in us. We know we are forgiven and adored by the God who runs the universe, because Jesus lives in us.

No, we are not yet what we one day will be. But we are not what we once were. By the grace of God, we are what we are—the children of God. The people who died to sin and are raised again to live every single day with Jesus.

Why be good if I'll be forgiven?

Pastor Daron Lindemann

How often do you wonder, "Do I have to be good today?" Yes, even Christians ponder that question, and sometimes our logic is: "Why be good if I'll be forgiven?"

Because sin changes things. It changes a person over time to become more uncontrollably addicted to bad behavior, to become more self-absorbed, to blindly miss how terribly he or she is hurting others and God. Unopposed sin changes from enemy to friend, like the serpent trusted by Eve.

Jesus changes things too.

Jesus is your life, and you are dead to sin. Dead people don't need anything. When Jesus your Savior gives you everything you need, you don't need what sin offers to give you.

Jesus is your Lord, and you are free from sin's control. Sin is not a giver but a taker. Jesus is Lord over every sin. Even the one you haven't controlled. Yet.

Jesus is your love, and you have true beauty in him. Acceptance. Desirability.

"Shall we go on sinning so that grace may increase? By no means! We are those who have died to sin; how can we live in it any longer? . . . Shall we sin because we are not under the law but under grace? By no means! You have been set free from sin and have become slaves to righteousness. . . . God's love has been poured out into our hearts" (Romans 6:1,2,15,18; 5:5).

A faith that saves you is a faith that changes you.

Come, Lord Jesus

Pastor Mike Novotny

Every few days, my family uses a common prayer before eating dinner. It starts, "Come, Lord Jesus, be our guest . . ." I like that line. I try to envision Jesus answering that prayer, walking into the room, and joining us with his life-giving, happiness-increasing presence. The thought of him makes me happier than the food at the table or the people sitting around it.

But that prayer is not reserved for just the evening meal. It's the deepest and most constant cry of every Christian heart. The Bible's second to last verse says, **"Amen. Come, Lord Jesus"** (Revelation 22:20). Because when Jesus comes in glory on the Last Day, everything bad and broken will have to leave. Everything we regret and fear will be dead and gone. Everything we long for and desire will be ours forever. Can you imagine life like that?

No more sadness, loneliness, or restlessness. No more disabilities, disease, or death. No grief, no fears, no phobias. No addictions, no compulsions, no obsessions. No PTSD, OCD, STD, or ADHD. No triggers, no trauma, no just trying to get by. Only glory. Only a happiness we have never felt. Only a rest that finally lets us sit and breathe and beam with joy. This is our hope. That is our for-sure future. It is going to happen. It sometimes feels like forever away, but soon and very soon we will see Jesus.

Amen! Come, Lord Jesus! Come quickly!

Remember to notice

Jason Nelson

This uplifting message is being brought to you by something good. I almost missed it because I was reading today's headlines. I'm conditioned to focus on bad news. I like to discuss it with others, which amplifies bad news. Any improvement in my attitude depends on seeing something good. There is a lot of good out there if we remember to notice it. **"Look, I've written your names on the backs of my hands. The walls you're rebuilding are never out of my sight. Your builders are faster than your wreckers"** (Isaiah 49:16,17 MSG).

Because sin tears down so much in our world, we are always rebuilding something. All of the rebuilding is under the supervision of God, whose arms are stretched over us to protect us and bless us. The rebuilding is in the hands of younger people who grew up hearing us gripe about misfortune but were quietly preparing for a better life for themselves. They should never be held captive to our burdens. We must not confine them to our grief or low expectations. God wants them to have their shot at happiness, hope, and a future.

When a remnant of God's chosen ones was overwhelmed trying to rebuild everything, God told them to notice something good. Young constructive people outnumbered and outworked negative people who tried to tear it all down. He said that's how **"you'll know then that I am God. No one who hopes in me ever regrets it"** (Isaiah 49:23 MSG).

Take it to the Lord

Sarah Habben

Grandma B. needs a cane and a friendly arm to hold in order to walk. Recently, I helped her get from church to the Bible study room. It was slow progress. Slow enough for her to recite several stanzas of "What a Friend We Have in Jesus" in a conversational sort of way, between painful steps. She wasn't about to bear any "needless pain" when she could take even this short walk to God in prayer.

Grandma B. shakes her head when she tells about a nephew who sat with her in the hospital. "Your doctor doesn't seem very confident," her nephew said, "—he was praying before your operation!" Her nephew didn't appreciate the privilege of prayer or the power of God who listens to prayer. Oh, what peace he was forfeiting!

What peace are *you* forfeiting by failing or forgetting—or fearing—to pray? How needless! **"The eyes of the Lord are on the righteous and his ears are attentive to their cry"** (1 Peter 3:12). When we cry out, Jesus doesn't turn away at the reek of our sin. He doesn't yawn over our problems. He doesn't dither over how to deliver us. With the alert love of a mom attuned to her child's cry, Jesus responds. He deposits our sins at his cross, lifts our cumbersome load of care, and supports our every step with the strong arm of his Word.

Whatever burdens you have, take them to the Lord in prayer.

As Grandma B. knows with all her might—you will find a solace there.

The chosen one
Pastor Mike Novotny

We love the idea of a "chosen one," don't we? Think of how many of our best stories involve the coming of some special person who will carry out a special mission and bring a special blessing to his people. Harry Potter, according to the prophecy, was chosen to fight against Lord Voldemort. Luke Skywalker, many believed, was the chosen Jedi who would restore balance to the Force. Neo from the *Matrix* and Aslan from Narnia were the same.

Why do we love those stories? Because they remind us of the greatest story of all—the true story of Jesus. On the night he was born, the angel said, **"Today in the town of David a Savior has been born to you; he is the Messiah, the Lord"** (Luke 2:11). The Hebrew title Messiah literally means, "the anointed one," but today we would say, "the chosen one." Jesus was chosen by God to take on human flesh, chosen to be anointed with the Holy Spirit, and chosen to bring a special blessing to his people, including you.

Because Jesus was the chosen one, you have been forgiven of that sin that you still struggle with (yes, that one too). You have an answer to every accusation of the enemy who claims you are not good enough to be loved, liked, and accepted by God (he never quits that claim, does he?). Because Jesus was the truly chosen one, you are one of God's chosen people.

God's judgment timetable

Pastor Mark Jeske

One of the sad features of our broken lives on a broken planet is that justice is often murky and delayed and sometimes seems absent altogether. It's bad enough to suffer injury from another, but it's worse when no one is apprehended, or someone is apprehended but not punished.

Even believers may fear that God isn't watching, or if he is that he doesn't care anymore. Ah, but he does. As Longfellow once wrote, "The mills of God grind slowly, but they grind exceeding small." An example: **"After Abimelek had governed Israel three years, God stirred up animosity between Abimelek and the citizens of Shechem so that they acted treacherously against Abimelek. God did this in order that the crime against Jerub-Baal's seventy sons, the shedding of their blood, might be avenged on their brother Abimelek and on the citizens of Shechem, who had helped him murder his brothers"** (Judges 9:22-24).

The Lord says that vengeance belongs to him; thus you and I can leave the judging and punishing to him. After all, we can be grateful that the punishment for our own evil words and deeds was put on Christ instead of us. In the meantime, we can expect injustices everywhere. Satan's lie to Eve that there would be no consequences for her disobedience is still persuasive to many, and they think they will get away with it all.

Give it to God and wait for him.

Face-to-face friendship

Pastor Daron Lindemann

"Here. Chew this."

How many people in your life—not including family—would you be able to walk up to, take the gum you are chewing out of your mouth, say that, and that person would do it without arguing?

That's a clue about the depth of friendship in the Bible where John writes, **"I hope to visit you and talk with you face to face"** (2 John 12).

The original Greek words that John used here literally say, "Talk with you mouth to mouth." As in, "I want to see your lips moving—trembling when you're sad, smiling when you're happy, frowning when you're angry. I want to talk and not just text or see your picture on my phone."

Just like pen and ink weren't enough for the apostle John to practice his friendship, Bible books and prophecies weren't enough for Jesus. Jesus needed to come and visit face-to-face. **"In the past God spoke to our ancestors through the prophets at many times and in various ways, but in these last days he has spoken to us by his Son"** (Hebrews 1:1,2).

God loves you so much that he meets you face-to-face, mouth to mouth, life to life in Jesus. You have his words, but that's not all. You have him.

Be that kind of friend to someone who needs you today.

Don't be troubled

Pastor Mike Novotny

What are you afraid of? Fear is the feeling that something will stop you from getting what you need to be happy. If you need a lot of money or a fulfilling job or a significant other or a healthy body or a prosperous country or anything else to be happy, fear is what you feel when something threatens those blessings.

And that's a legitimate feeling! In this broken world, God has not guaranteed that every Christian will be early retirement rich, perfectly employed, in love and loved, disease free, and blessed in the U.S.A. Every day, God's people lose their savings, their jobs, their marriages, their health, and their freedom. So, why wouldn't we all be afraid?

Jesus' answer? Because none of those threats can take away God. He told his quivering disciples on the night before he bled, **"Do not let your hearts be troubled. . . . My Father's house has many rooms; if that were not so, would I have told you that I am going there to prepare a place for you?"** (John 14:1,2).

Why not be troubled? Why not be afraid? Because God's house has plenty of room. A spot in the glorious presence of God is all you need to be blessed, to be eternally happy. And guess what? Jesus went to a cross and left a grave empty to prepare a place there for you. Tell that to your fears, and maybe your heart will be a little less troubled than it was before.

september

Set your minds on things above, not on earthly things.

Colossians 3:2

"Sacrament": Not in the Bible?

Pastor Mark Jeske

Thanks to the capital of California everybody knows this word, though it's not found in the Bible. But it is another example of valuable doctrinal shorthand to sum up what Scripture teaches and thus does not come under God's curse on biblical additions.

Sacrament comes from the Latin word *sacer*, which means "holy." The sacraments are holy rituals that Christ instituted, which use some kind of tangible material as a vehicle for God's Word and power and which bring the gospel of forgiveness to the receiver. It is a beautiful way of personalizing the Word by literally touching the person, so that there can be no doubt as to who is meant by God's forgiving grace. The washing of Baptism fits that definition, and so does the sacred Supper of the Lord: **"Whoever eats the bread or drinks the cup of the Lord in an unworthy manner will be guilty of sinning against the body and blood of the Lord. Everyone ought to examine themselves before they eat of the bread and drink from the cup"** (1 Corinthians 11:27,28).

The holiness of the acts of the Lord's Supper can be seen in this, that it is a direct encounter with the very body and blood of Christ himself. Thus St. Paul urges communicants to prepare themselves spiritually so that Christ will be worshiped and glorified and the recipient nourished and comforted.

How good it is to be washed and fed!

Wash me
Sarah Habben

The back window of our van often sports a scrawled, "Wash Me!" My neighbor's car, however, always shines. Even before sunrise, he kneels by his car with a bucket of soapy water, carefully sponging away dust and grime. A dirty vehicle can be cleaned with a modest amount of water and elbow grease. But what about a dirty conscience?

King David learned that concealing his guilt was about as effective as hiding a dead body under his bed. Out of sight was not out of mind. The reek of his sins awoke him at night and clung to him by day, sapping his strength. Finally, he dragged his sins into daylight and laid them before the Lord.

"Then I acknowledged my sin to you and did not cover up my iniquity. I said, 'I will confess my transgressions to the Lord.' And you forgave the guilt of my sin" (Psalm 32:5).

Thus unburdened, David cried out: **"Blessed is the one whose transgressions are forgiven, whose sins are covered"** (Psalm 32:1).

When David tried to cover up his sins, an elephant sat on his heart. When *God* covered his sins, David sang songs of joy.

When Satan scrawls accusing messages in the grime of your guilt, cry out, "Wash me, Savior!" And then remember your baptism. That water, connected to God's name and Jesus' blood, covers you. Cleanses you. Saves you. Sends you out new and shining into the world to do his will. Blessed are you through Baptism!

Reckless love

Pastor Mike Novotny

Musician Cory Asbury struggled to understand what God was like. But things changed when Cory had a son. Whenever he held his baby, he felt a love like nothing he'd felt before. And when he realized that his kid hadn't done anything, hadn't earned it, hadn't worked for it, Cory finally got the heart of God. He grasped the God who would do anything—climb a mountain, kick down a wall, plunge himself into the darkness—for the sake of just one person.

One day Cory wrote a song that became a favorite in many churches—"Reckless Love." It's about God's overwhelming and never-ending love. Love that can't be earned or deserved. That's the kind of love Cory felt for his son. That's the same love our Father feels for you.

Some Christians wondered if *reckless* was the right word to describe God's love. After all, God isn't foolish or reckless in his decisions, right? Cory responded with Jesus' story about a good shepherd. **"If a man owns a hundred sheep, and one of them wanders away, will he not leave the ninety-nine on the hills and go to look for the one that wandered off?"** (Matthew 18:12). Unconcerned with his own comfort or safety, willing to face a wolf or lay down his life for one sheep, Cory believed he had chosen the right word.

Thank God for that kind of love. Thank God that Jesus cared more about us than he did about himself. Thank God for the Good Shepherd who laid down his life for us, a display of his overwhelming, never-ending, reckless love.

Faith and obedience are good for business

Pastor Mark Jeske

There is a sad cynicism in our land that the entire world of work is rigged, that only privileged insiders profit, that hard work and thrift don't matter anymore, and that a tiny few people control everything and that everybody else basically gets the shaft.

The Bible shows that our God thinks differently. He watches us all the time to see if we are listening to him, learning his ways, trusting in his Word's wisdom, willing to do things his way first and wait for his reward. So are faith and obedience good for business? They certainly pay off in eternity, but do they pay off in the here and now?

King Hezekiah found out that they do: **"This is what Hezekiah did throughout Judah, doing what was good and right and faithful before the LORD his God. In everything that he undertook in the service of God's temple and in obedience to the law and the commands, he sought his God and worked wholeheartedly. And so he prospered"** (2 Chronicles 31:20,21). God's ways really do bring about prosperity. Put people first, act like a servant, tell the truth, study hard and learn your craft, keep your word, do what you say you will do, admit your mistakes, listen to people, live within your means, do quality work, exceed expectations—these have always been and will always be attitudes and behaviors that God will bless.

And that's good for business.

Anxiety & Jesus
Pastor Mike Novotny

Psychologist and professor Jean Twenge noted some factors connected to eighth graders feeling happier or more depressed. The leading habits connected with being sad—lots of time on social media and the internet. The leading habits connected with happiness—exercising and attending religious services.

It makes sense. Online we take selfies and find the filter that makes us look our best. We compare our lives to the highlights of their lives. But when we attend a worship service, we think about how much God is worth. We think about Jesus. Look in a mirror, and you'll see a sinner. Look at the cross, and you'll see a Savior. Look at yourself, and you'll always have to wonder if you're enough. Look at Jesus, and you'll never have to wonder, for he is enough.

Paul wrote about the life-giving power of focusing on the eternal God: **"Therefore we do not lose heart. Though outwardly we are wasting away, yet inwardly we are being renewed day by day. For our light and momentary troubles are achieving for us an eternal glory that far outweighs them all. So we fix our eyes not on what is seen, but on what is unseen, since what is seen is temporary, but what is unseen is eternal"** (2 Corinthians 4:16-18).

In this life, there are no quick fixes for anxiety and fear. But fixing our eyes on Jesus is the best way not to lose heart. Whether you are attending a worship service or meditating on this devotion, remember the eternal blessings that are yours because of Jesus' cross and empty tomb. Because faith is the best remedy for our fears.

Today

Jason Nelson

"The living, the living—they praise you, as I am doing today" (Isaiah 38:19).

Today you will take about 23,040 breaths, and you don't even have to think about it. You can hold your breath if you need to and catch your breath after climbing a hill. But today you will breathe.

Today your heart should beat about 115,200 times, give or take. If it is way off, you need to see your doctor. It will beat faster when you exercise and slower when you rest. But today your heart will beat.

Today you might stumble upon an opportunity or achieve something you always wanted to achieve, like getting in better shape so your heart keeps beating and you keep breathing.

Today is God's gift to you. It is wrapped in 1,440 minutes that add up but don't carry over to tomorrow. But, what you do with them today will.

If you live to be 80, you will have had 29,200 todays. That's a lot of breaths and a lot of heartbeats. And it is probably a lot of illnesses and recoveries, a lot of sadness and joy. It is seeing some things more than once and seeing some things for the first time. That's a full life.

Today you can shout, "Hallelujah!" Or you can whisper it if you don't want to wake a baby or a grandma from a nap. You can praise God for what he is doing today and what he did for you each day before this one.

Today you are living for a reason.

Counterculture
Pastor Mark Jeske

When you talk to baby boomers about their high school and college days, they may get a dreamy look in their eyes as they recall their involvement in the "counterculture." They are probably proud to have pushed back against the "establishment," advocating for civil rights and protesting the Vietnam War. The 1960s' counterculture also permanently changed America by its advocacy for recreational drugs and sexual promiscuity.

When Eisenhower was president, Christians were in the majority and Christian morality was the norm. Today there is a new normal. Christianity has a far smaller profile today. These days if you advocate publicly for something scriptural, you are part of a new counterculture—going against the crowd and its atheist and agnostic leadership.

The apostle Paul wants you to think that struggle is worth the stress: **"I tell you this, and insist on it in the Lord, that you must no longer live as the Gentiles do, in the futility of their thinking. They are darkened in their understanding and separated from the life of God because of the ignorance that is in them due to the hardening of their hearts. Having lost all sensitivity, they have given themselves over to sensuality so as to indulge in every kind of impurity, and they are full of greed"** (Ephesians 4:17-19).

It's nice to be in the majority. Today God calls you to stand with him, even when, especially when, it is uncomfortable.

Welcome to the Christian counterculture.

Don't call me Grandpa

Pastor Daron Lindemann

One of my early thrills of grandparenting was choosing a grandparent nickname.

Now, I called my own grandparents Grandpa and Grandma. Titles, really. So imagine my excitement when my son and pregnant daughter-in-law recommended that I choose a nickname as an improvement to Grandpa. Yes!

The selection process involved a Google search and eliminating grandparent nicknames existing elsewhere in our family. It was decided. Call me Papi (sounds like "poppy") and my wife Gigi (pronounced "jee jee"). I'm smiling right now just thinking about it.

A term of endearment offers something a bit more special than a title, doesn't it? Don't get me wrong. Titles aren't bad. They can promote a sense of respect and awe. That's a good thing. But not the only thing.

Jesus both respected his Father and also talked to him intimately, using a term of endearment. **"'Abba, Father,' he said, 'everything is possible for you. Take this cup from me. Yet not what I will, but what you will'"** (Mark 14:36).

Abba is an affectionate term easily pronounced by toddlers learning to talk, like *Papa*. It wasn't common in the Old Testament, considered by Jewish religious culture as a bit too chummy to be appropriate for the Lord God. That changed when the Son of God himself chose to use it. The Bible encourages us to use it too, enjoying intimacy and closeness with God (Romans 8:15).

Abba is smiling right now just thinking about it.

I want you
Pastor David Scharf

"I want you!" Maybe you've seen that slogan on a poster with Uncle Sam pointing his finger at you, recruiting you to serve in the U.S. Armed Forces. Uncle Sam was not the first one to express that. Matthew, the apostle, was once a tax collector, known for his cheating ways. Yet to his surprise, Jesus pointed to him one day and basically said, "I want you!" **"'Follow me,' he told him, and Matthew got up and followed him"** (Matthew 9:9).

Jesus wanted Matthew to be one of his followers. God would eventually use Matthew to record the life history of the world's Savior.

But it's not only Matthew whom our Savior wants as one of his followers. The Bible says that God *wants* all to be saved and to know the truth. To be wanted (unless it's by the police) is a great feeling. It boosts our confidence. It enhances our self-esteem. It gives us a sense of worth.

The ironic thing is that we weren't "worth" anything to God by nature. Worse yet, we were his enemies. Yet he still said, "I want you." Perhaps this attitude of God can be best depicted with how we usually picture our loving Lord calling us to follow him. We don't have a stern old man pointing at us who says, *"I WANT YOU"*; rather, we have a loving Lord who extends his open arms to us. What else can we do but follow him? What a beautiful thought to be wanted by God.

SLOPPY!

Jason Nelson

My light almost went out in first grade. For some reason, I never went to kindergarten. If you read Robert Fulghum's poem "All I Really Need to Know I Learned in Kindergarten," you'll understand that I was way behind. I started school in first grade. My teacher was a stern, unmarried lady. Her long gray hair hung from her head like seaweed on a clam. She made me nervous every day.

Miss S. was teaching us to print our letters, and they had to be perfect. She gave us whisper-thin manuscript paper and big fat pencils to use. I'm left-handed, and it was a right-handed world. I tried making good letters, but I knew they weren't good. I tried erasing them and rewriting them. All of a sudden Miss S. announced, "Times up." I turned in a paper that looked like it was used for target practice. It was full of holes and black smudges. The next day we got our papers back. Across the top of mine in big red letters for all the world to see was Miss S.'s judgment of me. S-L-O-P-P-Y! It was the first word I learned how to read.

I knew I was sloppy. What I didn't know was how not to be, and she never showed me. I have a message for all the Miss S.'s of the world: **"Anyone who withholds kindness from a friend** (or a first grader) **forsakes the fear of the Almighty"** (Job 6:14).

September 11

Father of grace

Pastor Mike Novotny

A few years ago, I heard a pastor and his son speak at a men's conference. The son told the story of when he got his fiancée pregnant, a fact he was very scared to tell his very religious parents. When he finally blurted out the news, the expecting mother burst into tears, afraid and ashamed. But the pastor and his wife looked at each other and knew exactly what to do. They showed the young couple grace. The pastor's wife embraced her grandchild's mother in a massive hug. Her husband told his son he loved him, he forgave him, and Jesus forgave him too. The couple had expected crossed arms and scowling judgment. Instead they experienced a glimpse of God's heart.

The apostle Paul would have applauded those parents. He once wrote, **"Fathers, do not exasperate your children; instead, bring them up in the training and instruction of the Lord"** (Ephesians 6:4). A massive, and often overlooked, part of training up children is giving them grace, declaring the gospel over them, looking them in the eyes, and reminding them they are loved by God—even post-sin.

Would you join me today and pray that more and more fathers remember the heart of their Father in heaven? We are desperate for a generation that loves and obeys the commands of God. But that will only happen when the good news of unconditional love has captured their hearts. Let's bring every child up to know the grace of God!

Rejection proof

Pastor Daron Lindemann

Jia Jiang knocked on the door of a stranger and asked if he could play soccer in the backyard. He also requested a "burger refill" at a restaurant.

Why? In order to overcome his fear of rejection.

Like most of us, Jia Jiang had experienced rejection, and it hurt. So each day for one hundred days, he asked a stranger something so ridiculous that that person would surely say no. He hoped that being rejected often enough would desensitize him to the pain. He ended up discovering much more.

I can't help but compare Jia Jiang's journey to the rejection Jesus experienced. Author Jia Jiang even mentions Jesus in his TED Talk about rejection along with Nelson Mandela, Ghandi, and Martin Luther King Jr.

These are great men who suffered rejection. But none of them were equals to Jesus.

Jesus experienced rejection—from the crowds, the Jewish and Roman authorities, his own friends, and even his Father in that moment of ultimate spiritual agony on the cross (Mark 15:34). Not to learn from it. Not to turn it into an opportunity for himself. Not to desensitize himself to its pain.

"He was despised and rejected by mankind, a man of suffering, and familiar with pain. . . . For he bore the sin of many, and made intercession for the transgressors" (Isaiah 53:3,12).

Jesus was rejected to suffer the painful punishment for your sins so that you will never be rejected in the same way.

Put a rock on it
Sarah Habben

I once read about a man who put a rock in his mouth to stop himself from speaking without thinking. Maybe he was on to something. Few parts of the Bible make me squirm more than James chapter 3, where the human tongue is called a fire, a restless evil, a tiny thing full of deadly poison. **"With the tongue we praise our Lord and Father, and with it we curse human beings, who have been made in God's likeness"** (James 3:9).

A world of evil balances on the tip of my tongue. In my Christian classroom, I can somehow manage to simultaneously praise the Good Shepherd and belittle his misbehaving sheep. In church, my tongue no sooner finishes with the final hymn before longing to restlessly wag over my fellow redeemed in the pews—*where was she all last month?* At the smallest invitation to gossip, I draw back my bow and release words like poisonous darts—*why can't he just follow through on a commitment?* At home, I can start a blazing fire by dropping a few choice verbal sparks.

I should just start the day with a rock on my tongue. No. Not *a* rock. *My* Rock. My Redeemer. In God's Word and promises, I find Christ's forgiveness. The Spirit's power. The desire to pray with King David: **"May these words of my mouth and this meditation of my heart be pleasing in your sight, Lord, my Rock and my Redeemer"** (Psalm 19:14).

Before I allow my tongue to speak, I can put my Rock on it.

Evidence of the Spirit: Kindness

Pastor Mark Jeske

It's not so hard to be nice to the nice. It's not so hard to dish back at people who give you guff. It's not so hard to go through life guarded and suspicious, assuming the worst in people. It's much harder to go first.

One of the unmistakable evidences that the Spirit of the Lord is living in people's hearts is that they treat other people better than they deserve: **"The fruit of the Spirit is . . . kindness"** (Galatians 5:22). Kindness is not payback; it's not treating others exactly as they deserve. In fact, it's just the opposite—it means extending yourself, being willing to give something of yourself away, taking the risk that your gift may be ignored or rebuffed.

Kindness means that you don't take out your bad day on the people who live with you. Kindness means you stay patient with a crabby customer and keep smiling. Kindness means that you don't keep score with your spouse. Kindness means that you choose not to hear some things and let them whiz past you. Kind people show kindness for its own sake, not as a preliminary maneuver to get something from somebody else.

Kind people are above-average aware of how kind God has been to them. Christ went first, essentially fronting us grace, mercy, and forgiveness, knowing we could never afford to earn it ourselves. What a joy to thank our kind Savior by showing kindness to the fools and sinners around us.

Who needs your mercy today?

Baby Jesus came to fight

Pastor Mike Novotny

I like to picture Baby Jesus with a sword strapped across his little back. Maybe a helmet on his tender head. And definitely some eye black under each of his piercing eyes. Does that make me weird? Actually, I think it makes me biblical.

Have you read Isaiah's prophecy about the child who would be born to us, the Prince of peace (Isaiah 9:6)? Do you know what comes just before those thrilling words? **"You have shattered the yoke that burdens them, the bar across their shoulders, the rod of their oppressor. Every warrior's boot used in battle and every garment rolled in blood will be destined for burning, will be fuel for the fire"** (verses 4,5). Boots, blood, and battles come right before the baby who would be born to us.

I love that image of Jesus. As God in human flesh, he is not some vulnerable, weak, cowardly kid who hides when something threatens your faith. No, he strides out onto the battlefield to fight for you. Like David marching out to drop Goliath, Jesus steps out in the name of the Most High God to win the victory on your behalf. And he started his fight from his first breath.

So, rejoice over your Jesus today. He is the warrior who fought for your forgiveness and brought home the trophy of your salvation. You are more than a conqueror through him who loves you (Romans 8:37).

I don't have to tell you to tell someone about Jesus

Pastor David Scharf

It scared children. It panicked parents. Other than the atomic bomb, it was the number-one fear of the time. Every summer, this stealer of children would come. It was a disease known as polio, and in the early 1950s this disease infected thousands, killing some and maiming others. The whole world was searching for a cure.

Then on April 12, 1955, it was announced that Jonas Salk had developed a vaccine that would prevent the dreaded polio disease. The news said it would work 100 percent of the time! Wow! One man described the country's feelings by saying this: *"It was as if a war had ended."*

Can you imagine how cool it would have been to be the one who got to announce that news to the world? This I guarantee: No one forced or guilted him into telling. No one needed to force anyone to tell news that big!

Friends, you have a solution to the gravest problems that this world faces, and his name is Jesus. You have the cure to the terminal illness of sin, and his name is Jesus. You have the peace, comfort, contentment, and joy that the world is searching for; and his name is Jesus. I don't have to tell you to tell someone. You have Jesus, the answer to what everyone is looking for. The truth is I couldn't stop you if I tried.

"The first thing Andrew did was to find his brother Simon and tell him, 'We have found the Messiah'" (John 1:41).

Preapproved

Pastor Daron Lindemann

A short tour through my house reveals how care-free life is for me.

Pretreated fabrics on my living room furniture resist stains without me worrying about it. Prewashed jeans allow me comfort and style without 16 cycles of washing and drying. Preseasoned pork tenderloin means no messy marinades. Preprogrammed apps think for me.

Except, somehow I manage to mess up some of this stuff. It's called "operator error."

There is one aspect of life that Christians can't mess up: following God's purpose for us. Succeeding in the role that God has for you today is preapproved by God himself.

"Before I formed you in the womb I knew you, before you were born I set you apart" (Jeremiah 1:5). That was God's promise to Jeremiah, a man he called to the role of prophet, and that is also God's promise to you for whatever role he has for you.

God set his own Son apart and called him to be your Savior. God has also set you apart, given you his approval, and gifted you with the ability to obey his purpose for you. Your "operator error" is corrected by his perfect grace.

Face your responsibilities and relationships with confidence today. **"Your labor in the Lord is not in vain"** (1 Corinthians 15:58).

All believers have a priestly ministry
Pastor Mark Jeske

For a long time there has been some confusion around the word *ministry*. It is generally reserved to describe the job that pastors have. But I think it would be better to call the pastors' job "representative ministry," meaning that they exercise an authoritative teaching function *on behalf of a group.* Only a few function in that kind of ministry.

In Old Testament times, the word *priest* was reserved for the sons and grandsons of Moses' brother, Aaron, who had a hereditary role as intercessors and offerers of sacrifices between God and his nation of Israel. They personally represented Jesus Christ, the Great High Priest. But in the New Testament era, God calls *all* believers his royal priests, and as such they too have a ministry *as individuals.* God gives people gifts for that service, as well as opportunities and his permission to get started.

Many centuries before the outpouring of the Holy Spirit on the Day of Pentecost, the great prophet Joel looked ahead to the way in which all of the believers would enthusiastically share the gospel message: **"And afterward, I will pour out my Spirit on all people. Your sons and daughters will prophesy, your old men will dream dreams, your young men will see visions"** (Joel 2:28).

Our confused and broken world has too many hurting people for just the clergy to tend to. They need you and the priestly message of salvation you can bring them.

That's the one!
Pastor Mike Novotny

What do you think when you see a group of teenagers all sitting at the same table, staring at their phones? Or when your nephew boldly posts something anti-Christian on social media, knowing that you are a devoted follower of Jesus Christ? Or when the neighbor girl next door wants to transition to being the neighbor boy next door? Or when you hear the statistics about how many college students pray or even believe in God at all?

Confusion? Frustration? Despair? Before you give in to those feelings, check out how Jesus feels: **"What do you think? If a man owns a hundred sheep, and one of them wanders away, will he not leave the ninety-nine on the hills and go to look for the one that wandered off?"** (Matthew 18:12). When the Good Shepherd loses just one sheep to its wandering ways, how does he feel? Concerned. Compassionate. Brokenhearted.

As America becomes an increasingly non/anti-Christian culture, we Christians must not forget Jesus' words. Those who are far from God need our hearts to be broken, broken enough to leave our comfort zones, broken enough to love them by listening, and broken enough to look for ways to bring them back to the only Shepherd who can save them from danger.

So, when you see someone who's far from God, remind yourself, "That's the one!" That's the one whom Jesus talked about. That's the one whom God still longs to bring home.

Trusted with grace

Jason Nelson

For a long time, the relationship between God and people was a transaction. It was always *quid pro quo,* this for that, tit for tat. **"'I have loved you,' says the Lord. . . . 'If I am a father, where is the honor due me?'"** (Malachi 1:2,6). The return the Father expected for his love was more than just a little respect.

Then out of the blue God trusted us with grace. It was no longer a two-sided transaction. He made it only *quid*; he made it only *this.* **"They will be my treasured possession. I will spare them, just as a father has compassion and spares his son"** (Malachi 3:17). He sent Jesus, who showed us love going one way only. Jesus nudges our response away from ourselves in the direction of how we treat each other.

We are used to bartering with each other. It is embedded in everything we do in business, government, and ministry. Our interactions with each other are mostly matters of give-and-take, and often they need to be: taxes for services, money for goods, donations for books. But what happens when we trust each other with grace the same way God trusted us? What if we didn't try to assess if others are worthy of love? What if we didn't care if they wanted love for the right reasons? What if we didn't ask for anything in return? What if we just loved people? I have a strong feeling they would love us back.

The husband who went to war

Pastor Mike Novotny

My colleague Tim has a tattoo of an obscure but powerful passage in the Bible. **"[The LORD] will take great delight in you; in his love he will no longer rebuke you, but will rejoice over you with singing"** (Zephaniah 3:17). Isn't that incredible? God does not just put up with you or love you because he is obligated to. Just the opposite. He delights in you. Even better, he takes "great delight" in you. Everyone who trusts in Jesus makes God so happy that he busts out in song, rejoicing over us with singing. Like a head-over-heels teenager falling in love, God can't help but smile when he pulls out a picture of his church.

But I never knew how Tim's passage began until recently. Before the delight/rejoicing part, Zephaniah 3:17 begins, **"The LORD your God is with you, the Mighty Warrior who saves."** How can God delight in you? Because he is the Mighty Warrior who died to deliver you. How can God sing when he sees you? Because he first suffered to save you. The image of Jesus as a happy husband only comes after seeing him as the wounded warrior.

The balance of that imagery is powerful. The tough picture of a soldier at war. The tender picture of a devoted husband. Everything our hearts want and need is found in Jesus.

The world we long for
Jason Nelson

I'm writing this devotion after innocence was shattered one more time. Children were killed at school. It seems disrespectful to call them children because they stared death in the face. No one remains a child who stares death in the face. I was inspired by the maturity of young survivors and dismayed at the ineptness of older people responsible for their safety. I long for a better world for children.

Isaiah also longed for a better world. Read Isaiah chapter 11 and ask yourself if he is describing the world you long for. In the midst of a society torn apart and taken captive, he looked ahead to the coming of the Messiah. The Messiah is at the center of the world we long for. It's a place where **"the wolf will live with the lamb, the leopard will lie down with the goat, the calf and the lion and the yearling together; and a little child will lead them"** (Isaiah 11:6). But must we wait for the Messiah's return to have a better world? Can't we improve the one we have?

Long before the Messiah became a victim of violence himself, he called for the end of violence. What a childish approach to life. It is the kind of childishness that should dwell in our hearts forever. Jesus can change people. **"They will neither harm nor destroy on all my holy mountain, for the earth will be filled with the knowledge of the Lord"** (Isaiah 11:9).

Say, "mercy"

Pastor David Scharf

Did you ever get pinned down by your older brother or sister? Or perhaps you were the one pinning him or her. If that's the case, do you remember what you made them say before letting them up? More than likely you said, "Say, 'uncle'" or "Say, 'mercy.'"

The word *mercy* is scattered throughout the Bible. Mercy is undeserved love that generates in God's heart because he sees our weakness. It's similar to the reaction you might have for someone who is struggling with a disease. When you see someone's hurting, your mercy prompts you to see how you can help.

Do you ever feel like you're pinned down on your back in life? Like the troubles of life, whether marital or financial or work related, have you flat on your back? Well, what's the solution? Say, "mercy."

In life, sometimes the only time we see God is when he allows us to be knocked flat on our backs. And that can be good because what do we see when we're on our backs? The only place to look is up. **"Our eyes look to the Lord our God, till he shows us his mercy"** (Psalm 123:2).

We see God, who is with us and sees our hurts, our struggles, and our needs. We see Jesus, who showed us his great mercy by suffering and dying on a cross so that we can be in heaven with him someday. We see our God, who shows mercy.

A hiding place

Pastor Mark Jeske

Do you have a location in your life where you always go when you are stressed? have a really tough decision to make? took some abuse? suffered a defeat? Maybe there are woods where you like to walk. Maybe you get in the car and drive somewhere. Anywhere. Maybe you go down in the basement with the lights off and think in the dark. Maybe you head for the bedroom, burrow under the covers, and go into the fetal position.

There is also a place in your mind where you can always go when life is overwhelming you. Through your faith in Christ, the great power behind the universe has adopted you as his son or daughter. When you come to him humbly, dragging your burden, you will always find a warm welcome, a listening ear, and heavenly omnipotence at your service. **"The Lord is good, a refuge in times of trouble. He cares for those who trust in him"** (Nahum 1:7).

Just talk to him. Your prayers don't have to be long or flowery and eloquent or formal or perfect. Just talk to your Daddy, commander of the angel armies, chancellor of the treasury, Ancient of Days. Talk to his Son, Jesus, crusher of the head of the serpent, firstborn from the dead, lion of the tribe of Judah. Call on the Spirit, Counselor and Giver of heavenly gifts.

Give it all to him, and then let it go.

What Batman wants for Christmas

Pastor Mike Novotny

Do you know what Batman wishes for at Christmas? During an interview with *USA Today* about his role as Batman in the movie the *Justice League*, actor Ben Affleck asked, "Wouldn't it be nice if there was somebody who could save us from all this, save us from ourselves, save us from the consequences of our actions, and save us from people who are evil?"

Amen, Batman. That would be nice. In fact, it is nice. Or maybe I should say *he* is nice. One day Jesus will return from heaven to save us from "all this"—from the political squabbles, the burdensome tasks at work, the family drama, the return of cancer, and the weight of grief. But Jesus has already saved us from ourselves, from the spiritual consequences of our actions, from the penalty of our sins. The author to the Hebrews stated, **"Christ was sacrificed once to take away the sins of many; and he will appear a second time, not to bear sin, but to bring salvation to those who are waiting for him"** (9:28). One day, hopefully soon, Jesus will rescue us from the danger of sickness, pain, and frustration. But today we find peace in the fact that our sins are "taken away," removed from us entirely. When God looks at you, there is not a single sin hanging over your head. There are zero reasons for God to reject you or turn away from your prayers.

Sounds nice, doesn't it? It is. Maybe someone should tell Batman.

Blame game

Pastor Mark Jeske

It would be funny if it weren't so tragic and true. What was the first thing Adam and Eve did when confronted with their catastrophic rebellion against God? They blamed somebody else. Eve blamed the serpent, and Adam managed to blame both Eve and God. Satan was laughing as he slithered away. Since he blamed God for his fiery fall from heaven, it doubtless brought him sick pleasure to see God's children turning against him too. It is now part of his permanent strategy for keeping people confused and spiritually sick.

People like to set up tests to prove the existence of God or to prove whether or not he loves them or has as much power as advertised. When things don't turn out as desired in these "tests," people feel justified in drawing conclusions about God's power, love, competence, or all of the above. They may not have noticed that their dilemmas are largely of their own making: **"A person's own folly leads to their ruin, yet their heart rages against the Lord"** (Proverbs 19:3).

Our "nonjudgmental" culture feeds that delusion. People who are prone to commit domestic violence or engage in drug abuse, sexual abuse, or alcoholism are classed as "victims" of "diseases," and thus absolved of personal responsibility. People who have dropped out of school complain bitterly about the meager job opportunities available to them.

When you have the right opportunity, speak the truth in love to your friends who talk like this. Or to yourself.

Time well spent

Jason Nelson

Since our relationship with God is all taken care of, what should we do with our time? No smile toward the heavens will make us more charming to God. No penance can make up for recent wrongdoing. We have nothing God needs, nor can we give up something so he can have more of it. Beating ourselves up more severely won't convince him we recognize how unworthy we are. More time at the fitness center won't make us more attractive to him. We can't show him anything he doesn't already see. Even reading several of these devotions every day won't persuade him we really want to be holy. Not one of the many moments God gives us needs to be spent making ourselves right with him. We are saved by grace. It is finished. So, what in all the world should we do with our time?

"Be generous with the different things God gave you, passing them around so all get in on it: if words, let it be God's words; if help, let it be God's hearty help. That way, God's bright presence will be evident in everything through Jesus" (1 Peter 4:10,11 MSG).

This is hard to keep straight, but what God wants us to do with our time is to turn it completely outward. He wants us to bend the arc of every day away from ourselves toward others. He wants us to spread his love around so everyone gets in on it.

When church hurts

Pastor Mike Novotny

It might just be one of the hardest commandments in the entire Bible to keep. Jesus said, **"If your brother or sister sins, go and point out their fault, just between the two of you. If they listen to you, you have won them over"** (Matthew 18:15).

Do you know why this is so agonizing? Why your palms leak like 1940s plumbing and you delete your text before your thumb pushes the blue arrow to send it? Why you decide to talk about someone who hurt you instead of to the person who hurt you? Because the devil knows the power of forgiveness. Over the millennia, the enemy has seen the power of peacemakers. He's witnessed that one step—going and showing—that clears up so many misunderstandings, builds so much empathy, and offers a chance to forgive in Jesus' name. The reason it feels so hard is because it is so holy.

Is there a hard conversation you need to have today? Has someone sinned against you, causing two parts of Christ's body to become disjointed? If a name or a face pops into your head during this paragraph, can I encourage you to trust Jesus' wisdom and start a conversation? Don't worry if you don't want to. That's just the devil whispering in your ear.

For the sake of your heart, that person's soul, and Jesus' church, go and show the sinner his or her sin. I will pray that the Holy Spirit helps your words win that person over. I will pray for a restoration of unity in your church.

Life or death

Pastor Mark Jeske

All of us are a bundle of opinions on great movies we've seen, restaurants we like, favorite foods, coolest cars, and politics. These opinions are all over the place, and though people love to argue passionately about them, they are neither right nor wrong.

Some people would add religious beliefs to that mix and add that everybody's religious opinions are just as valid *for them* as every other opinion. Religious "intolerance" is very unfashionable these days. Christianity, however, is not a religion or philosophy. It is *reality*, like gravity or the rotation of the earth. It is not one of many honorable points of view. Its teachings are not true for some and not for others.

Moses' last words to the Israelites impressed on them what was at stake in their treatment of God's revelation to them: **"Take to heart all the words I have solemnly declared to you this day, so that you may command your children to obey carefully all the words of this law. They are not just idle words for you—they are your *life*"** (Deuteronomy 32:46,47). The whole world is caught up in a titanic struggle between light and darkness, good and evil. You are either with the God of the Bible or against him. It is life or death.

The Bible is not just an ancient and interesting piece of literature. It connects you to Christ, who holds the keys to heaven and hell, and you will spend eternity in one or the other.

Don't blend in!

Sarah Habben

On our island home, it's easy to spot a tourist. It's not just their white skin that gives them away. It's their straw hats and sunburns, their shorts and sandals, their bottled water and beach bags. The cruise boats encourage these tourists to disembark and enjoy the local people and surroundings . . . but to avoid drinking the water. Even a small number of foreign microbes could wage war in their guts and ruin their trip.

Believers are tourists too—temporary inhabitants of a sinful world. And God doesn't want us to blend in. He says, **"I urge you, as foreigners and exiles, to abstain from sinful desires, which wage war against your soul"** (1 Peter 2:11). With our final, heavenly destination in mind, God warns us: *Don't* blend in! Abstain from the local brew!

But the world serves temptation on a fancy tray. Satan's waiters bustle about with their menus of sin, promising to quench our thirst for happiness. All around us, people tip back tall, tinkling glasses of desire. And look! They seem powerful. Popular. Beautiful. Privileged. If that is the result of blending in, what does it matter if I cheat a little, lie a little, give someone a bad name?

It matters because those "harmless" sins battle for our souls: souls that belong to God. He chose us. Showed us mercy. Paid for our adoption with the blood of his Son. Equips us to stand out as joyful servants in a dog-eat-dog world.

We are foreigners with a heavenly home. *Don't* blend in!

october

My grace is sufficient for you,
for my power is made perfect in weakness.

2 Corinthians 12:9

God so loved the world

Pastor Mike Novotny

Have you ever paused long enough to meditate on the staggering meaning of John 3:16? **"God so loved the world that he gave his one and only Son, that whoever believes in him shall not perish but have eternal life."** Let's break that famous verse down.

God. Do you know what God is like? He is absolutely self-sufficient. He's good without you (no offense). God has never said to anyone, "You complete me." He is complete already. If the entire world would have perished in hell and no one would have gotten eternal life, God would have been just fine. He's God, after all.

And yet—this should mess with you—God so loved. He chose to love us even when he didn't need us. He thought of our needs (to not perish) even if it cost him his very best (his one and only Son). Love always involves a sacrifice, and God's love required the greatest sacrifice of all—Jesus.

And whom did God love so much that he sent his only Son? (Brace yourself for this!) The whole world! Black and white and every shade of brown. Rich and poor. Male and female. Married and single and divorced. Good people, bad people, prodigals, and Pharisees. Me, thank God. You, praise God. Grace is love with no strings attached, and this love wasn't based on history, morality, or potential. It was pure. It was undeserved. It was for everyone. It was for you too. It still is.

What a verse! What a God!

It is well with my soul

Sarah Habben

The Great Chicago Fire of 1871 left Horatio Spafford in financial tatters. Shortly after, while crossing the Atlantic, all four of Spafford's daughters drowned in a collision with another ship. His wife, Anna, survived and sent him a telegram that read succinctly—heartbreakingly—"Saved alone." Several weeks later, as Spafford's own ship passed near his daughters' watery grave, he wrote these words to his famous hymn: "Whatever my lot, thou hast taught me to say, it is well, it is well with my soul."

What beautiful words! Believers across generations and denominations sing this confession of hope in the midst of heartache.

But it didn't stay well with Spafford's soul. Sometime later, he started a cult, calling himself "the Branch" and his wife "the Bride." They received "divine" revelations, denied marriage and hell, affirmed purgatory, and taught that all would be saved, including Satan. They set a date for Christ's return and were disappointed. They believed they wouldn't die and were disappointed again.

Lord, keep me from the lie that it's *well with my soul* apart from Jesus, apart from your Truth. Forgive me for tweaking your will and Word in order to justify my wrongful habits. Keep me from willfully squirming free of your arms of grace. Let 1 Thessalonians 5:23 be my daily prayer: **"May . . . the God of peace, sanctify** [me] **through and through. May** [my] **whole spirit, soul and body be kept blameless at the coming of our Lord Jesus Christ."**

And teach me to say, "It is well with my soul."

Dearly loved children

Pastor Mike Novotny

When the students of the area Christian high school in my city head out to their cars each afternoon, a Bible passage catches their eyes. **"Be imitators of God, therefore, as dearly loved children"** (Ephesians 5:1 NIV84). Those words are engraved over the exit doors, lifted up so that every teenage eye can see them.

As much as I love the challenge of the first phrase (to imitate the God of love), I adore the final words even more. We are "dearly loved children." It would be incredible to be called the children of God. Even more incredible to be called the beloved children of God. But Paul insists that we Christians are dearly loved children! That is the most incredible truth of all!

The love among the Father, Son, and Spirit overflows and gushes out into our lives. In the same way, God wants our love for one another to overflow out the doors of the church and flood our communities, schools, and workplaces. This is what Paul urged the Ephesian Christians to do, and today our calling is still the same.

Imitating God's love is no small activity, but thankfully we have a solid identity through faith in Jesus. We are the dearly loved children of a glorious Father in heaven.

What goes before a fall?
Pastor Mark Jeske

Things had been going so well. King Uzziah had been enjoying the Lord's favor, and military security and economic prosperity followed. But Satan never quits. He was ready with Plan B. **"After Uzziah became powerful, his pride led to his downfall. He was unfaithful to the Lord his God, and entered the temple of the Lord to burn incense on the altar of incense. Azariah the priest with eighty other courageous priests of the Lord followed him in. They confronted King Uzziah and said, 'It is not right for you, Uzziah, to burn incense to the Lord. That is for the priests, the descendants of Aaron, who have been consecrated to burn incense. Leave the sanctuary, for you have been unfaithful; and you will not be honored by the Lord God'"** (2 Chronicles 26:16-18).

Are you proud? Might you be proud of your humility? Would the people around you say that pride is a problem for you? Are you stubborn? Do you listen well? Can you admit it when you're wrong? Do you allow people strong enough to rebuke you to be around you?

Realize that Satan would like to twist your thoughts into knots. Even when you've won some temptation battles, he is already plotting his counterattack. Stay vigilant. Stay in the Word so that you can hear the clear voice of the Master above the din of your life's battles.

You would do well to keep a mentor around who will tell you when you're getting too full of yourself.

Why not just ask?

Jason Nelson

"Our Father in heaven . . . give us today our daily bread" (Matthew 6:9,11).

I have prayed these words thousands of times. Not once did I think, "He knows what I need. I shouldn't have to ask." But when my big, strapping kids were lying on the couch and the sidewalk needed to be shoveled, that is exactly what I thought: "They know what needs to be done. I shouldn't have to ask."

Asking isn't generally a sticking point between us and God. It is the essence of our communication with him. We do it all the time without feeling resentful. But it can be a trouble spot among people, especially between parents and their teenage children. Sometimes we expect more omniscience and sovereign willpower from awkward humanoids fighting their way through puberty than we expect from God himself. We think they should routinely quiet their hormones, focus their distracted thoughts, overcome the exhaustion they feel from growing so fast, and simply volunteer to do what needs to be done.

That is an unfortunate mind game we don't need to play. So, the next time the dishwasher needs to be unloaded or a load of their undies needs to go into the washing machine, fight the urge to say something sarcastic like, "Your clothes aren't going to wash themselves." Muffle the exasperated voice in your own head. If the ultimate goal is getting them to do something you want done—again—why not just ask?

I knew that would happen

Pastor David Scharf

How good are you at predicting the future? When asked who's going to win a sporting event between two evenly matched opponents, usually people will be cautious in their answers because it's anybody's game. Ask them after the game, and they will say, "I knew that would happen" and then give you all the reasons for that opinion. Hindsight is 20/20.

We know from experience that if we predict something beyond a shadow of a doubt, we oftentimes end up looking foolish. In 1773 King George II said that the American colonies had little stomach for revolution. Whoops! The *Titanic* was declared to be unsinkable. Whoops! In 1939 the *New York Times* said that TV wouldn't succeed because Americans don't have time for it. Whoops!

The moral of the story is this: "Don't predict the future unless you know it." None of us does. But is that true? **"You spoke by the Holy Spirit through the mouth of your servant, our father David"** (Acts 4:25). Jesus spoke through the mouths of the prophets hundreds of years before he came. When he came, everything happened just as he said it would. That was not dumb luck! Jesus fulfilled God's promises—all of them! Now, when all of Jesus' predictions in the New Testament come true, including that he will come and take you to heaven, you can say, "I knew that was going to happen!"

In fact, the most comforting thing about it is . . . you can say it now!

A lot in common
Jason Nelson

We Americans have a penchant for seeing ourselves as God's chosen people. That's the mentality our Puritan forefathers and mothers handed down to us. They thought that out of the wilderness they could carve a Christian utopia. So, the most secular issues were viewed as having existential implications. Later, President Andrew Jackson didn't just make a fiscal argument for eliminating Nicholas Biddle's monolithic national bank; he made a spiritual one. He likened the giant bank to the golden calf and warned that God would punish America like he punished Israel if the country continued to bow to it.

Spiritual imagery is part of our national consciousness because of our history and because Christianity and democracy have much in common. They both give people broad liberties and wonderful opportunities. We can direct our own lives and freely express our own faith in God. I think African Americans understand the parallels better than most. Their enslaved ancestors sang about it in their hope-filled songs.

Oh, let us all from bondage flee, Let My people go!
And let us all in Christ be free, Let My people go!
—Anonymous

"It is for freedom that Christ has set us free. Stand firm, then, and do not let yourselves be burdened again by a yoke of slavery" (Galatians 5:1). Let us all in Christ be free. Let us use our liberty to expand his kingdom by all possible means so Jesus can set people free everywhere.

I just want to be liked

Pastor David Scharf

"You want me to do what?!" Ever been intimidated by a job that you felt was just too far over your head? Welcome to the prophet Jeremiah's world. The Almighty God called Jeremiah to be his spokesman to God's people of Israel. If you know nothing else about Jeremiah's ministry, you should know this: He was faithful; and because of it, he was persecuted and disliked. There had to have been times that he thought, "I just want to be liked."

The truth is that we all want to be liked. But because God has called on us to be his witnesses to the ends of the earth and teach everything that he commands, that means that not everyone will listen. If we're faithful, there will be times that people don't like what we have to say. As a church that remains faithful to the Word of God and as individuals who strive to do the same, sometimes, tired from the "battle," we slump over and think, "I just want to be liked!"

At those times, remember that Jesus loves you even when rejected. He knows you. He has set you apart. As you remain faithful as his witness, he likes you . . . he really, really likes you.

Just look to his cross for proof! Let his words in commissioning Jeremiah to be his prophet comfort you as you strive to be his witness: **"Before I formed you in the womb I knew you, before you were born I set you apart"** (Jeremiah 1:5).

Life's a song

Jason Nelson

My three-year-old granddaughter, Addison, has the lead role in her own musicals. Her life is filled with songs. She's in a very happy head space. She doesn't just ask questions. She sings them. One of my favorites is a soulful Sunday-morning classic: *"When can I get my church dress on?"* She holds out the last note in a heartrending vibrato. When she does get her church dress on, she concludes her performance with interpretive dance that features lots of twirling and graceful arm extensions. Thanks to Addy, I know what cherubs look like. Addy gets ready to worship God the way his people did a long time ago. She starts before she ever gets to church. **"On your feet now—applaud God! Bring a gift of laughter, sing yourselves into his presence"** (Psalm 100:1 MSG).

Can you imagine a church parking lot where people pile out of their SUVs and start skipping and singing on their way into the gathering space because their lives are filled with songs? Maybe we should let the children go in first and show us how to do it. Children express joy with their singing and dancing, and in a miraculous way their singing and dancing sustain their joy. It is the joy of always living in the presence of God. It is the joy of still being near enough in time to your first breath that you just assume God has everything covered. So why not just sing?

Worship is proclaiming

Pastor Mark Jeske

Have you ever been dating someone who wants to keep your relationship on the down low? Who doesn't want to go anywhere publicly with you? Who won't claim you on Facebook, still pretending to be "single"? As the weeks slide by, don't you start to wonder if there's a future with this person? Why won't he or she acknowledge you publicly?

Can you imagine how God feels when people seem to want the forgiveness and immortality that he promises, seem awfully glad to have his gift pass into heaven when they die, but they won't acknowledge him in front of their friends? Don't settle for an invisible relationship. Go public! Be proud of your Savior and King! Wear the colors! Stand with the team! **"Give praise to the Lord, proclaim his name; make known among the nations what he has done"** (1 Chronicles 16:8).

Worship is *proclaiming*. Worship shows the world that you are proud to be one of God's children and servants, Jesus' brothers and sisters, joyful members of his PR and communication team. In a world full of confusion, ignorance, and brokenness, worship shows that you believe the words of the Bible to be true. You can most certainly worship God quietly in your home. Do that too. But let the world see you go to church, assemble with other believers, participate in a joyful and loving fellowship, and bring value to your community.

Public worship shows that you are proud to be called a *Christ*ian.

Thank you for the privilege
Pastor David Scharf

"So you also, when you have done everything you were told to do, should say, 'We are unworthy servants; we have only done our duty'" (Luke 17:10).

Do Jesus' words here strike you as unJesus-like? Wouldn't you expect him to talk about the rewards of grace for doing what he asks like he explains elsewhere in the Bible? But here, Jesus is stressing the privilege of being a servant. He is also stressing that we earn nothing from our service. Rather, a servant does what he is told.

If we think these words are negative, we need to look at it from Jesus' perspective. In love, he became man to live a perfect life for you and die for you. In love, he took great pains to make sure you heard the good news about him. In love, though he is all-sufficient without us, he condescends to use us in carrying out the task of telling others about him. In love, he gives us his powerful means to carry out that task through his Word and sacraments. The point? What a privilege to be his servant! What a blessing to be part of kingdom work, unworthy servants that we are! What a privilege to come from the throne room of the great King with an urgent message to share with the world! All glory is his. . . . We have only done our duty. I guess these words aren't so unJesus-like after all. These words drip with his love! Thank you for the privilege, Jesus!

Everything we do teaches

Jason Nelson

The King of kings and Lord of lords, with every supernatural power at his disposal, said his disciples should go into the whole wide world and convert all nations to Christianity. It would be a monumental undertaking. And he put just one tool in their toolbox: **"teaching them to obey everything I have commanded you"** (Matthew 28:20). He didn't say legislate people into the kingdom of God or bribe them into it or argue with them about it or scare the hell out of them. He said go and teach. That is the power he gave us. He gave us the incredible power to teach the whole counsel of God as he revealed it to us in the Bible.

That is still the church's purpose in the world. To teach everything Jesus did and said via everything we do and say. Everything about us teaches: from the clarity of our message to the tone in our voices, to the looks on our faces, to the forms we follow, to the demographic makeup of our gatherings. Everything we do sends a message to all nations about our take on the Savior.

Here is the good news: What we teach people about us-and-Jesus tends to stick with them. Here is the bad news: What we teach people about us-and-Jesus tends to stick with them. The question of reckoning is, "What do we want to stick with people about us-and-Jesus?" That is what we should teach.

Wail no more

Pastor Mike Novotny

Every day in Jerusalem, Jewish people gather at the Wailing Wall. Ever heard of it? It's the western wall of the Temple Mount, the big box that the Jewish temple used to stand upon. In Jesus' day, the temple represented the presence of God, but in A.D. 70, the Romans ravaged the entire complex, tossing every stone down on the streets below. For the last 1,950 years, the Jews have wailed, missing the place where their God used to live, aching to be reunited with the holy presence of their Lord.

But Christians don't have to wail. The night before he died, Jesus promised, **"I will ask the Father, and he will give you another advocate to help you and be with you forever—the Spirit of truth"** (John 14:16,17). According to Jesus, there is a new holy place—you. Your body is a temple of the Holy Spirit, the God who is in you and with you forever.

All the wisdom, strength, and power you need to honor God is at your disposal. All the courage to fight against temptation and all the faith to find peace in Jesus' cross are closer than your breath. Because our Father gladly answered the prayer of his Son and gave you the Spirit of truth. So do not be timid and do not be afraid. You are walking with God!

Nobody knows
Christine Wentzel

"Nobody Knows the Trouble I've Seen" is an old African American spiritual song that was sung in the days of slavery way before its publication in 1867. Sorrow was their intimate shadow, but hope led its footsteps.

The devil's arsenal of weapons includes the temptation into isolation, to permanently separate us from the only One who personally knows our troubles.

The writer and singers of this spiritual knew that truth well. They finished their lament with pure gospel: "Nobody knows the trouble I've seen. Glory hallelujah!" It rings out the virtues of hope-filled believers: long-suffering, patient, with joyful endurance through which we declare our identity in Christ. As Jesus suffered, so do we.

"Not only so, but we also glory in our sufferings, because we know that suffering produces perseverance; perseverance, character; and character, hope. And hope does not put us to shame, because God's love has been poured out into our hearts through the Holy Spirit, who has been given to us" (Romans 5:3-5).

Repeat the rescue: God's love is poured into our hearts through the Holy Spirit! We are no longer slaves to our sufferings!

We are free to believe the lie of isolation—curling around our troubles, staring inward through our tears—or look up and see our Savior's pierced hands holding ours. Unwind in his presence.

GLORY HALLELUJAH!

You've got a different view (Part 1)

Linda Buxa

As I'm writing this, I'm sitting in the window seat of an airplane. The woman in the middle seat has been looking out the window too. So far, I've randomly mentioned, "Oh, check out that wind farm" and "That water is such a unique color" and "Look, we're finally reaching the mountains."

Each time, she's said, "I can't see it."

It's hard to comprehend that someone sitting right next to me—after all, it's an airplane and we're practically on top of each other—could have such a different perspective.

This world is like that too. You're surrounded by so many people who are so close to you, and yet they have different perspectives. They can't see what you see—hope, peace, perseverance, gentleness, self-control, for example—because they don't have the window seat to the gospel.

"The god of this age has blinded the minds of unbelievers, so that they cannot see the light of the gospel that displays the glory of Christ, who is the image of God" (2 Corinthians 4:4).

This doesn't have to be how the story ends, however.

When my seatmate sat a little taller, leaned in a bit, or waited just a little bit longer, then she could see what I saw. So don't stop talking about what it looks like from your seat. Invite the people around you to check out the view. There's still time.

You've got a different view (Part 2)
Linda Buxa

(A four-hour flight means I've had plenty of time to mull over just how different the view is from my window seat as opposed to the people in the middle and aisle seats. Check out yesterday's devotion to catch up.)

As I sit in the window seat of an airplane, the person in the aisle can crane his neck to get a look outside. That person can see the mountains vaguely, but he really has no idea of how great the view really is.

When the Bible says, **"Now I know in part; then I shall know fully, even as I am fully known"** (1 Corinthians 13:12), it makes me realize that I'm in the aisle seat of life and faith. I don't know or see it all—and I won't as long as I'm on the earth. Oh, I know just what I need to know to build my faith and grow my faith. But I can't always see the way God's going to work through my friends' struggles. I can't always see how he's going to work things for my good. And I certainly don't know everything about what's ahead.

But because I know the Pilot, I trust that he's going to get me safely through this ride. And at the same time, I'll look forward to the best view when the time is right.

Chores for God's children
Pastor Mike Novotny

Since my bride is a beautifully organized woman, she has created a color-coordinated chore chart for our children. Every morning our daughters see the work that needs to be done before the day's end. I suppose there are two ways for them to see those charts. They could see them as chores, as regrettable labor that must be done to escape parental punishment. Or they could put the emphasis on "children's" chores, as proof that they are part of a loving family. In either case, there is work for them to do. But only the second point of view is inspired by gratitude and fueled by love.

How do you view the "chores" the Father has commanded you to do, that list of laws that God wants obeyed? Jesus framed it like this: **"As the Father has loved me, so have I loved you. Now remain in my love. If you keep my commands, you will remain in my love"** (John 15:9,10). Notice that Jesus has commands (not suggestions) for you to keep. Yet, which word dominates the context? *Love.* Jesus wants you to know that he loves you as much as the Father loves him—perfectly and constantly. The delight that the Father feels for his Son, Jesus feels for you.

You might struggle with a certain aspect of the Christian life—forgiveness, contentment, purity, etc. But please start where Jesus did—with the divine love your Savior feels toward you. Yes, there are chores to be done. But it feels much less like a chore when you believe you've been chosen as a child in the Father's family.

When they hate you

Pastor Mike Novotny

There is an odd passage printed on the wall next to the main doors of the church where I serve. It reads, **"If you belonged to the world, it would love you as its own. As it is, you do not belong to the world, but I have chosen you out of the world. That is why the world hates you"** (John 15:19). That's a weird thing to leave church with, isn't it? "People will hate you!" Couldn't we choose something more inspiring? Some Pinteresty quote like "Live, Laugh, Love"?

Actually, no, we can't. Jesus spoke those words the night before he died so that you would be prepared for the days and nights of real life. So that when you attempt to be full of grace and truth (like Jesus—John 1:14), you are ready for the world to unfriend you. When the sting of rejection comes, Jesus doesn't want you to backtrack and give up your beliefs just so you can belong to the world. Instead, he wants you to remember that you belong to God. God, in his love, has chosen you out of the world, made you one of his own, and blessed you with the spiritual humility to submit to his divine authority.

In a world that loves to call the shots and define truth for itself, a Jesus who insists on being Lord will not be loved. But don't panic. Instead, praise the Savior who called you out of the world and chose you to be his own.

The evangelistic power of love

Pastor Mike Novotny

How much money would you pay for a "+1 pass" to heaven? If you could be guaranteed that your best friend or your brother or your son or your daughter or your mother or your father or whoever would believe in Jesus and be with him and you forever, how much would you give? If you love people like I do, I bet you'd give anything.

Obviously, you can't pay for another person to get faith. But there is something you can do. Listen to Jesus—**"I pray also for those who will believe in me through their message, that all of them may be one, Father, just as you are in me and I am in you. May they also be in us so that the world may believe that you have sent me"** (John 17:20,21). Jesus wants the world, your non-Christian friends included, to believe he is the Christ, the chosen one. And how might that happen? If we who currently believe would "be one." If Christian love could make us one, our friends might know he's *the* One.

That is a fresh thought for my faith. Often I think of outreach as how I treat my friends who don't go to church. But Jesus thinks that how I treat my friends who do go to church is just as magnetic. If the world can watch a church that is defined by love—the kind of love that gives up its time, energy, and preferences—they might wonder what kind of Savior can make people so selfless.

How could you love your fellow Christians today? What uncommon love might the world witness at your local church?

He changed the world forever
Karen Spiegelberg

Chances are you will use some communication device today that was inspired by Steve Jobs, the founder and genius of Apple Inc. Most people have been a beneficiary of his gifted mind through technology in some way. At his passing, the news headlines stated, "He changed the world forever!"

The apostle Paul likely thought the same thing about Jesus as Paul sat imprisoned in Rome, penning letters to the early Christian church. Paul didn't have an extravagant device to communicate with the young believers in Ephesus or Corinth or elsewhere. He had the power of the Word, given to him through the Holy Spirit, to share the most important information that anyone could receive—full and free salvation through our Lord and Savior Jesus Christ! That is not only world changing; that is eternity changing.

Steve Jobs created and invented helpful and life-changing gadgets, the likes and complexity of which most of us cannot even fathom. But in his prayer in Ephesians 3:20,21, Paul sums up credit and glory to God for the more far-reaching importance of what Jesus did:

"Now to him who is able to do immeasurably more than all we ask or imagine, according to his power that is at work within us, to him be glory in the church and Christ Jesus throughout all generations, for ever and ever! Amen."

Jesus Christ—He *truly* changed the world forever.

Someone hold my hand

Jason Nelson

This may not seem very manly, but sometimes I just need someone to hold my hand. I need affection. That's what I love about my grandchildren. When I take them somewhere and extend my hand, they always hold it. It never fails. They hold my hand until they let it go so they can run ahead to something they can't wait to get to. It's one of the things I love about my wife. When we go for a walk and I extend my hand, she holds it. We have been walking together for a long time, and she never fails to hold my hand whenever I extend it to her.

Ladies and gentlemen, boys and girls, we need to take care of each other. We need to look out for each other. We need to lower the barriers that keep us apart: racial tension, religious separatism, cultural warfare, partisan politics, sports rivalries, generation gaps, gender divides, you name it. Sometimes we just need to stop talking and hold each other's hands. If we don't look out for each other, who in this world will?

Maybe I sound like an old hippie. I don't care. Sometimes I don't know what to say and don't want to hear any more divisive rhetoric. I just need someone to hold my hand. I need the touch of people and the touch of God in my life to feel it's all right. **"Into your hands I commit my spirit; deliver me, LORD, my faithful God"** (Psalm 31:5).

What would you do?

Pastor David Scharf

Hypothetical questions can be dangerous, but I'll ask this one anyway. What would you be willing to do for 10 million dollars? In a recent poll, two-thirds of Americans would agree to at least one if not several of the following: would abandon their entire family (25%); would abandon their church (25%); would become a prostitute for a week or more (23%); would leave their spouse (16%); would withhold testimony and let a murderer go free (10%); would kill a stranger (7%); would put their children up for adoption (3%).

You may look at this list and say, "I'd never do that!" But look at what Jesus said: **"Watch out! Be on your guard against all kinds of greed; life does not consist in an abundance of possessions"** (Luke 12:15). His point? "Don't be so certain. Greed can creep into anyone's life." That's true for me just as it is for you. Greed is perhaps one of the biggest blind spots for Americans. What concessions have we made to get more stuff? Neglecting our faith? Neglecting our families? Neglecting the work of the Lord? All of these are true temptations . . . and sins.

What's the remedy? Take your greed to the cross in repentance. There at the cross you see you have everything you need in your Savior. There at the cross you find true contentment in your forgiveness. Earthly wealth is meaningless apart from Christ. With Christ, you see any wealth you do have as a gift from God to be used to his glory.

Idolatry seems to work

Pastor Mark Jeske

It's not too hard to mock the Israelites for their seemingly endless fascination with worshiping Baal, the storm god of the Canaanites, and his sister-wife Asherah, the queen of heaven. The Canaanites seemed to the Israelites to have a much better life, and so it made sense to the Israelites to appeal to Baal for similar help. Any prosperity that then came to them *must have come from Baal*, right?

This is what God was hearing from his people: **"We will burn incense to the Queen of Heaven** [i.e., Asherah] **and will pour out drink offerings to her just as we and our ancestors, our kings and our officials did in the towns of Judah and in the streets of Jerusalem. At that time we had plenty of food and were well off and suffered no harm. But ever since we stopped burning incense to the Queen of Heaven and pouring out drink offerings to her, we have had nothing and have been perishing by sword and famine"** (Jeremiah 44:17,18).

With deep disappointment, God had his prophet Jeremiah announce the judgments that would be coming upon his faithless children. He describes himself without apology as a jealous God, one who will not share worship with anyone or anything else in all creation. Their perceptions of Baal as the divine cause of good things in their lives were illusions of the devil.

Anything we love, trust in, or fear more than God is an idol, and any perceived benefit from that idol is a devilish lie.

A long obedience
Christine Wentzel

"Fat" is a label that many of us put on ourselves without having any help from the peanut gallery of body-shamers. We can't hide our bad habits. We need to get to the root of the real problem. This insight about our faith walk may tip the scales in our favor: "It's a long obedience in the same direction."

"After fasting forty days and forty nights, [Jesus] was hungry. The tempter came to him and said, 'If you are the Son of God, tell these stones to become bread.' Jesus answered, 'It is written: "Man shall not live on bread alone, but on every word that comes from the mouth of God"'" (Matthew 4:2-4).

Jesus stayed in perfect obedience to his Father while the devil pecked at him in his hunger. It's a food temptation only the Son of God could resist. He understands our temptation of living to eat instead of eating to live.

Jesus, Son of Man, willingly made his earthly life a long obedience in the same direction for the joy of our salvation. We, in turn, follow him in thankful, willing obedience for the same reason—that's it!

Living a long obedience is not easy. However, it's a process assisted by the Holy Spirit, making the experience of becoming healthier fruitful and less stressful. This lesson is followed by many Jesus people learning to eat from the mouth of God first. Let's dine with them!

Evidence of the Spirit: Self-control

Pastor Mark Jeske

Comedian Jim Carrey has a line I love. He's about to go crazy, and then he hollers out with a smirk, "Sssomebody ssstop me!" Isn't it fun to assume that it's someone else's job to restrain our bad behaviors? Like the lost boys in *Peter Pan,* we don't really want to grow up. We'd like to stay children forever. Somebody else has to do the hard work of acting like a grown-up.

Do you expect God to take responsibility for your life? I know some people who actually believe that God controls their every move—it's a weird form of piety. Perhaps they think that they are giving God honor. In fact, they are not listening closely enough to his Word. God created us to be junior versions of himself, with *his* value system, *his* attitudes, and *his* agenda. He did not make us to be his marionettes, helplessly hanging limp until he twitches our strings.

We aren't helpless. Our Father and our Redeemer, Jesus, have given us their Word and Spirit, all with the goal of leading us to grow in discernment and making good choices. The power of personal restraint is one of them: **"The fruit of the Spirit is . . . self-control"** (Galatians 5:22,23). You can learn not to blurt out whatever flies through your mind. You can say no to sexual temptation. You can take charge of your food and alcohol consumption.

You can focus on important goals, complete your tasks, and value your relationships.

Love compels us

Pastor Mike Novotny

Back in the early 1700s, a rich and powerful man named Nikolas saw a painting that changed his life. As a 19-year-old, he visited a museum in Dusseldorf and saw a moving painting of Jesus' suffering. There, crowned with thorns and being led off to the cross, Jesus looked out from the painting with magnetic eyes, a gaze that stopped viewers in their steps. On the bottom of the piece, the artist added two lines: "All this I did for thee. What doest thou for me?" Those words gripped Nikolas' soul, comforting him with the selfless sacrifice of Jesus and compelling him to live a life of sacrificial love. From that day forward, he used his considerable influence and wealth not for himself but for the good of God's kingdom.

The apostle Paul would have summarized that painting with these words: **"Christ's love compels us"** (2 Corinthians 5:14). It is love, not the law, and grace, not guilt, that compel Christians to do good works. Yes, you need a clear path of commands as you walk with God. But, even more, you need the fuel to take another step toward obedience. That fuel is love. And your Savior Jesus has more than enough of it for you.

So if you struggle to be kind, to be gentle, to be selfless, or to be pure, spend some time staring at your Savior. Let his love warm your heart and compel your soul to walk with God.

A-Z grace
Pastor Mike Novotny

"God so loved the world that he gave his one and only Son, that whoever believes in him shall not perish but have eternal life" (John 3:16). There are many amazing words in that classic verse, but please don't miss this one—*whoever*.

Whoever includes everyone who trusts in Jesus, the A-Z list of sinners. Angry, boastful, critical, doubting, evil-doing, foulmouthed, gluttonous, homophobic, irresponsible, jaded, know-it-all, lying, mean, nasty, obscene, proud, quarrelsome, rude, self-righteous, thin-skinned, uncommitted, vicious, worrying, xenophobic, yawning, zoned-out sinners. Feel free to swap your ugliest sin into that list, because God's grace still applies.

If some type of sinner wasn't on God's list, we could never sleep in heavenly peace. But since God's love is for the world and *whoever* means *whoever*, we can sleep soundly under the warm blanket of grace. So tell the devil to pack up his accusations and take a hike. His flaming arrows, meant to pierce us with shame, can't get past the sturdy shield of John 3:16 and its impenetrable word—*whoever*.

I don't know everything you've done, but I do know this. God loved the entire world so much that he sent his Son, Jesus. And the world includes you, whomever you are.

Wretched. Rescued.

Sarah Habben

John Newton knew something about guilt. It shackled his heart. And young John had seen plenty of shackles as the captain of a slave ship from 1750 to 1754. He once witnessed one hundred sick slaves thrown overboard and a baby tossed to the waves because he wouldn't stop crying. At least one of Newton's voyages included delivering slaves to the shores of Antigua. There he learned that slaves rarely lasted nine years before they were worked to death.

Two centuries later, I worship with descendants of those slaves. We frequently sing a hymn that Newton wrote after turning his back on the slave trade and becoming instead an Anglican priest and abolitionist: "Amazing grace, how sweet the sound, that saved a wretch like me."

Does your heart call you a wretch? A wretched, impatient mother? A wretched, cheating husband? A wretched, thankless child? We *are* wretches, despite our best efforts. We thrash in a sea of guilt. And Satan, our slave master, loves to hold us underwater. But there is rescue! Newton was saved. We are too—when we cling to the plank of wood that is Christ's cross, trusting in him as our Savior.

"If our hearts condemn us, we know that God is greater than our hearts, and he knows everything" (1 John 3:20).

God knows our sins better than we do. He paid for them with his Son's life. Every day he hauls us ashore and pulls us to our feet to follow him anew. God is greater. And his grace is amazing.

The victory fosters peace

Jason Nelson

Friends of Jesus in every generation, peace be with you. What Jesus did two thousand years ago is still bringing peace because it turns each one of us into peacemakers. Not peacekeepers. Peacemakers.

"Let the peace of Christ rule in your hearts, since as members of one body you were called to peace. And be thankful. Let the message of Christ dwell among you richly as you teach and admonish one another with all wisdom through psalms, hymns, and songs from the Spirit, singing to God with gratitude in your hearts. And whatever you do, whether in word or deed, do it all in the name of the Lord Jesus, giving thanks to God the Father through him" (Colossians 3:15-17).

The peace of Christ rules our hearts and gives us very strong wills. We are thankful people but not passive people. The gospel lives among us and asserts itself through us. The peace of God is not peace and quiet. We make peace by teaching each other and redirecting each other with the wisdom of God's Holy Word. We put serious energy into that wisdom with loud singin' and prayin' because we are one big body of believers. The war-torn gates of hell can't stand up to the commanding peace Jesus brings.

Spirit of the living Lord Jesus, rule in our hearts. Unite us and make us a force for good and makers of peace. This is our faith. This is our hope. This is our victory. Amen.

Parental torment
Pastor Mark Jeske

It always tore me up inside to see my children sick, especially when they were small. Feeling their little foreheads burning with fever, cheeks hot, listless, moaning—what a nightmare. Worse—several couples I know have children who regularly suffer seizures. When our kids are sick, we are sick at heart with them.

Imagine the plight of this man, who once cried out to Jesus: **"Teacher, I beg you to look at my son, for he is my only child. A spirit seizes him and he suddenly screams; it throws him into convulsions so that he foams at the mouth. It scarcely ever leaves him and is destroying him"** (Luke 9:38,39). It seems that when Satan realized that the Son of God was on the surface of the earth, he sent his demons there too, invading people's minds and spirits, showing his true colors by tormenting them. God had allowed that parental torment to go on for a while. But at just the right time, Jesus spoke his word of power and the demon had to flee.

When we see our children struggle and suffer, let's give their needs to Jesus and settle down to wait in patience. Jesus loves our children even more than we do, and their misery won't last a minute longer than he has determined. He will make their pain work for them and the family. At the time of his choosing, he will bring relief.

Even the demons of hell have to obey him.

No creepy stuff allowed

Diana Kerr

My mom made everything a celebration growing up. I remember putting up decorations for several holidays a year, including Halloween. Until one year, when my mom said we weren't decorating for Halloween anymore. We were allowed to trick or treat like we always had, but we couldn't dress up as witches or zombies or anything creepy.

My mom's change of thought on Halloween came from reading more about the origins of the holiday. I respected her stance, but I noticed that, within my small Christian school, each parent had different guidelines. Some kids were gung ho about spooky Halloween stuff. Another one held an autumn "costume party" every year but couldn't trick or treat. One kid wasn't allowed to participate at all.

Which parents were right? Halloween gets a lot of debate each year from the Christian community. Jesus didn't give us a handbook of trick-or-treating guidelines. He did, however, give us the handbook of his Word, as well as the freedom to use his Word and faith-filled discernment to make good choices. Like Elihu encourages in Job 34:4, rather than listening to what others say (on Halloween or anything else), let's consult God's truth to form our stance: **"Let us discern for ourselves what is right."**

In the case of Halloween, I think "what is right" is going to look different from one Christian to another, especially among parents of young ones. I admire each Christian parent who makes a thoughtful, informed choice on Halloween, regardless of their differences.

november

All this is for your benefit, so that the grace that is reaching more and more people may cause thanksgiving to overflow to the glory of God.

2 Corinthians 4:15

Pray for the persecuted church
Pastor Mike Novotny

According to Open Doors USA, an organization that tracks Christian persecution around our planet, 245 million believers face threats, violence, and death every day because of their connection to Jesus. That's 1 in 9 global Christians. Like Leah who was abducted in Nigeria with one hundred of her classmates for refusing to convert to Islam. Or Maizah whose conversion to Christianity meant she was beaten and forced to become the fourth wife of her abuser unless she wanted to watch her family die. Or the Christians in rural China whose neighbors are now offered money by the atheistic government for reporting any followers of Jesus that they know.

What can you do? Pray. Paul wrote, **"If one part [of the church] suffers, every part suffers with it"** (1 Corinthians 12:26). Pray for the persecuted church. Right now these suffering Christians are somewhere thinking something. Pray that Leah thinks of the eternity of pleasure Jesus has promised and not the brutal pain that will one day end. Pray that Maizah remembers the sermons she has heard and the passages she has believed. Pray for every church that gathers on Sunday with the threats of their neighbors in their ears. Pray they would not be afraid of those who can only kill the body. Pray they would fix their thoughts on Jesus, the Savior who has promised that those who stand firm will receive the crown of life.

Jesus, come quickly and rescue your church! And help us to pray for each other until that day comes!

This faith of ours
Jason Nelson

This faith of ours is a warm hug from Jesus. It is a gift of his Holy Spirit that enables us to embrace God for ourselves. We can say, "I have faith" because he gave it to us in a way that allows us to possess it. I don't remember a time I didn't have mine. I do know that over the course of my life it has ebbed and flowed. It has been strong and weak. It has been an active and passive force in my life. I have studied the Bible and gone to church to maintain it and build it up. But it has always been there, and I really don't know how to live without it.

C. S. Lewis said, "I believe in Christianity as I believe that the sun has risen: not only because I see it, but because by it I see everything else." He lost his faith in adolescence and then found it again later in life. He cherished his faith because he tried life without it and then saw everything in life was better with it. He distinguished himself defending this faith of ours.

The psalms consistently attach suffixes like *ful* and *fulness* to the word *faith* because faith isn't static. It is a dynamic force that determines our ability to love God and love others in a trustworthy way. Inner faith makes us outwardly faithful. **"Love and faithfulness meet together; righteousness and peace kiss each other"** (Psalm 85:10). This faith of ours is everything.

Connect the dots

Pastor Mark Jeske

When you were a sophomore in high school, do you think you had the maturity and wisdom to rule a country? I sure didn't. Uzziah was only 16 when he became king of Judah, and though he might have been as raw as I was, he was blessed to have a wise, believing mentor who guided his development and royal decisions.

Zechariah showed the king how to connect the dots, i.e., see cause and effect between obedience to God and the peace and prosperity the nation enjoyed: **"Uzziah was sixteen years old when he became king, and he reigned in Jerusalem fifty-two years. . . . He did what was right in the eyes of the LORD, just as his father Amaziah had done. He sought God during the days of Zechariah, who instructed him in the fear of God. As long as he sought the LORD, God gave him success"** (2 Chronicles 26:3-5).

Can you connect the dots in your life? Have you lived long enough, are you perceptive enough, do you listen to others enough, do you know Scripture well enough to see that God still blesses people who care about his will and consult him? Do you believe that the Lord of the universe actually intervenes in human history and changes things in your favor as a blessing for your obedience?

Okay, so you know that. Now comes the hard part—will you act on that knowledge and live that way?

There is no pedestal

Jason Nelson

Hierarchies are things of the past. They are vestiges of societies that placed a premium on having privilege. Hierarchies reflect an old covenant way of thinking about God and world order. God is up there, and we are down here. High priests are in the Most Holy Place, and plain-old Levites are down here doing the grunt work. Lords are up there in the castle, and peasants are down here on the grimy side of the moat. Preachers are up there in ornate pulpits, and churchgoers are down here on hard wooden benches. But when **"the Word became flesh and made his dwelling among us"** (John 1:14), God upended all of it. He obliterated hierarchies.

The new covenant is about undeserved love and has nothing to do with trying to earn privilege. Let the Scriptures interpret the Scriptures. Let the Spirit of Christ put everything in perspective. Let the incarnation of Christ be the grace note that sets the tone for our relationship with God and our relationships with one another. **"So in Christ we, though many, form one body, and each member belongs to all the others"** (Romans 12:5).

The way forward is in awareness that we belong to one another. If we could think like Jesus thought, we could break down every barrier and shatter every glass ceiling because there is no pedestal. So there's no point for anyone to try to climb to the top of it.

You must be born again

Pastor Mike Novotny

Once upon a time, there was an old, repetitive preacher who thundered his favorite refrain Sunday after Sunday: "You must be born again!" On Christmas Eve, he cried, "You must be born again!" On Easter morning, he repeated, "You must be born again!" One day a courageous church member approached him. "Pastor," he asked, "why do you always say I must be born again?" The preacher looked back and smiled, "Because, my friend, you *must* be born again."

He was right. **"Jesus replied, 'Very truly I tell you, no one can see the kingdom of God unless they are born again'"** (John 3:3). In order to see the kingdom of God (i.e., to get into the place where Jesus rules as King), you must be born again. In order to be with Jesus, you must be given a new kind of life—a life under God's authority, a life motivated by God's love, and a life directed toward God's glory.

Every biology student knows how people are born, but how can we be born again? James answers, **"[God] chose to give us birth through the word of truth"** (James 1:18). The reason we are so passionate about preaching, Bible reading, and sharing the message is because God uses the Word as "the seed" that gives people an entirely new kind of life in the kingdom of God. Take note of that truth because, as that old preacher said, "You must be born again!"

Plan to reflect God's glory
Christine Wentzel

There are basically two extreme types of planners: the long-ranger with Post-it Notes all over the house, car, and work; and then the fly-by-the-seat-of-your-pants type who thinks time is a magazine title.

Planning is a good and necessary thing. Better yet, God-dependent planning is a responsible and rewarding part of Christian living.

Our King's glory is so awesome that we tend to shine it only on the big plans of our lives: medical procedures, selling or buying high value items, employment, etc. Here our total dependence on his guidance is a no-brainer.

"So whether you eat or drink or whatever you do, do it all for the glory of God" (1 Corinthians 10:31).

But how about reflecting his glory on the seemingly insignificant plans in our lives? As you stand in front of a mirror, what will your wardrobe choices reflect? As you plan meals, will the food choices harm or keep your body healthy? As you plan to attend the next social gathering, will your words float on the wings of virtue or sink with the weight of dishonor? As you plan your next shopping trip, will it fit within your means? Is God's glory reflecting so brightly in these areas that you're glowing like Moses at the burning bush?

There's no time like the present to reconfigure where needed and get out those sunglasses!

Get help

Jason Nelson

The local news reported that the suicide rate among farmers is now higher than it is among veterans and that farmers are becoming addicted to drugs. When commodity prices are low, farmers struggle to survive financially. The independence farmers enjoy also leaves them feeling isolated when trouble strikes. Rather than reach out to others, they stay quiet and turn inward. That is the formula for a mental health breakdown. Pillars of our society are breaking down: farmers, veterans, clergy, parents, and many others who feel isolated and turn inward.

You can check me out on this, but I think most of Jesus' healing miracles were performed on people who were looking for help. For example, **"Two blind men were sitting by the roadside, and when they heard that Jesus was going by, they shouted, 'Lord, Son of David, have mercy on us!'"** (Matthew 20:30). Even these blind men knew enough to look for help.

Sometimes it is difficult to know where to look for help. But there are solutions to problems that don't include ending one's life. If you are struggling with depression, anxiety, and despair in any way, I am pleading with you to get help. Join a support group of people who are going through what you are. Find a qualified therapist who can help you improve your outlook on life. Ask a doctor to prescribe the right medication to rebalance your brain chemistry if that is necessary. And always cry out to Jesus, "Have mercy on me!"

Grudges
Pastor Mark Jeske

I know exactly why people hold grudges (got a few myself right now). Nursing a grievance instead of resolving it gives me a fake sense of moral superiority. I can look down at the person and feel wounded and righteous. Holding a grudge helps me justify my own bad behaviors. It helps me justify my own laziness and failures by constructing a mental narrative that I am always the victim of other people's neglect and cruelty. If I have to risk talking to the individual about his or her faults, I know I will then open myself up to that person's pointing out mine. If I never start that conversation, I won't have to confront my own weaknesses.

All understandable thoughts, but all poisonous. Jesus Christ himself taught his followers that a spirit of mercy toward other people is not just a nice accessory but *central* and *indispensible* to the Christian life. We despise God's mercy to us if we fail to show it to other people. St. Paul heartily agreed: **"Bear with each other and forgive one another if any of you has a grievance against someone. Forgive as the Lord forgave you"** (Colossians 3:13).

In those words you'll find the power to break out of your "grudgy" ruts. God's steady, unconditional mercy to us, based on his decision and not our worth, warms our hearts and thoughts.

What are you stewing over today? Let it go.

Love defined:
Fist bumps, handshakes, and hugs

Pastor Mike Novotny

The night before the cross, Jesus prayed that Christians would love each other. **"I pray also for those who will believe in me through their message, that all of them may be one, Father"** (John 17:20,21). So what exactly does that look like? Three things—the fist bump, the handshake, and the hug.

A fist bump requires two fists, two hands held together tightly. That's like our beliefs from the Bible. When you and I hold tightly to God's Word, we have true spiritual unity under God's divine authority. A handshake requires two open hands from two people. When you and I relax our personal opinions about worship songs or what we wear to church or a thousand other issues, we can remain united instead of raising two fists to fight. A hug requires us to be close but not closed. When we stay close by doing life together and being real with one another, we are one. Time and honesty allow us to love one another in personal and powerful ways.

How closely do those three aspects of love align with your experience at church? Is there anything you could do today to increase the love among the Christians in your life?

Here's the good news—Jesus doesn't just want that. He also prayed for that. He personally prayed for you and me to love one another. With God's answer to his Son's prayer, love like that is absolutely possible.

The #1 reason people reject Jesus

Pastor Mike Novotny

When you were a teenager, did your mom ever rudely open the blinds in your room while you were still sleeping? Do you know why that was so painful? When a room is dark, your pupils dilate to absorb every bit of light they can. But when the lights are suddenly flipped on, so much light floods your dilated pupils that its muscles spasm and hurt. You squeeze your eyes shut, wanting to go back to the comfort of the darkness.

That is the same reason why most people don't want the real Jesus, the Light of the world, in their lives. John chapter 3 says, **"This is the verdict: Light has come into the world, but people loved darkness instead of light because their deeds were evil. Everyone who does evil hates the light, and will not come into the light for fear that their deeds will be exposed"** (verses 19,20). When someone listens to Jesus' teachings—his definition of a godly, obedient life—it is painful. Deeds and lifestyles get exposed. Change is demanded. And it hurts.

Maybe you know people who have turned from Jesus for that very reason. They didn't want to feel judged. They didn't want to change. Don't be surprised by such reactions. Ninety-nine percent of the crowds who met Jesus personally did the same thing.

But I pray you stay in the light. After your eyes adjust to him, you'll start to see that Jesus is the place where peace and joy and growth are found. So come into the light and do not be afraid of the pain of repentance.

Sleepless nights

Linda Buxa

You would think that David, the king of Israel, would have had it easy because he had servants and officials. (I'm pretty sure a chef and a maid would make my life so much easier.) But that's not what David said. Instead, he wrote that he was exhausted because of the problems he faced. **"I am worn out from my groaning. All night long I flood my bed with weeping and drench my couch with tears. My eyes grow weak with sorrow; they fail because of all my foes"** (Psalm 6:6,7).

Maybe you don't have enemy armies fighting against you the way David did, but you're in the middle of a spiritual battle (and you will be your whole life here on earth). This means you know what sleepless nights are like.

For some it's not being able to fall asleep at night, and others wake in the middle of the night. It's because nighttime seems to be when our minds flood with worries about bills, loneliness, children, work, finances, relationships, and health.

This is when you most need the reminder that your Jesus hasn't left you hopeless or alone. Because he already fought your biggest battle on your behalf, he is your safe place to rest in the middle of the rest of your battles.

Then, just like David, you get to say, **"In peace I will lie down and sleep, for you alone, Lord, make me dwell in safety"** (Psalm 4:8).

The victory is ours now

Jason Nelson

Friends of Jesus in every generation, the victory is ours right now. We don't have to wait to be thrilled by the spectacular events that will accompany our returning Champion. We are already raised with Christ. We can set our hearts on things above. We can set our minds on things above. We can have big hopes, big plans, and big dreams for ourselves and our children. We can rise above anything that is unworthy of the living Lord of everything and beneath the dignity of victorious Christians.

"Therefore, as God's chosen people, holy and dearly loved, clothe yourselves with compassion, kindness, humility, gentleness and patience. Bear with each other and forgive one another if any of you has a grievance against someone. Forgive as the Lord forgave you. And over all these virtues put on love, which binds them all together in perfect unity" (Colossians 3:12-14).

Spirit of the living Lord Jesus, fill our hearts with love. Thank you for making us your chosen people. Take charge of our thoughts and help us control our impulses. Help us defeat lust, evil desires, greed, rage, lies, and anything else that should be discarded remnants of our old selves. Help us put on our new selves, renewed in the image of our Creator where Christ is all in all. Help us wear love for others outwardly like Jesus did. Love creates unity. This is our faith. This is our hope. This is our victory. Amen.

Persistent love
Karen Spiegelberg

Raise your hand if Hosea is your favorite book of the Bible! I have a feeling there aren't many hands going up. I felt the same way until recently.

In the past, I've glossed over Hosea thinking, "Whatever. Those silly Israelites. Will they never learn?" But, for a short book, Hosea packs a big punch with a beautiful reminder of God's persistent love for us. The longer God gives me on this side of heaven, the more I appreciate that type of love. Like a father has for a child. Despite our continual sin and Israel's rebellion, God exhibits patience. Oh, he shows consequences for sin as a loving parent should, but he never gives up on the people of Israel or on us.

"When Israel was a child, I loved him, and out of Egypt I called my son. But the more they were called, the more they went away from me. They sacrificed to the Baals and they burned incense to images. It was I who taught Ephraim to walk, taking them by the arms; but they did not realize it was I who healed them. I led them with cords of human kindness, with ties of love. To them I was like one who lifts a little child to the cheek, and I bent down to feed them" (Hosea 11:1-4).

Although it can be a troublesome book, give Hosea another glance and feel with me the persistent love of our amazing Father God!

The Lord hears
Sarah Habben

Joseph Scriven was born in Ireland in 1819. He grew up, earned a degree, and fell in love. The night before his wedding, his fiancée drowned. Soon after, the 25-year-old Scriven emigrated to Canada.

There Scriven taught and did farm labor. On lunch breaks he read his Bible aloud to the railway workers. At 36 he fell in love again. Shortly before his wedding, his second fiancée caught pneumonia . . . and died.

What tragedies in *your* life make you wonder if God is really in control . . . if he hears your midnight prayers . . . if he's still worth following?

If Scriven had those doubts, they only made him dig deeper into God's Word. Inspired, he wrote a collection of Christian verses, including a poem for his dying mother. Some know it today as a hymn called "What a Friend We Have in Jesus."

Scriven dedicated the rest of his life to serving others. He worked without pay for the disabled and destitute. He died in poverty at age 66. It sounds like a sad ending, until you read one of his verses:

> "But oh, our sweetest hope
> Is that the Lord will come,
> And death in life be swallowed up,
> When we shall all go home."

Don't just wonder if God cares. Open your Bible and find Jesus, your dear Friend and Savior. Pour out your prayers. And hear the promise, for now and forever: **"The righteous cry out, and the Lord hears them; he delivers them from all their troubles"** (Psalm 34:17).

Born again?

Pastor Mike Novotny

Have you ever heard the phrase "born again"? To some people, born again is a certain type of Christian who tends to vote in a certain type of way, but is that true? What did *born again* mean to Jesus when he used it years ago?

When you were born, two things happened: You were (1) passively pushed into (2) a new kind of life. You were passive, because your mom did the painful pushing. And when that happened, you entered a new kind of life. You had life before, life in the womb, but this life was different. You got to see and experience a whole new world.

The same two things help us understand Jesus' metaphor. When you are born again, you are passively pushed; that is, you receive life due to the pain and work of another (Jesus/the Holy Spirit). As Jesus himself taught, this is a life you are given, not one that you work for or automatically get from your parents (John 1:13). And what a life it is! After becoming a Christian, everything is different. You see everything with new eyes—your purpose, your time, your money, your body, your work, your behavior, your death, your entire life.

This is what it means to be born again. That is what it takes to see the kingdom of God. **"No one can see the kingdom of God unless they are born again"** (John 3:3).

Cut it off
Jason Nelson

This is a very tough choice: **"If your hand or your foot causes you to stumble, cut it off and throw it away. It is better for you to enter life maimed or crippled than to have two hands or two feet and be thrown into eternal fire. And if your eye causes you to stumble, gouge it out and throw it away. It is better for you to enter life with one eye than to have two eyes and be thrown into the fire of hell"** (Matthew 18:8,9). Jesus is addressing the fact that evil likes convenience. Evil looks for a glide path from easy access to something to someone misusing it. That's why we don't let children play with matches.

We face difficult choices as a society (**so-ci-e-ty** *noun*: the aggregate of people living together in a more or less ordered community). When should we restrict access to something because it is disordering us? Overprescribing opioid painkillers led to the heroin epidemic that seems intractable. Availability of military weapons to the general public made it easier for madmen to kill lots of people. What do we think legalizing pot will lead to? I know. There's money to be made.

Not everyone with two hands steals with them or with two eyes looks at pornography. Not everyone who needs to take a pain pill becomes addicted. Not everyone who owns guns wants to shoot people. But when the prevalence of something destabilizes everything, it may be time to cut some of it off.

Listen to me

Christine Wentzel

Chatty strangers are put on this earth to test impatient-bent Christians. Whether they catch us on a good or bad day, there seems to be an underlying urge to avoid them, or be annoyed by them.

What makes a stranger open up to another stranger? We all desire a sense of connection. We all know what it's like to feel lonely or tuned out in rudeness, anger, or indifference. But, in this age of everyone standing on their personal soapboxes, it's so much easier to speak than to listen!

"Remember this, my dear brothers and sisters: Everyone should be quick to listen, slow to speak, and should not get angry easily" (James 1:19 GW).

Note that the apostle James mentions "everyone" in his reminder. That means we all can be quick to listen if we prayerfully work at it. And listening isn't only hearing, but it's "listening" to body language as well. We know the physical cues of people in need. Let's slow down and listen. Let's acknowledge their presence with Jesus' presence in us—giving them our full attention and some precious time.

Doesn't even a small moment of real human connection ring true for both parties and bring God glory?

I think I can. . . . I know God can

Pastor David Scharf

"I think I can. . . . I think I can. . . . I think I can," said the little engine that could. All he had to do was believe in himself, and he could make it over the mountain.

What are the mountains in your life right now that you need to get over? You know, the mountains of problems or sins or tasks that you've employed "little engine" theology to get over. So often in our lives we meet these mountains and say, "I think I can get over them." But so often on our own, what happens? We go rolling backward down the mountain, unable to muster the strength in ourselves.

Want to get over the mountain? Ask for help. Trust in God's great power. The same Savior who is so strong that he defeated death by rising from the dead still lives, and he lives to serve you! Want proof that he lives to serve you? Just look to the cross and see how he died to serve you. God is big! God is strong! God loves you! Trust in his great power in your life. Your mantra isn't, "I think I can" but, "I know God can!" And he will.

"If any of you lacks wisdom, you should ask God, who gives generously to all without finding fault, and it will be given to you. But when you ask, you must believe and not doubt, because the one who doubts is like a wave of the sea, blown and tossed by the wind" (James 1:5,6).

Grow your vocabulary: Sanctification

Pastor Mark Jeske

When you were first connected to Jesus Christ and received the amazing outpouring of his gifts to you, the gifts of love, forgiveness, hope, and promise of immortality, it was the best thing that ever happened to you. But that isn't the end. You are not merely existing here on earth. This planet is not a huge station where you are just killing time waiting for the train to take you to heaven.

You were saved for a purpose *now*, not just for your later passage into heaven. The day you became a believer the Holy Spirit took up residence in your brain and heart and the personal transformation began. The Spirit has a double agenda: 1) to change your thoughts, words, and behaviors to be more like Christ, and 2) to make you useful to God's agenda to help and convert other people. This process is called sanctification, saint-making. St. Paul knew that he had been converted, not just for himself but so that he could in turn become a blessing to many others: God **"gave me the priestly duty of proclaiming the gospel of God, so that the Gentiles might become an offering acceptable to God, *sanctified* by the Holy Spirit"** (Romans 15:16).

The sanctification process (i.e., transforming you to act like a saint instead of a sinner) is gradual and incomplete. Not until heaven will you be 100 percent free from sin. But in the meantime, you can enjoy the Spirit's power, renewing you constantly and giving you the dignity of usefulness.

The victory is still won

Jason Nelson

Friends of Jesus in every generation, the victory is still won. It has not been reversed or overturned. It will never be reversed or overturned. The life, death, and resurrection of Jesus removed our sins, subdued the power of the devil over us, and turned the moment we die into a very brief pause on the way to eternal life with him. His teachings are the road map for the life he wants us to live. This is our faith. This is our hope. This is our victory. We are victorious every day because the Holy Spirit revives our spirits and changes how we think and act for the better.

"And if the Spirit of him who raised Jesus from the dead is living in you, he who raised Christ from the dead will also give life to your mortal bodies because of his Spirit who lives in you" (Romans 8:11).

Spirit of the living Lord Jesus, come live in us. Come into our hearts today as we read your words. Stay in our hearts every day as we think about what we have learned from the Bible. Give us mere mortals the extraordinary power to live the victorious lives Jesus won for us. And since we also have eternal souls, give us confidence that we will live forever with you, saints, angels, and other great things we don't even know about. This is our faith. This is our hope. This is our victory. Amen.

Live like a farmer
Pastor Mark Jeske

In the 21st century, only a small percentage of our citizens are employed in agriculture or farm-related businesses. Most of us don't see farming happening from day to day, and we need to travel a bit to get the flavor (and the smell) of these things firsthand.

There is a seasonal rhythm for growing food that farmers ignore at their peril. They must also do things in the right order. There is a window of opportunity for plowing, planting, weeding and watering, and finally comes the harvest (hurry before the frost gets it). The prophet Hosea lived in an agrarian society and used images he knew well to teach believers about life: **"Sow righteousness for yourselves, reap the fruit of unfailing love, and break up your unplowed ground; for it is time to seek the Lord, until he comes and showers his righteousness on you"** (Hosea 10:12).

Even city people can live like farmers. Hosea's encouragement is that we do the right things, even when they're hard and even when there seems to be no reward, in confident anticipation that the harvest will come later. Repenting of our sins, telling the truth, helping other people, and keeping our promises sometimes have a delayed payoff. In an age of instant gratification, we need to teach our children and grandchildren to be patient, to sacrifice now, to learn discipline, and to look forward to the Lord's showers of blessings later.

There will be a harvest if we do the plowing and planting first.

Imagine love

Pastor Mike Novotny

The night before he died, Jesus prayed that the world would witness uncommon unity and love among Christians. **"I pray also for those who will believe in me through their message, that all of them may be one, Father"** (John 17:20,21).

Can you imagine if the Father answered his Son's prayer among us this week? Like . . . "Mom, who are the flowers from?" "Some friends at church. They remembered that your dad died four years ago this month." "Really?"

Or . . . "Dude, why are you driving that sorry excuse for a truck?" "Honestly? I gave my car fund to a family from church that's struggling." "Really?"

Or . . . "Wait, you and your ex go to the same church?" "Yeah, we couldn't work it out, but we forgive each other and both need our church friends right now." "Really?"

Or . . . "Who are you texting?" "A buddy from church. He's struggling with an addiction, and we try to encourage each other to stay strong." "Really?"

That kind of love would be weird and wonderful. Maybe the world would know that Jesus is more than another religion. Maybe they'd wonder if he's the One. Wouldn't it be wonderful if the church was not known for its music or its ministers but for the way we love one another? Thankfully, we have a listening Father, a forgiving Jesus, and an empowering Spirit to help us do that very thing.

So, brothers and sisters, let the light of Christian love shine brightly today!

We get the award
Linda Buxa

After actress Kate Winslet won an Oscar in 2009, she decided not to keep the trophy on a shelf or in a display case. Instead, she kept it in her guest bathroom. What? Why?

She did it so that when friends came over, they could hold the award and make an acceptance speech in the mirror.

Yes, when the woman who worked at her craft and suffered rejection throughout her career finally won a coveted award, she decided to let others act as if it were theirs.

Sounds familiar.

Jesus is the one who lived a perfect life. He stood strong in the face of every temptation by the world and by Satan. He followed every single command given by the Father. Still, he suffered the Father's rejection, which should have been ours. Then, when he finally rose from the dead on Easter morning, he won and got to make his victory speech: **"After being made alive, he went and made proclamation to the imprisoned spirits"** (1 Peter 3:19).

Then he put the award in the guest bathroom for us. We didn't earn or deserve it, and yet we get to act like it's ours: **"But thanks be to God! He gives us the victory through our Lord Jesus Christ"** (1 Corinthians 15:57).

We get to look in the mirror and make our acceptance speeches humbly, because we know that God sees us as award winners—all because Jesus gladly shared his trophy with us.

Who would hate Jesus?

Pastor Mike Novotny

If Jesus was full of grace, if he never sinned and always loved, why did so many people hate him? Jesus actually answered that question: **"The world cannot hate you, but it hates me because I testify that its works are evil"** (John 7:7). The world hated Jesus, even the church people hated him, because he told them what they were doing was evil. When he insisted they change, they called for the cross.

That's still the issue today. There's something we all have in common—church people, not church people, everyone. We all hate being judged. That's in our DNA, isn't it? When someone says or even suggests that we need to change, we swing back hard. We defend ourselves or accuse our accusers. Even if they're quoting Jesus. The reaction we see in toddlers who are told no is the same reaction we see in drivers who hear the horns of other cars. We get angry. And it gets much worse with moral behavior and personal beliefs.

So where's the grace in today's message? Simply this—If you repented today, if you apologized to God for your sins, you have vivid proof that the Holy Spirit is working in your heart. That deep desire to be corrected and be better is not in human nature. It's a gift of God.

So even if you're struggling and falling short today, praise God even for your remorse. It's proof that you love the real Jesus, the Jesus who calls himself your Lord.

If God himself be for me

Sarah Habben

He grew up in Germany during the Thirty Years' War, which caused more than eight million casualties thanks to a hot pot of conflict, famine, and disease. Midway through this period, Paul Gerhardt earned a theology degree, but the ongoing conflict prevented him from being ordained until he was in his 40s.

In his sermons, he spoke against false doctrine and was deposed for his efforts.

He knew what it meant to suffer for the truth. His wife and four of his five children died. He understood emptiness and loss.

And despite that, or because of it, Gerhardt also understood what the apostle Paul meant in Romans 8:39, that *nothing* **"will be able to separate us from the love of God that is in Christ Jesus our Lord."**

For Gerhardt, that promise was personal. He wrote, *"No danger, thirst, or hunger, no pain or poverty, no earthly tyrant's anger shall ever vanquish me. Though earth should break asunder, you are my Savior true; no fire or sword or thunder shall sever me from you."*

For Christians in places like Sri Lanka, where the 2019 Easter bombings annihilated over 250 churchgoers, this promise is personal. Violence can't sever us from God's love.

For Christians who know brokenness and loss, this promise is personal. God's love in Christ glues us back together.

For Christians dismayed by our decaying world, this promise is personal. Earth *will* break asunder—but our heavenly home awaits.

Confusion over cause
Pastor Mark Jeske

It may be that some roosters think they cause the sunrise because *every time* they crow, the sky gets lighter. The real reason for the coming of day, of course, is that the Maker of the universe set the planet spinning during creation. But roosters don't know that.

The prophet Hosea had a message from God for the Israelites, here called by God's affectionate nickname "Ephraim" (one of the patriarch Abraham's great-great-grandsons). God needed to have a conversation on that same subject of cause and effect. God absolutely loves to give his children things, and there were stretches in Israelite history when the nation was secure and prosperous. Maybe too secure and prosperous, because it went to their heads. They must have assumed that their military genius and business acumen got them there. God was heartbroken that his gifts were not recognized: **"It was I who taught Ephraim to walk, taking them by the arms; but they did not realize it was I who healed them"** (Hosea 11:3).

When God listens to your comments to other people and when he listens to your communications to him, do you suppose he gets the idea that you think you built everything in your life? Does he hear gratitude from your lips for the family, friends, education, work opportunities, angelic protection, skills, and talents that have prospered you?

Or does he think you sound like a rooster?

Top ten reasons to go to church
Pastor David Scharf

Why do you want to go to church? As a parish pastor, every year I would have a "Help the Pastor Write His Sermon" week in eighth-grade religion class. Matthew 21:16 reads, **"From the lips of children and infants you, Lord, have called forth your praise."** And that's precisely what happened time and again through this activity.

One year, as a part of the project, I had the class give their own "top ten reasons to go to church." Look at what they wrote: #10—To sing praises to the Lord; #9—To hear God's Word; #8—To strengthen our faith; #7—When we go to church, it helps others grow in faith; #6—To learn about what God has done for us; #5—to hear the law and see our sins; #4—To see Jesus' love in the gospel; #3—So that we learn new things about the Bible; #2—To join with fellow Christians in worship; #1—Church is awesome!

Wow! If that's what goes on every week in worship, it's going to be a great week! Who could need more reason than that?

"We will tell the next generation the praiseworthy deeds of the Lord, his power, and the wonders he has done so the next generation would know them, even the children yet to be born, and they in turn would tell their children" (Psalm 78:4,6).

A heart to hear
Linda Buxa

Sometimes when I don't know what to pray for, I take the advice of Jesus' brother James: **"If any of you lacks wisdom, you should ask God, who gives generously to all without finding fault, and it will be given to you"** (James 1:5).

I know I'm not completely wise, and if God said he'd give it to me, I might as well pray for it. After all, doesn't wisdom equal smart and knowledgeable? Who doesn't want that? Then I read Solomon's view of wisdom.

One night, the Lord appeared to Solomon in a dream and said, **"Ask for whatever you want me to give you."** Solomon didn't ask for riches or honor, but instead said, **"Give your servant a discerning heart to govern your people and to distinguish between right and wrong"** (1 Kings 3:5,9).

In Greek, "a discerning heart" means Solomon asked for "a heart to hear." Solomon's view of wisdom leaves less opportunity to display my knowledge and more opportunities to display my love. A heart to hear means that in all my interactions with people, I'm asking for more patience, more awareness of their needs. It means I take the time to listen, which leaves less time to talk and display my wisdom. It means I have compassion to see where other people are hurting and find ways to serve them. A heart to hear requires more of me, because it's not about me.

Ask for a heart to hear, and it will be given to you.

Farewell Moses
Jason Nelson

Among the most poignant stories in the Bible are those dealing with the last days of great leaders. No leader loomed larger than Moses did. He was the lawgiver and recorded the earliest history of mankind. He was out front of a moving mass of humanity and led them from captivity to the Promised Land. He performed miracles. He is beloved by Christians and is important to the majority of people on our planet right now. God dearly loved him. **"Since then, no prophet has risen in Israel like Moses, whom the Lord knew face to face"** (Deuteronomy 34:10). Only about David and Jesus did God say something similar.

The run-up to Moses' death was a spectacle that impressed upon Israel one more time what God had done for them. Moses renewed their covenant relationship with God. He reminded them of the blessings that come from obeying God and the consequences of disobedience. He reviewed laws he brought down from Sinai. He endorsed Joshua as his successor. He sang one last long benediction over them. Then this 120-year-old man with good eyesight and God's vigor climbed the mountain where he would die. He looked over a land his life was all about but would never set foot in. And then it was over. The people grieved over him as they should have. God buried him somewhere. To this day no one knows where that is. We do know that **"no one has ever shown the mighty power or performed the awesome deeds that Moses did"** (Deuteronomy 34:12).

Christmas is a time for war

Pastor Mike Novotny

How would you finish this sentence? Christmas is a time for _____. I bet I could predict the top answers—Peace. Hope. Joy. Love. Family. But how many would say Christmas is a time for war? Um . . . I'm guessing zero.

Except Luke. Did you catch the word Luke chose to describe the glorious scene out in the shepherds' fields? **"Suddenly a great company of the heavenly host appeared with the angel"** (Luke 2:13). Do you know what the word *host* means? My dictionary says, "someone who entertains guests," like the family that hosts a Christmas party. But an older use of the word, the one Luke refers to here, is "army." On the night Jesus was born, a great company of the angel army appeared. Erase the images of dainty, frail, pale angels. Insert barrel-chested, sword-wielding, black ops heavenly soldiers.

Why would Luke choose that word? Why not "heavenly choir," given their upcoming rendition of "Gloria"? Because, as the rest of Luke's gospel will prove, Jesus came into this world to fight, not to sing. General Jesus was born to direct the armies of God against all the forces of hell.

And that's good news for you. Because on the days when you're losing the fight against worry or jealousy or bitterness, you can turn to the Jesus who fought for you. When you don't have the strength to fight off your demons, you can call upon the name of the wounded warrior who bled, died, and rose to conquer every threat to your salvation. **"The Lord will fight for you; you need only to be still"** (Exodus 14:14).

december

God so loved the world that he gave his
one and only Son, that whoever believes
in him shall not perish but have eternal life.

John 3:16

Christmas happened!
Pastor Mike Novotny

Christmas is the season of stuff that didn't actually happen. A magical snowman with a button nose. A bullied reindeer with a heartwarming story of acceptance. A mischievous elf who delights children and exhausts parents throughout the holidays.

But Christians' Christmas is different. Just ask Dr. Luke, the man who wrote the longest version of the Bible's Christmas history. In the original Greek, Luke began his account with the words, "It happened." Literally, **"[It happened] in those days that Caesar Augustus issued a decree"** (Luke 2:1). That same phrase, "it happened," appears four more times in Luke 2:1-20. The point? This isn't a heartwarming story, an ancient myth, or the stuff of legend. This is fact. History. Truth.

And that's really good news. It means that there's a real Jesus, a real Savior, and a real hope for the real stuff you are going through. Frosty and Rudolph can't help you through cancer, grief, and fractured relationships, but the real Jesus can. Santa and his elves can't forgive you for the sins of the past year (or the past day), but the real Jesus has. Holiday emotions are not strong enough to support you through the storms of life. But the history of these holy days is the rock upon which our faith is built.

So the next time you see a manger or Mary with child, smile and say with Dr. Luke, "It happened!"

Breaking branches

Christine Wentzel

There's a scene in the movie *National Lampoon's Christmas Vacation* where Aunt Bethany's cat is gnawing on a string of lights. The cat ends up as a blackened outline forever burned into the Griswold's carpet. It brings to mind our tendencies to play with the "pretty" things that could eternally burn us.

Let's look at our pet sins. Really look at the ones so familiar to us that we're going blind to the fact that we're chomping away at the branch that gives us true life. We need to pause for a moment to see how close we are to the devil yelling, "Timberrrrr!"

"I am the vine; you are the branches. If you remain in me and I in you, you will bear much fruit; apart from me you can do nothing" (John 15:5).

No pet sins are too strong to be broken. We feel the strength of their claws dig into us like phantom pain. But their real hold was clamped on to the Lamb of God at the cross. As a result, with our daily repentance, we have the Holy Spirit's renewal and our Christian community for cultivating God-pleasing lives.

Dear Jesus, thank you for grafting me into your life-giving vine. Forgive me for growing numb toward the sins I keep. Open my eyes to its true harm. Help shift my desire into actions that bear good fruit in your name. Amen.

The waiting game
Diana Kerr

What are your pre-Christmas memories from your childhood? I remember coming in from afternoon recess at school, getting settled in my desk, and my teacher lighting a candle on an Advent wreath before opening up a worn-out book to read our afternoon devotion. I *loved* the time before Christmas and cherished that season.

This time was filled with lots of waiting and anticipation as a child. Where has that gone? As adults, most of us have more anxiety than anticipation as the deadline of Christmas draws near.

Because we're adults, though, this time should be even sweeter than it was when we were kids. With each year of life, we experience more pain and burden, and we sin more sins. We need a Savior. We need rest from our burdens, and that rest can come only through a special little baby.

What would it take for you to *truly* anticipate the peace of Jesus' birth this season? What would it take to be still and rest in God's presence, rather than be a busy, frantic ball of stress? What would it take to set aside some of the earthly stuff and focus on waiting for the Lord? Whatever it takes, it's worth it. The writer of Lamentations, amidst overwhelming challenges, encourages us in this situation: **"It is good to wait quietly for the salvation of the Lord"** (3:26).

In this time before Christmas, quiet the outside noise and slow down. Slow down enough to enjoy the waiting game of anticipating salvation's coming in human form.

Christmas or chaos-mas?

Karen Spiegelberg

It's the most wonderful time of the year! Or is it? I haven't started my Christmas cards or my shopping, and I've got strings of lights tangled so badly I'd rather throw them out than mess with them. Maybe the Grinch had the right idea about Christmas. I think I'll go live in a cave on Mount Crumpit.

Does this sound familiar to you as you prepare for Christmas? Since many preparations fall on women, we often act more like Martha of the Bible than Mary, her sister. We get so wrapped up in the holiday chaos and expectations. That's when we need to listen to Jesus' wise words to Martha when she questioned him in frustration about her sister's lack of household help. **"'Martha, Martha,' the Lord answered, 'you are worried and upset about many things, but few things are needed—or indeed only one. Mary has chosen what is better, and it will not be taken away from her'"** (Luke 10:41,42).

There's nothing wrong with having some Martha aspect to our lives. Christmas preparations and traditions can be a lot fun and be blessings to our families. But, when we start to feel all "kerbobbled" like Cindy Lou Who, we then should stop and take time to sit at the feet of our Master by being in the Word. The one thing needed. With renewed hearts, we can see more clearly the priorities of the season and simplify the demands we place on ourselves. Then we can have a Mary Christmas!

Is sorrow good or bad?

Pastor Mark Jeske

Well, this is a no-brainer, right? Who on earth would ever *want* to be sad? We don't have to go looking for sadness. It comes and finds us, whether we like it or not. Millions of Americans take antidepressant medication to help them cope with their dark moods. Nobody wants to be sad.

And yet. There *is* a good sorrow—the spirit of repentance when we have been in rebellion against God. We *need* to be shocked at our own carelessness and stupidity. We *need* to feel a sizzle of fear that we were dumb enough to flirt with spiritual suicide. We *need* to be mindful of the people whom we've hurt: **"Godly sorrow brings repentance that leads to salvation and leaves no regret, but worldly sorrow brings death. See what this godly sorrow has produced in you: what earnestness, what eagerness to clear yourselves, what indignation, what alarm, what longing, what concern, what readiness to see justice done"** (2 Corinthians 7:10,11). Paul's warnings in his first letter were heeded. The people in the Corinthian congregation listened and changed their ways.

Daily repentance is like respiration for Christians. When we stop repenting, we've stopped breathing. Godly sorrow is good when we see our words and actions for the acts of rebellion they are and back away from them . . . rethink our values . . . repair what we've damaged . . . form a new plan . . . and commit to bringing God's Word to the front of our thought process.

What needs work in your life today?

Good news for black sheep
Pastor Mike Novotny

Did you know that, according to many rabbis who lived around the time of Jesus, shepherds were the black sheep of the Jewish family? With little oversight or accountability, these drifters were tempted to steal sheep from other flocks or graze their flocks on private land. One Jewish father listed *shepherd* next to *tax collectors* as the most-despised occupations. Another wondered why God would call himself a shepherd in Psalm 23 if all the shepherds he knew were so ungodly.

Are any of you the black sheep in your family or your church? The person who stands out from the others due to your past choices or your present behavior? If so, have you ever wondered where you stand with God? If it's too late to make things right with him? If you've lost your chance to be called his son or his daughter?

If so, listen to what God's messenger said to the black sheep of Jesus' time: **"Do not be afraid. I bring you good news that will cause great joy for all the people. Today in the town of David a Savior has been born to you"** (Luke 2:10,11). Did you count the "yous" in that news? The good news that causes great joy is for all people, shepherds and you too. Jesus, the Savior, was born so that the most messed-up, sinful, broken, backward people could come back to the Good Shepherd and find a happiness that only God can provide. Will you call out to him today? He would love to welcome you home and lead you to the green pastures of forgiveness and peace.

Take my life
Sarah Habben

Young Frances walked with her head down. A clever girl, she'd memorized Bible passages when she was only four and started writing poems at seven. But Frances was afraid of hell. She begged God to save her but feared she wasn't saved.

Hymn writer Frances Havergal was born in 1836 in England, the daughter of an Anglican clergyman. She mastered six languages by her teen years. And it was a Greek verb tense in 1 John 1:7 that finally broke fear's stranglehold on her: **"The blood of Jesus, his Son, *purifies* us from all sin."**

Puri*fies*. Not puri*fied*. Jesus' blood *keeps on* cleansing us of our wrongs. This truth lifted young Frances' head—directing her hymns and the rest of her life. When illness confined her, she fixed this passage to the foot of her bed. When she died at age 43, it was inscribed on her headstone.

Lord, rouse my conscience! The wrongs that should make me beg for mercy I instead wear like a badge of honor: my ear for juicy gossip, my "witty" sarcasm, my mama-bear nature that roars into action when my child is in any way slighted.

But when those wrongs crush me, Lord, reveal your comfort! Jesus' blood wasn't a temporary fix, like a $20 car wash. His precious blood purifies me over and over again. It leaves me brimming with forgiven joy and singing with Frances Havergal: "Take my life and let it be consecrated, Lord, to thee. Take my moments and my days; let them flow in endless praise."

Good news for bad days

Pastor Mike Novotny

Every Christmas when I was a kid, my church made me memorize and recite the words of Luke 2:1-20: **"In those days Caesar Augustus issued a decree . . ."** I droned out the words, counting the minutes until church was done and the present-opening extravaganza could begin.

But in my monotonous recitation, I missed something massively important—*God does good things during bad days*. Just think about the words in Luke's account. "Those days" were hard days for God's people. The Romans ruled with an iron fist. Tax collectors bled them dry. Herod the Great murdered anyone who looked at him the wrong way. Caesar Augustus, the first Roman emperor, considered himself divine, a son of the gods. He "issued a decree." He demanded that humble men like Joseph take days off of work to travel and pay taxes to make Rome stronger and the rich richer.

In other words, those were bad days. And yet God was up to a good thing. The birth of the Savior. The start of Jesus' perfect human life that would end in his innocent death, which would lead to an empty grave and the forgiveness of every one of your sins.

Remember that when the headlines tell you these are bad days. We have our own Herods and Caesars and decrees, as you know too well. But we also have a God who is at work through it all, working out his plans and purposes. Now that's good news!

E is for empathy

Jason Nelson

If you're a young adult wrestling with the idea of going to church and attaching yourself to organized religion, I want you to know that I get it. I understand. Many of the options out there might seem a little strange: somber people sitting quietly in dark spaces. And they light candles. Older Christians can relate to all that talk of the end being near. But, I imagine that when you have your whole life ahead of you and want direction for it, hearing that everything is broken including you is a little off putting. You already knew the world was messed up when you stepped away from it to look for hope and inspiration for your life. Be assured the message of Jesus isn't gloom and doom. Jesus is about making everything whole again, including you.

Being a Christian is having a faith relationship with Jesus Christ. His life is an open book—the Bible. If you follow him around for a while in that book, you will come to love him deeply. Notice where he was willing to go and who he was willing to befriend. Think about what he taught with his stories and sermons. Watch him pray. I like watching him deal with those entrenched in their religion. Above all, understand that his self-sacrifice defines love.

No matter what you may have heard, please take Jesus at his word. **"I have come in order that you might have life—life in all its fullness"** (John 10:10 GNT).

Praying for others
Linda Buxa

I'm editing a book for a friend. She started the project to tell her story, even though she really wasn't a writer—though with time and persistence she is developing those skills. Frankly, I have no experience editing a book—though with time and persistence, I am developing those skills.

We both agree that our inexperience is good because whatever success we might have means we can only give God the glory. Still, our inexperience means we could use some help. That's why she immediately texted a photo of us to her closest friends and asked them to pray for the project. And I promptly forgot about it.

About a year later, I was introduced to one of the pray-ers. Her eyes opened wide, she pulled me into a hug, and said, "You're the one I've been praying for—for over a year." She released me. Then hugged me—again and again.

Whoa.

There's no privilege quite like hearing that a sister in Christ, who is a perfect stranger, has been persistently praying for me!

It is a privilege to pray for others and a blessing to hear that others are praying for you. So today let's remember to **"pray in the Spirit on all occasions with all kinds of prayers and requests. With this in mind, be alert and always keep on praying for all the Lord's people"** (Ephesians 6:18).

Then call, text, or email them to let them know.

This is only a test

Pastor Mark Jeske

King Hezekiah was a phenomenal leader of the Israelite people and provided godly and inspired leadership that saved the country from annihilation. King Hezekiah was a vain fool who couldn't resist showing off his kingdom's wealth to envoys (really spies) from Babylon. Q: Which statement is true? A: They both are.

God could have stopped the Babylonian spies, but he didn't. Why not? Because he was testing Hezekiah: **"But when envoys were sent by the rulers of Babylon to ask him about the miraculous sign that had occurred in the land, God left him to test him and to know everything that was in his heart"** (2 Chronicles 32:31). Doesn't God know everything, including what's in people's minds and what they are going to do? Of course. But here's the paradox: Scripture also describes God's work in *real time*—going moment by moment, waiting to see what we are going to do.

Remember that God's whole purpose behind the creation of the human race was not to manufacture mindless puppets whose every move he would control. God made us to be miniature versions of himself, with the idea that we would exercise judgment to choose what is good and shun what is evil. Thus he left Hezekiah alone not to abandon him but to give him the chance to use his God-given wisdom and life experiences to do the right thing. Does that mean that God uses our life dilemmas to test our maturity and self-control? *Hmm.*

Christmas is a time to seek

Pastor Mike Novotny

How fast do you think the shepherds ran at Christmas? Once the angels had delivered God's mail and told the shepherds that the Savior of the world was in Bethlehem, what pace do you think those guys clocked on the way there? Luke's gospel records, **"So they hurried off and found Mary and Joseph, and the baby, who was lying in the manger"** (Luke 2:16). They ran.

And why wouldn't they? If the angelic rumors were true, they were just a few steps from the promised Savior from sin, from God in human flesh. But since baby Jesus wasn't Amazoned to their pasture, they had to seek him. They had to take a step.

Sounds like life, doesn't it? There are glorious promises connected to Jesus: He forgives and cleanses and saves and guides and prepares a place for you. He is the Good Shepherd, the Bread of life, the Light of the world, the Vine that helps Christians produce the fruit of love, peace, and joy. But, just like in that famous field in Bethlehem, Jesus is not visible right here. His voice isn't echoing off the walls of the place where you are. No, we have to seek him. To open the Bible and seek the real Jesus in the Word. To follow his footsteps through the gospels until we find the only one who can satisfy our souls.

But he's so close. Just a step or two away. So, seek him today. Spend some time running off through his Word. Trust me; he's worth hurrying off to find.

Christmas is a time to smile

Pastor Mike Novotny

I have a pet peeve with most nativity sets. Some pastors are bothered by the wise men around the manger, since they technically didn't arrive until Jesus was back at Joseph's "house" (Matthew 2:11), but my issue is bigger than that. I'm bothered by how bored everyone looks.

Seriously, have you ever seen a happy nativity set? Ever seen ceramic shepherds with massive smiles on their faces or Joseph looking like he's going to burst from joy? Probably not. Instead, we get Mary, Joseph, shepherds, and sheep all looking like they're watching Bethlehem's 17th annual paint-drying contest. Their expressions are quietly thoughtful at best and glazed-over bored at worst.

But that's not the real story. Luke's gospel gives us good news of great joy, angels lifting up voices in praise, shepherds hurrying off to find Jesus (and spreading the word once they do), bystanders who are amazed at the message, and a whole bunch of loud verbs like **"praising"** and **"glorifying"** God (Luke 2:10-20). The only quiet one in the story seems to be Mary, who treasures up all these happy moments and ponders them in her heart.

So don't fall into the nativity set trap. Remember that what happened in Bethlehem is worth smiling about. It's worth shouting and singing and dancing about. A Savior has been born for you. He is the Messiah, the Lord!

Christmas is a time to think

Pastor Mike Novotny

Have you ever heard of Sakichi Toyoda? He was the father of the man who became famous for his car company. Sakichi himself was a wise businessman who is known in the leadership world for his "5 Whys," a method of thinking deeply through complex problems and confusing situations. Mr. Toyoda found that when he forced himself to ask *why?* five times in a row, he would often discover powerful solutions to his problems.

I wonder if that's what Mary did on that first Christmas night. **"But Mary treasured up all these things and pondered them in her heart"** (Luke 2:19). Jesus' mother treasured up all these things—the cries of her baby, the shouts of the wide-eyed shepherds, and the smell of the barnyard where the birth happened—and she pondered them in her heart. Mary thought deeply about what had all happened in Bethlehem and what it meant for God's people.

That's a wonderful way for you to think too. Treasure this season up and ponder it all. Dig deeply into words like *hope*, *peace*, and *joy* until their true meanings get to your heart. Make each verse of the Christmas story sit on a metal chair at the Pondering Police Station and interrogate it with Mr. Toyoda's questions—Why was Jesus born? Why did we need to be saved? Why is sin such a big deal? Why is heaven worth getting to? Why is being with God the best thing imaginable? By the end of that pondering, you might end up with the good news that causes great joy, just like the angels promised.

When I grow up
Pastor David Scharf

"When I grow up, I want to be weak and scrawny!" Nobody would ever say that! We don't want any part of our lives to be weak and scrawny. We want to be strong both physically and spiritually. How does God give that strength to us? By feeding us.

Every parent knows what to say to a six-year-old who complains, "Why do I need to eat my peas?" The answer? "Because they'll help you grow up big and strong." God gives us the same answer for spiritual strength from his Word.

Imagine a world-class chef comes over to your house and says he will make you your favorite meal from scratch. All day long you smell the delicious aroma of the food being prepared in the kitchen. You're getting hungry! Finally, he's done preparing your meal and gives you a fork full. It's the best thing you've ever eaten in your life. Would you tell him, "Thanks for the bite. I don't need anymore"? No! In fact, you probably wouldn't want anyone watching you devour the rest. Why would you act that way? Because you tasted how good it is!

You've experienced how good Jesus and his promises of forgiveness, life, and salvation taste. You crave it! **"Like newborn babies, crave pure spiritual milk, so that by it you may grow up in your salvation, now that you have tasted that the Lord is good"** (1 Peter 2:2,3).

Keep eating your whole life! It's how Jesus makes you strong.

This child will trouble us

Jason Nelson

Our thoughts of baby Jesus make us glad like Mary's did for her: **"My spirit rejoices in God my Savior"** (Luke 1:47). It is nice knowing God is with us. This child stirs us like the finger of God churned the pool of Bethesda so the lame, blind, and paralyzed knew it was time to jump in and be healed. This child troubles us because he wants in.

Come into our hearts, Lord Jesus, and disturb our complacencies. Move us to find healing for our ills of body and of soul. We will go where you lead because it's no trouble if you are with us.

Our thoughts of baby Jesus challenge us like Simeon's challenged him: **"This child is destined to cause the falling and rising of many"** (Luke 2:34). It is unsettling to think about Jesus' destiny as we approach his cradle. This child would grow up and die on a cross. Do we believe in him or not? When he comes into our hearts, we commit ourselves to a life with serious implications. We collapse under the weight of our sins to be lifted up again in this child's grace. He has the power to calm the storms we create for ourselves like he stilled the Sea of Galilee later in his life. This baby wants into troubled hearts.

Come into our hearts, Jesus, and convince us that we will always be better off because you are there.

At the manger
Karen Spiegelberg

It's that time of year when we enjoy the lights and Christmas decorations neighbors have displayed in their yards. I particularly love any outdoor nativity scene. My deep appreciation for nativity scenes goes back to when I was a child. We lived just blocks from our church, and it was an annual tradition for my dad to walk our family to see the rustic stable with Joseph, Mary, and baby Jesus. I remember staring in at that tiny "baby" and wondering what it would have been like to be one of the shepherds on that most holy night.

Oh, how I would have loved to have been there when the angels announced the birth of the Messiah, the One who was promised to come! However, my time on this earth was not meant to begin until the late 1950s. But why should my mission be any different than the shepherds of long ago? I should also feel as in Luke 2:17 where we read: **"When they had seen him, they spread the word concerning what had been told them about this child."** Amen and hallelujah!

In these last days before Christmas, my prayer for you is that you take time to peer closely at that baby and then "spread the word" with family, friends, coworkers, and anyone at your holiday gatherings or events. Isaiah's prophecy is fulfilled! The Prince of peace was born for you and for me and for all people!

The source of Christmas joy

Pastor Mike Novotny

If you had to describe Christmas with an emoji, what would it be—the red angry face, the blue tearful face, or the yellow smiling face? The answer, according to our culture, is the last one. Count the number of "joys" in cards and commercials and you'll run out of fingers and toes. Note every "Merry" Christmas and "Happy" Holidays and you'll need a book for all those notes. Sing "*Joy* to the World." Or "God Rest Ye *Merry* Gentlemen." Or "Shepherds, why this *jubilee*? Why your *joyous* strains prolong?" It seems everyone everywhere is telling us to rejoice at Christmas.

But that's only possible if your happiness is in the right source. Put your happiness in the perfect presents and you might end up like that angry emoji, frustrated over what your family didn't buy. Put your happiness in the presence of your preferred people, and you might be sad when friends and family have to work, travel, or pass away. But put your ultimate happiness in the perfect present, the presence of the eternal and glorious God, and you will always have a reason to rejoice. **"I bring you good news that will cause great joy for all the people. Today in the town of David a Savior has been born to you"** (Luke 2:10,11). Great joy! Explosive happiness! Why? Because Jesus was born. Because the Savior has come. Because Immanuel—God with us—is always true for those who trust in Christ. Now that is a reason to rejoice!

The gift that keeps on giving

Karen Spiegelberg

Most likely you've heard the phrase, "It's the gift that keeps on giving." It was first coined in the 1920s and promoted radios. The whole slogan read, "You will recognize them as the gift that keeps on giving."

Fast-forward a hundred years, and I doubt if those radios are still "giving." Every earthly thing eventually wears out, becomes obsolete, or goes out of style. At Christmas, we celebrate the only gift that truly keeps on giving—the undeserved and unconditional love of God, who sent his Son to earth to bear our sins and take them to the cross assuring us of eternal life.

In return, I want to give him a life lived in gratitude, but what do I mostly give him instead? I pathetically give him my failures, my weaknesses, and my sorrows all wrapped up into one neat and unattractive package. Now *that's* a gift I bet you didn't have on your wish list this year! But that very gift is on God's wish list, *and* he wants us to give it to him. When we do, we receive his pardon, strength, and joy all wrapped up in the love of our Savior Jesus Christ—the gift that keeps on giving . . . and giving . . . and giving!

"This is love: not that we loved God, but that he loved us and sent his Son as an atoning sacrifice for our sins" (1 John 4:10).

Lies: I have to be perfect or I'm a failure

Pastor Mark Jeske

All our lives we need to seek balance—balance between work and play and family, our needs and the needs of others, wealth accumulation and generosity, pride and humility, criticism and praise, conflict and peacemaking.

One of the most important life balances to think through is how to aim high, to drive yourself, to achieve big things, but yet not torment yourself with becoming perfectionistic. Perfectionists are hard on people and on themselves—nothing is ever good enough. It's hard for them to praise other people because they see all the flaws too clearly, and those flaws spoil any sense of celebration or gratitude. In their minds if they fail to be perfect, they are failures.

It's a lie to think you have to be perfect before you can like yourself. Be realistic: **"We all stumble in many ways"** (James 3:2). You carry around sinful brokenness and limitations in your thinking, willpower, and capacity. It is the forgiveness that Jesus has bought for you that frees you from the terrible pressure to achieve your own worth by yourself.

Knowing that you are loved and forgiven unconditionally means that you are set free to serve God and serve other people. You can celebrate what you've achieved today and let go of unfinished business for tomorrow. You can clap and cheer for other people's achievements, knowing how much they've overcome, without nitpicking their shortcomings.

Only God is perfect, after all.

Just imagine
Pastor David Scharf

Imagination is on the decline. With the rise of TV watching and the decline of book reading, you don't need to imagine anymore. Someone will show you how to picture it! I still remember growing up and imagining myself on a professional basketball floor playing with and outshining the greats. . . . It never happened, but it was fun to imagine!

Imagine what you would like most in life. Go ahead and come up with a list. Perhaps health, love of family, wealth, or respect made your list. Those are great, but now dream bigger! Imagine a life of total peace. Imagine your life with no regrets and no blemishes. Imagine your life as a journey to the best vacation of all time. You don't have to imagine. You *have* those and so much more!

Just try to wrap your mind around the love of Jesus that went to the cross for you—total peace! Because of that you now live in a state of constant forgiveness—no blemishes! Now look up to the sky. That billion-star resort awaits you—best vacation of all time!

If you think that's good, Jesus can and does do even more than you can imagine. **"Now to him who is able to do immeasurably more than all we ask or imagine . . ."** (Ephesians 3:20). Maybe I will never "shine" on the basketball court, but because of the wonders that Jesus has performed and still performs each day for me, I shine through him.

Even if they roll their eyes

Jason Nelson

There were some *eye rollers* around my dinner table. They had my surname and were eating my food. Whenever I took that occasion to do some re-parenting, they would rotate their corneas as far north as they could get them. It didn't bother me that they acted like they heard it all before. There were lots of signs that the wisdom I needed to impart to them hadn't sunk in. My job as a parent was to make sure it did. I was determined to outlast their indifference. The sweet justice of it all is that my eye rollers now have eye rollers of their own. And they have the gall to complain to me about their children's attitudes. I just say, "I don't feel sorry for you."

Parenting is the most repetitive undertaking any of us will ever engage in. Full stop. Don't even ask them, "How many times do I have to tell you?" Teaching children the will of God and how to be decent human beings is a matter of repeatedly reinforcing God's message to them. Faith comes from hearing that message. Even when it seems they are not listening, they are still hearing. They develop Christian consciences because they have heard it often enough. They learn the way they should go and will stay with it when they are older because they know it so well. Here is the payback for your efforts: **"May you live to see your children's children** [roll their eyes]**"** (Psalm 128:6, adapted).

december 23

We've got a lot to pray about
Pastor David Scharf

Jesus had the salvation of the world on his shoulders. He was about to give his life on a cross. Jesus was praying for all people. He had a lot to pray about! But Jesus knew that his Father is big enough to help. And the Father made Jesus' prayer matter!

We've got a lot to pray about too! I have a friend struggling with cancer, a relative who is straying from Jesus, a coworker who's been hospitalized for weeks, and dozens more (literally!) on my prayer list. That's just my list! What about yours? We've got a lot to pray about!

Let's just appreciate that. Let's appreciate that we know the power of prayer—that we get to go to the Almighty in prayer and know that he answers. Let's appreciate that no matter how big our prayer list, we have an even bigger God who promises to make our prayers matter and answers them perfectly. Let's appreciate that when we pray, our minds and hearts are taken away from the frenzy of life and are focused on the very reason for our existence, our good and gracious God. Let's appreciate that prayer is another very special way that God has given to his children only to be able to help, heal, and serve others. Let's appreciate what a wonderful blessing it is . . . that we have a lot to pray about!

"[Jesus] **took Peter, John and James with him and went up onto a mountain to pray"** (Luke 9:28).

Great joy for all people
Christmas Eve
Pastor Mike Novotny

Are you ever shocked by the shepherds in the Christmas history? When you see those staff-grasping men around the manger, do you gasp? When you drive by the front-yard nativity scene, are you stunned to see shepherds kneeling next to our Savior?

You should be. Some scholars say that most shepherds in the first century did not just carry crooks; they were crooks. Sheep-stealing, lie-telling, good-for-nothing men. The rabbis wouldn't let shepherds testify in court due to their reputations for not telling the whole truth . . . or even part of it. And even if that scholarship is slightly exaggerated, we know that shepherds were common men, third-shift workers and not first-shift rulers.

But that makes Luke's words all the more stunning: **"But the angel said to** [the shepherds]**, 'Do not be afraid. I bring you good news that will cause great joy for all the people. Today in the town of David a Savior has been born to you; he is the Messiah, the Lord'"** (Luke 2:10,11). Catch that? Good news for "all the people." Even shepherds!

Even you. You might not be impressive by the world's standards. You might be a third-shift worker, a nameless neighbor, or a sinner who messed up in very public ways. But the angel declared good news for all people, which logically must include you. So, rejoice today! A Savior was born to you!

Jesus is a big baby
Christmas Day
Pastor Mike Novotny

It's hard for a baby to be a big deal. As much as I adore my two daughters, I realize that only a tiny percentage of the world's population shares my affection for them. How many people remember their birthdays? Maybe a few dozen? That means approximately 99.9999999 percent of human beings don't know and don't care about their births.

But Jesus is different. Today more than two billion people celebrate Christmas. Even those who don't trust in Jesus as their Savior are aware of the day marked to remember his entrance into our world. Based on what the angel said to the shepherds, that enthusiasm is not mistaken: **"Today in the town of David a Savior has been born to you; he is the Messiah, the Lord"** (Luke 2:11). A Savior to rescue us from the danger of sin. A Messiah chosen by God himself to reconcile us to the Father. A Lord, a powerful authority, who flexes his divine power to protect his people.

That's a big baby! So praise the name of Jesus from Christmas to Christmas (and all the 364 days in between). Sing songs of worship and praise to him today. Call upon his name whenever life troubles you, depresses you, or keeps you up at night. Take your shame to the manger so you can leave like the shepherds with great joy. Look at the child in the manger, smile at your Savior, and say, "That's a big baby!"

Jesus' little friend

Pastor Mark Jeske

Jesus' disciples on occasion were a little too full of themselves. Jesus was a child magnet—they loved his tone and presence—but the disciples viewed the children as a nuisance and tried to shoo them away. They thought that discussing the faith was grown-up business.

Jesus saw children as his champions: **"He called a little child to him, and placed the child among them. And he said: 'Truly I tell you, unless you change and become like little children, you will never enter the kingdom of heaven. Therefore, whoever takes the lowly position of this child is the greatest in the kingdom of heaven'"** (Matthew 18:2-4).

Jesus praised child-faith for two powerful reasons: 1) Its *simplicity*. Children haven't yet learned all the scientific reasons why the Christian faith is unbelievable. They don't stall and argue. They just accept it. 2) Its *humility*. Children are used to being marginalized and ignored by adults, and so they don't think too highly of themselves. Jesus' tone was sharp with his disciples. Not only *could* children have saving faith, but their faith was to be a *model* for adults. In fact—outrageous concept—without childlike faith it is impossible to enter the kingdom! Not only do children bring value to God through their service; their humble posture is to be a *model* for big people.

Does Jesus have any child champions in your life who can inspire and guide your mind-set?

The glory of the Lord
Pastor Mike Novotny

If a kindergartener asked you what *glory* meant, could you explain it? When you pray, "The kingdom and the power and the glory are yours now and forever," do you know what you're praying? When you sing "Gloooooooria" at Christmas, do you know what you're saying? When you read, **"An angel of the Lord appeared to** [the shepherds]**, and the glory of the Lord shone around them, and they were terrified"** (Luke 2:9), do you understand what you're reading?

If not, let me help. In the Bible, the word *glory* is used to describe King Solomon's royal robes (Matthew 6:29), bright starry nights (Psalm 19:1), and Jesus seated on his throne (John 12). So, what do those three things have in common? My one-word answer—Wow! Glory is when something is jaw-dropping, stop-and-stare stunning. When yawning is impossible and wanting to take a picture is natural. That's glory.

On the night Jesus was born, God's glory appeared. A holy angel lit up the night, and the shepherds were wowed, then scared of their sins, and eventually thrilled by the news of God's grace.

And this is my prayer for you—that Christmas, no matter how many times you have celebrated Jesus' birth, would still "wow" you. That every time you'd see God in a manger, you would be stunned at his humility and mercy. That you would never get used to God reaching down to you simply because he wanted you to be part of his family. Wow . . . isn't God glorious?

Evidence of the Spirit: Goodness

Pastor Mark Jeske

"Sincerity is the main thing. Once you've learned how to fake that, you've got it made."

I laughed at those words on a poster when I first saw them, but then I winced. How painfully true! How we lie to each other . . . How we feign interest in people though we're really feeling only boredom or disdain . . . How crushing to our spirits when we realize painfully that someone was only pretending to like us.

But how soul-refreshing it is to be helped by someone who has nothing to gain! Here is another of the sure evidences of the Holy Spirit's influence in human hearts: **"The fruit of the Spirit is . . . goodness"** (Galatians 5:22). In a business world rotted out by greed, manipulation, and cheating, how encouraging is it to realize that the person you're doing business with actually cares about your well-being? That his word is true? That she intends to keep her promises?

What a great way for you and me to give glory to the One who never lies to us and who is always working for our good! The gospel of Christ changes how God looks at us. The Spirit of the Lord working through that gospel also changes how we look at other people—not as competition, annoyances, obstacles, and idiots but as redeemed and valuable souls with whom we can share life in heaven. We are vessels of God's goodness.

God is good all the time. All the time God is good!

Catch anything?
Pastor David Scharf

You've been in the boat all day, frustrated that all you've gotten are a few nibbles by little fish whose mouths aren't big enough to get over your hook OR a few chomps by big fish that took the bait but got away as you were reeling them in. All you want to do is go back and relax on shore. As you approach the dock, your family or friends call out, "Catch anything?" Which only adds to your frustration.

Isn't that how you feel sometimes as a Christian? You keep throwing your gospel lines into the water to the people around you. A few seem to nibble, others chomp down but then release themselves; finally, there are those who don't seem to come close to the boat. And it's frustrating, especially when the "fish" you're trying to catch is someone close to you. Then to add to your frustration, you have to answer negatively to those who ask, "Catch anything?"

But don't let your frustration keep you from fishing. Jesus said, **"'Let down the nets for a catch.' Simon answered, 'Master, we've worked hard all night and haven't caught anything. But because you say so, I will let down the nets.' When they had done so, they caught such a large number of fish that their nets began to break"** (Luke 5:4-6).

Continue to "fish" for people, simply because your Master says so. And as you do, Jesus will shine through you.

Just an ordinary year
Jason Nelson

I thought I would do a retrospective on the past year. Here is my checklist for this year in review.

- Did I get some woodworking projects done, and do I still have all of my fingers? *Check.*
- Did two more back surgeries reduce the pain at least a little? *Check.*
- **"As long as the earth endures, seedtime and harvest . . . summer and winter, day and night will never cease"** (Genesis 8:22). *Check.*
- Did I learn something new so my brain won't shrivel up? *TBD*
- **"'For I know the plans I have for you,' declares the Lord, 'plans to prosper you and not to harm you, plans to give you hope and a future'"** (Jeremiah 29:11). *Check.*
- After over 40 years of trying, did my wife finally win a prize from Publishers Clearing House? *Not a chance.*
- Will she stop trying next year so we can save a little money on postage? *Not a chance.*
- Was everything smooth sailing? *I wish, but we're still sailing.*
- **"No temptation has overtaken you except what is common to mankind. And God is faithful; he will not let you be tempted beyond what you can bear. But when you are tempted, he will also provide a way out so that you can endure it"** (1 Corinthians 10:13). *Check.*

Looks like this was just an ordinary year. God is faithful.

Christian resolutions
New Year's Eve
Pastor Mike Novotny

Did you know January was named after the Roman god Janus? Janus had two faces, one looking backward and the other forward, which is where the tradition of New Year's resolutions comes from.

While the apostle Peter wasn't interested in worshiping Janus, he was very passionate about resolving to grow from year to year. He wrote, **"Make every effort to add to your faith goodness; and to goodness, knowledge; and to knowledge, self-control; and to self-control, perseverance; and to perseverance, godliness; and to godliness, mutual affection; and to mutual affection, love. For if you possess these qualities in increasing measure, they will keep you from being ineffective and unproductive in your knowledge of our Lord Jesus Christ"** (2 Peter 1:5-8). Peter wanted those of us who have faith to "make every effort" in order to "add" the listed qualities to our current faith.

As you look over Peter's list, which one is God urging you to add to your faith? What would it mean to make every effort in order to do so? Can I encourage you to think carefully about those questions and to share your thoughts with a fellow Christian? After all, resolutions are more likely to become reality when you share them with others.

And please don't forget Jesus. Many resolutions fail because they're based off of grit and willpower, but we believe Jesus' mercy is new every morning and his grace endures from year to year. So, make every effort and know that Jesus is there to catch you when you fall.

Devotions for Special Days

Be merciful
Leap Year | February 29
Pastor Mark Jeske

"Lord, have mercy!" Do you ever say that? I hope you do, and when you say it, I hope you mean every word of it. We are utterly dependent on the Lord's mercy for our spiritual life and hope. Mercy means to be shown kindness that we do not deserve. Mercy comes from goodness in the heart of the giver, not merit on the part of the receiver.

You and I are bathed in mercy from God, and it is our privilege to be reflectors of it to other strugglers and stragglers. God would like us to treat others in their time of weakness in the same way that he has treated us. **"Be merciful to those who doubt; save others by snatching them from the fire; to others show mercy, mixed with fear"** (Jude 1:22,23).

What sin have you ever seen in other people that you yourself were not also once guilty of? Doubt? Rebelliousness? Meanness? Deceit? Cruelty? Adultery? Theft? Hypocrisy? Christ Jesus allowed himself to be blamed for all of your sin, and its guilt is attached to you no more.

A believer who is fully aware of being treated better than he or she deserves finds joy in being merciful to others.

Do you tremble at the words of God?
Good Friday
Pastor Mark Jeske

Every Holy Week, amid the sad and somber stories of the crucifixion of Christ, our congregation sings the old spiritual "Were You There?" Do you know it? Each stanza includes the phrase, "Oh, sometimes it causes me to tremble, tremble, tremble."

I had to ask myself, though, "Does it really? Do I really tremble?" How about you—do you seriously *tremble* at the words of God? Are you 100 percent convinced that you owe your very existence to God? . . . that you owe God full and perfect obedience to his will? . . . that his threats of anger and judgment are not for other evil people but for you too? . . . that the torments of hell are real and permanent? Ezra the priest and the leaders of Israel came to realize with shock how far the Israelite people had fallen: **"Everyone who trembled at the words of the God of Israel gathered around me because of this unfaithfulness of the exiles. And I sat there appalled until the evening sacrifice"** (Ezra 9:4).

When the terror and reality of God's solemn words of law and condemnation sink in, there is only one place for sinful tremblers to go: to the cross of Christ. It is for just such rebels and sinners as you and me that the Son of God chose to come to earth, live a sinless life as our substitute, and offer that life as a replacement victim.

Do you tremble also with relief and joy to know that Christ Jesus has bought you sweet forgiveness, divine favor, and life forever?

Easter sets us free from death's sting
Easter Sunday
PastorJeremy Mattek

Richard was on an airplane eating his lunch when he felt something land in his hair. He rubbed his head, which caused the scorpion that had fallen from the overhead bin to fall onto his dinner plate. When he tried to shoo the scorpion, it stung him. The flight attendants caught the scorpion and flushed it down the toilet.

How many of you would choose to fly if you believed you would be stung by a scorpion? I bet there's at least one situation in which all of us would.

Would you rather fly on an airplane and be stung by a scorpion or would you rather feel the sting of someone's death?

Some of you know the answer because you've felt that sting recently. For others, it's been a while, but your heart doesn't hurt any less despite the time. For some, the pain is sporadic; it doesn't hurt as much when you distract yourself with other things. But then suddenly you're reminded of that person and the sting is painful. It's a pain that stings the hearts of every age and every race. And it's a pain that we face head-on on Easter morning.

Jesus had died too. His friends and family had been stung by death very deeply. But on the third day, Jesus rose. He had been stung by death but not defeated by it. This is why the apostle Paul wrote in 1 Corinthians 15:55: **"Where, O death, is your victory? Where, O death, is your sting?"**

Death doesn't get the final say in a person's life. The risen Jesus does.

Last word
Memorial Day
Pastor Mark Jeske

Military cemeteries are some of the most eerie and moving places anywhere on earth. All those headstones are exactly alike—thousands of them in neat rows, all engraved with a branch of service, all stating a military rank. In a military cemetery, you can almost hear the ghostly boom of artillery and the rattle of rifle fire.

But it's actually quiet there. Memorial Day is a great time to reflect on the sacrifices made by so many men and women in defense of their country and in bringing order and peace where there had been chaos. It's a time to reflect that many of those warriors never came home—their bodies rest in Europe or Asia. How grateful we the living can be!

The machines and technology of war remorselessly charge forward. The insane power of today's aircraft, submarines, missiles, and nuclear weaponry will make the next big war a global nightmare. But as you ponder those military graves, be comforted that God has the last word. He is mightier than any human weapons, and he steers and guides the affairs of nations toward his redemptive mission: **"The valiant lie plundered, they sleep their last sleep; not one of the warriors can lift his hands. At your rebuke, God of Jacob, both horse and chariot lie still. It is you alone who are to be feared. Who can stand before you when you are angry? From heaven you pronounced judgment, and the land feared and was quiet—when you, God, rose up to judge, to save all the afflicted of the land"** (Psalm 76:5-9).

Thank God for the Holy Spirit
Thanksgiving Day
Pastor Mike Novotny

Do you ever find it difficult to keep Jesus' commands? Me too. I love the idea of being patient, forgiving, and humble, but when my kids are taking too long to get out the door or someone jumps to conclusions about my motives or a critical comment comes my way, doing what Jesus says feels almost impossible.

I think that's why Jesus offered to help. The night before he died, Jesus said, **"If you love me, keep my commands. And I will ask the Father, and he will give you another advocate to help you and be with you forever—the Spirit of truth"** (John 14:15-17). Jesus asked the Father to send the Spirit, the entire Trinity working together to help us prove our love for Jesus by keeping his commandments.

What a promise! The Spirit is "with you forever," right at your side when you are tempted. He is an "advocate," a voice that speaks to your heart about the love of Jesus and how supremely worthy he is of your obedience. And he is called "the Spirit of truth," the one who points you back to the Truth, Jesus, whose constant forgiveness is just what you need to free you from shame and empower you to try to keep his commands again.

Yes, being patient, forgiving, and humble is hard. But you are never alone when you try. Thank God for the Holy Spirit!

About the Writers

Pastor Mike Novotny has served God's people in full-time ministry since 2007 in Madison and, most recently, at The CORE in Appleton, Wisconsin. He also serves as the lead speaker for Time of Grace, where he shares the good news about Jesus through television, print, and online platforms. Mike loves seeing people grasp the depth of God's amazing grace and unstoppable mercy. His wife continues to love him (despite plenty of reasons not to), and his two daughters open his eyes to the love of God for every Christian. When not talking about Jesus or dating his wife/girls, Mike loves playing soccer, running, and reading.

Linda Buxa is a freelance writer and Bible study leader. She is a regular speaker at women's retreats and conferences across the country, as well as a regular blogger and contributing writer for Time of Grace Ministry. Linda is the author of *Dig In! Family Devotions to Feed Your Faith*, *Parenting by Prayer*, and *Made for Friendship*. She and her husband, Greg, have lived in Alaska, Washington D.C., and California. They now live in Wisconsin, where they are raising their three children.

Pastor Matt Ewart and his wife, Amy, have been blessed with three young children who keep life interesting. Matt is currently a pastor in Lakeville, Minnesota, and has previously served as a pastor in Colorado and Arizona.

Sarah Habben is a freelance writer and a remedial teacher for grades 1-6 at St. John's Church and School in Antigua, where her husband, Dan, has been a pastor since August 2017. Before moving to the Caribbean, the Habben family lived in Alberta, Canada, for 18 years. They are still thawing out. Sarah and Dan have four daughters. Sarah is the author of *The Mom God Chose:*

Mothering Like Mary (2015, Northwestern Publishing House) and the coauthor of *The Bloodstained Path to God* (2012, Northwestern Publishing House).

Pastor Mark Jeske brought the good news of Jesus Christ to viewers of *Time of Grace* for 18 years. He is currently the senior pastor at St. Marcus Church, a thriving multicultural congregation in Milwaukee, Wisconsin. Mark is the author of several books and dozens of devotional booklets on various topics. He and his wife, Carol, have four adult children.

Diana Kerr is a certified professional life coach on a mission to help go-getter Christian women break free from overwhelm and design their time and life for what matters most. Diana lives in Milwaukee with her husband, Kyle, and their son, Harrington. Visit dianakerr.com to learn more about Diana and explore her free tips and resources on intentional living.

Pastor Daron Lindemann is pastor at a new mission start in Pflugerville, Texas. Previously, he served in downtown Milwaukee and in Irmo, South Carolina. Daron has authored articles or series for *Forward in Christ* magazine, *Preach the Word*, and his own weekly Grace MEMO devotions. He lives in Texas with his wife, Cara, and has two adult sons.

Pastor Jeremy Mattek has been married to Karen since 2000. God has blessed them with five children (three girls and two boys). Together, they find great joy in encouraging souls with the gospel of Jesus Christ. Jeremy is currently a pastor in Greenville, Wisconsin, and is a regular speaker for Grace Talks.

Jason Nelson had a career as a teacher, counselor, and leader. He has a bachelor's degree in education, did graduate work in theology, and has a master's degree in counseling psychology. After his career ended in disabling back pain, he wrote the book *Miserable Joy: Chronic Pain in the Christian Life* (2007, Northwestern Publishing House). He has written and spoken extensively on a variety of topics related to the Christian life. Jason has been a contributing writer for Time of Grace since 2010. He has authored many Grace Moments devotions and several books. Jason lives with his wife, Nancy, in Wisconsin.

Pastor David Scharf served as a pastor in Greenville, Wisconsin, and now serves as a professor of theology at Martin Luther College in Minnesota. He has presented at numerous leadership, outreach, and missionary conferences across the country. He is a contributing writer for Time of Grace and a speaker for Grace Talks video devotions. Dave and his wife have six children.

Karen Spiegelberg lives in Wisconsin with her husband, Jim. She has three married daughters, two grandsons, and has been a foster mom to many. Years ago she was encouraged to start a women's ministry but felt it wasn't the right time. Then, when her brother died suddenly, it hit her hard—that we can't wait until the time seems right for our ministry; the time is now. And so in 2009, A Word for Women was born. Karen finds great comfort in Psalm 31:14,15: "But I trust in you, O LORD. . . . My times are in your hands." www.awordforwomen.com

Christine Wentzel, a native of Milwaukee, lives in Norfolk, Virginia, with her husband, James, and their fur-child, Piper. After two lost decades as a prodigal, Christine gratefully worships and serves her Salvation

Winner at Resurrection in Chesapeake, Virginia. There she discovered latent talents to put to use for the Lord. In 2009 she began to write and create graphic design for an online Christian women's ministry, A Word for Women, and now serves joyfully as a coadministrator for this ministry. www.awordforwomen.com

About Time of Grace

Time of Grace connects people to God's grace—his love, glory, and power—so they realize the temporary things of life don't satisfy. What brings satisfaction is knowing that because Jesus lived, died, and rose for all of us, we have access to the eternal God—right now and forever.

To discover more, please visit timeofgrace.org or call 800.661.3311.

Help share God's message of grace!

Every gift you give helps Time of Grace reach people around the world with the good news of Jesus. Your generosity and prayer support take the gospel of grace to others through our ministry outreach and help them experience a satisfied life as they see God all around them.

Give today at timeofgrace.org/give or by calling 800.661.3311.

Thank you!

Made in the USA
Middletown, DE
19 November 2019